The WHOLE WORLD Loves CHICKEN SOUP

BOOKS BY MIMI SHERATON

The Seducer's Cookbook
City Portraits
The German Cookbook
Visions of Sugarplums
From My Mother's Kitchen
Is Salami and Eggs Better Than Sex? (with Alan King)
Mimi Sheraton's The New York Times *Guide to New York Restaurants*
Mimi Sheraton's Favorite New York Restaurants
New York's Best Restaurants 1989

As Historical Food Consultant:
The Horizon Cookbook: An Illustrated History of Eating and Drinking Through the Ages

MIMI SHERATON

THE

WHOLE WORLD

L·O·V·E·S

CHICKEN SOUP

Recipes and Lore to Comfort Body and Soul

WARNER BOOKS

A Time Warner Company

I am grateful to all of the following for allowing me to reprint quotes, recipes or adaptations of recipes, and information previously published or unpublished:

Sekou Diabate for descriptions that were the basis for the Ivory Coast recipes *Pepper Soup, Potato Soup,* and *Gumbo Soup*; Bobby Flay and the Mesa Grill for the recipe *Green Chili Chicken and Posole Soup*; Alan King for the memoir on page 45; Christer Larsson and Christer's restaurant for the recipe *Christer's Chicken and Savoy Cabbage Soup;* Ismail Merchant for the recipe *Chicken Ginger Soup;* Giancarlo Quadalti and the erstwhile Amarcord restaurant for the recipe *Passatelli or Passetini;* Charles Ritzberg, author of *Caribfrikan Portfolio* and *Classic Afrikan Cuisines,* for quotes and the basis for the recipe *Caribbean Chicken Pepper Pot Soup;* Douglas Rodriguez and the Patria restaurant for the recipe *Ajiaco Colombiano;* Theo Schoenegger and the San Domenico restaurant for the recipes *Ristretto di Cappone, Tortellini,* and *Wine Soup;* Arraya Selassie and The Blue Nile restaurant for his version of *Spicy Chicken Soup;* Michael Tong of Shun Lee and Shun Lee Palace for the recipes *Banquet or Best Taste Soup, Black or Silkie Chicken Soup, Basic Chinese Chicken Soup,* and *Hot and Sour Soup;* Dr. Douglas Torre for his poem "Chicken Soup"; Anne Tyler for the recipe *Ezra Tull's Gizzard Soup,* from *Dinner at the Homesick Restaurant* (New York: Alfred A. Knopf, 1982) and Dr. Jay F. Rosenberg for the original recipe from *The Impoverished Students' Book of Cookery, Drinkery, & Housekeepery* (Portland, Oregon: Reed College Alumni Association, 1965); Jean-Georges Vongerichten and the Vong restaurant for the recipe *Chicken, Galangal, and Coconut Milk Soup;* Gene Young and Juliana Koo for the recipe *Steamed Chicken Custard Soup.*

Warner Books, Inc., 1271 Avenue of the Americas, New York, NY 10020

Ⓦ A Time Warner Company

Printed in the United States of America
First Printing: October 1995
10 9 8 7 6 5 4 3 2 1

Library of Congress Cataloging-in-Publication Data

Sheraton, Mimi.
The whole world loves chicken soup : recipes and lore to comfort
body and soul / Mimi Sheraton.
p.   cm.
Includes index.
ISBN 0-446-51737-2 (hardcover)
1. Soups. 2. Cookery (Chicken) I. Title.

TX757.S44 1994
641.8' 13—dc20

95-13372
CIP

Cover and book design by
Kathleen Herlihy-Paoli,
Inkstone Design
◆
Illustrations by Yvonne Buchanan

*This book celebrates all the mothers of the world
who season their chicken soup with love*

ACKNOWLEDGMENTS
·········◆·········

No book of this scope could be the work of only one person. Indeed, I would truly have been in the soup were it not for the generous help and guidance of the chefs, restaurateurs, scholars, and friends who are mentioned throughout the text, along with their valuable contributions of scientific data, lore, family memories, and recipes. To all of those, I say a very heartfelt thank-you for their enticing contributions.

But there are several others whose cooperation was invaluable and sustaining. Above all, I must again thank my beloved and supportive husband, Richard Falcone, not only for moral uplift but for his enormous help with original research, his translations of obscure, antique Italian cookbooks, his aid in shopping, and his cheerful (well, almost always) willingness to accept yet another chicken soup for lunch or dinner. Best of all, perhaps, was his enduring my endless harangues and observations about chicken soup, especially through the blizzards of 1994, when we were snowed in and I kept crying out for more chickens.

In a sense, this book was born at Michael's, the New York restaurant favored by publishers. I was having lunch with Pamela Bernstein, then my agent at William Morris, and after introducing me to Laurence J. Kirshbaum, the president of Warner Books, who jokingly said he would buy whatever we were discussing (as it happened, not a book at all), she challenged me to come up with an idea. A knock-down-drag-out worldwide encyclopedia of chicken soup had long intrigued me as a sort of crazy, wonderful project, and so this book took shape. I am grateful to both Pam and Larry for their brave faith in the idea. In addition, I must thank Owen Laster, who took over on my behalf when Pamela left to start her own agency, and to his assistant, Helen Breitwieser.

I owe unmeasured gratitude to Olivia B. Blumer at Warner Books, who stepped in to become the patient, impeccably exacting, and organized editor of this book, and who became a good friend along the way, no small feat in an editor-author relationship. Because of her work, there are far fewer obfuscations, oblique instructions, and just plain errors, all of which she diligently caught.

Others at Warner who made this work a coherent reality are the patient and efficient Caryn Karmatz, the exacting and organized managing editor, Harvey-Jane Kowal, and Carole Berglie, who did meticulous copyediting. The combination of Diane Luger as art director, Kathleen Herlihy-Paoli of Inkstone Design who designed the book, and Yvonne Buchanan who illustrated it, accounts for its handsome appearance.

I am grateful to Nadine Brozan who writes the Chronicle column in the *New York Times*, for leading me to information on Yasir Arafat's favorite chicken soup. And also to Richard Z. Chesnoff of *U.S. News & World Report*, who shared that soup with the P.L.O. Chairman and described it to me in detail.

One of my most valued former editors, Byron Dobell, made me realize I had the title of this book inside my head, but didn't know it.

Jessica B. Harris not only provided many explanations of African products and cooking techniques, but also added inspiration with her books *Iron Pots and Wooden Spoons, Tasting Brazil,* and, the newest, *The Welcome Table.*

Meryle Evans, a friend, writer, and diligent food historian, shared some recipes for the chicken soups of North Africa, and especially Tunisia.

Helpful nutritional data on the efficacy of chicken soup came from Dr. Marion Nestle, Professor and Chairperson, Department of Nutrition, Food and Hotel Management at New York University.

Geoffrey Beene, a dear friend who keeps me looking well put together, led me to Dr. Torre, whose charming poem appears on page 7.

Similarly, I thank Dr. Stuart I. Springer, another good friend and magically gifted orthopedic surgeon, who helped in my research for soups of African origin.

Richard Sheppard, a dear former colleague at the *New York Times* and a language and New York folklore scholar, guided me to sources for explanations on the semantics of Jewish chicken soup.

For his valuable help in researching books of many countries, I am indebted to Nach Waxman, whose cookbook shop, Kitchen Arts and Letters, is a mecca for food writers and researchers.

Although I tested almost all of the recipes myself, Sandy Gluck provided relief from the tedious work with dumplings and noodles, which she did skillfully, cheerfully, and precisely.

To all named here and throughout the text, I raise a toast not in mere champagne but in the purest, golden chicken soup. May you always know its comforts and its sweetly fragrant joys.

◆◆◆

CONTENTS

CHAPTER 7

.........◆.........

CHAPTER 8

.........◆.........

CHAPTER 9

.........◆.........

CHAPTER 10

.........◆.........

CHAPTER 11

.........◆.........

INTRODUCTION

········◆········

"It is my favorite! I have it every day. It is chicken soup!"

Had this been said by Yitzhak Rabin it would hardly be news. Jews, after all, are famous for loving chicken soup, so why not the Israeli prime minister? However, because it was said by the P.L.O. chairman, Yasir Arafat, it was worthy of mention in the "Chronicle" column of the *New York Times*.

When he was served chicken soup as Arafat's lunch guest in Tunis, Richard Z. Chesnoff, senior correspondent for *U.S. News & World Report*, asked his host if he knew that chicken soup is called Jewish penicillin because it is so popular with Jews. Arafat smiled but said he had never heard that, making him, quite possibly, the only person in the world who had not. But his smile indicated his appreciation of the irony: two bitter enemies, who until recently appeared to agree on almost nothing, share a love of chicken soup. Had President Clinton known of that common ground, he might have followed the historic handshake of September 1993 with a lunch of golden broth, perhaps ladled out of one big tureen, to seal the accord. And in the full-flavored spirit of compromise, the White House chef might have garnished the soup with the chicken, rice, and parsley (see page 165) that Arafat prefers, as well as with matzoh balls to honor Rabin.

In a way, the Yasir Arafat factor explains why I wrote this book. You really don't have to be Jewish to love chicken soup, and that is the wonder of it. No matter what the rendition, there is something almost universal in the gentle appeal of its limpid sheen, its soul-warming flavor, and the myriad enchantments of its garnishes. There is even the reassuring promise of nourishment, both physical and emotional, from its delicate but unmistakably meaty aroma as it simmers away at a "smile," the cheerful level of cooking deemed technically correct by true connoisseurs.

I cannot remember when my own love affair with chicken soup began, for having grown up in a Jewish, Eastern European family, I probably imbibed it along with mother's milk. Surely it was the lubricating elixir of our family life and my mother's proudest culinary accomplishment. In case we weren't paying attention to the things that really count, she herself would point out how clear, how golden, how rich the week's version would be, and the next day, how thoroughly the leftover soup had gelled, another mark of quality, indicating that it had been made with the right proportion of water to chicken and bones.

My mother also tended to evaluate women on their soup, and her ver-

---

smile: *(smīl) n. The cheerful level of simmering of chicken soup deemed correct by true connoisseurs.*

dict that "She can't even make decent chicken soup" left no room for doubt about the unfortunate woman's worth in other areas. In our home, chicken soup was the answer to everything, never mind the question. It appeared to celebrate triumphs and it brought comfort in sadness. It was offered when we were in blooming health and when we were ill, yet it was special enough to distinguish wedding dinners.

Sometimes when cooking chicken soup, I feel my mother speaking through me, as I repeat her litany of self-congratulations. But what surprised me as I began to travel and discover other cuisines was how much of the world shared what I thought was a Jewish passion. In fact, there seems to be almost universal agreement on the esthetic and efficacious virtues of chicken soup. Even the sophisticated Four Seasons hotel chain tantalizingly advertises that its hotels offer, among other comforts, homemade chicken soup at midnight.

That widespread appeal of this soup is due at least in part to the high status generally accorded white foods, among them, chicken. As explained by the culinary anthropologist Margaret Visser in *Much Depends on Dinner*, white food is associated with mildness and soothing innocence, "and has often been thought especially appropriate for sick people, children, and women," she writes. The same baseless but persistent delusion shapes our attitudes toward white bread and sugar, and even to the costliest honey that is known as water-white. Currently, there is a fashion for white spirits— vodka, rum, gin, and wine—though none is truly lighter in calories or alcohol content than its more colorful counterparts. In her later book, *The Rituals of Dinner*, Visser says that chicken has long been considered festive, an assessment shared by the Chinese.

The ancient Romans also held this belief, according to Alexis Soyer, the French chef who made his reputation in Victorian London, and who wrote in his history of food, *The Pantropheon*, that "according to learned physicians, the flesh of these birds is good for weakly persons as well as those who are convalescent." Soyer also cites Aristotle, who thought that because air is less dense than earth, poultry ought to stand higher in estimation than quadrupeds. In the early ages of the Christian church, Soyer continues, poultry in general was regarded as food fit for the most sacred fast days because in *Genesis* it is said that birds and fishes were created on the fifth day, whereas quadrupeds were created on the sixth. Therefore, apparently, the meaty johnnies-come lately are less exalted.

So much for chicken, but how about soup? Margaret Visser declares it a symbol of love in *The Rituals of Dinner*. Claude Lévi-Strauss, in his essay "The Roast and the Boiled" as it appears in *The Anthropologists' Cookbook*, agrees and adds the thought that boiling is the more private, family-oriented

Among the inventive bouquets several New York florists send to convalescents are bouquets that include packages of dehydrated Campbell's Chicken Soup.

type of cooking, and that it is more advanced because it requires a vessel, which is a cultural object and therefore proof of civilization. He cites the continuing references in folklore to the cauldron of immortality, but never the spit of immortality. Put all of that in your soup pot and see what a heady broth results.

How then can anyone resist the combination of love, strength, healthfulness, and celebration, all conveniently contained within a single bowl? No wonder chicken soup is considered the best food to strengthen mothers after childbirth in countries as far apart as Denmark and Ethiopia, Italy and China!

I think that chicken soup appeals not only because it is pale, and therefore symbolically pure, but also because it is golden, a color that traditionally has been prized in many dishes for its intimations of opulence and prosperity. Part of that mystique may also be psychological, if not downright metaphysical. In the dull, gray winter of regions such as Eastern Europe, golden flecks of fat glinting on the soup's surface may suggest sunlight so long absent from a leaden sky. In some cultures, the golden color of chicken soup is heightened by the addition of many carrots or sweet potatoes, or by saffron or the less expensive annatto seeds, or by browning the onions in their skins before adding them to the soup.

Practical considerations also account for the near-ubiquitousness of chicken soup. However extravagant chicken may or may not be in a given culture, the types traditionally used for making soup always represent an economy, as they do not make pleasant eating in other preparations, and protein, of all nutrients, cannot be wasted. Old roosters who have either outlived their usefulness in the barnyard or who were the losers in cockfights, and hens past their egg-laying prime, are rendered edible only by long, slow, wet cooking that moistens the meat while extracting its flavor and nutrients. Smaller chickens are fine in stews such as *coq au vin*, where their meats can gain succulence as they produce condensed, flavorful gravies, but the tougher, older birds are better simmered in soup pots where their juices leach out slowly, turning water into a golden elixir, comparable perhaps to the miracle at Cana, at least to those who value soup as much as wine.

Fortunately, not all of the world's chicken soups are alike. Some are almost as clear as spring water, albeit with a sunny shimmer, while others are richly opaque and bound with cream and egg yolks or are thickly flecked with vegetables, okra, dumplings, tortillas, noodles, rice, or barley. They may be soigné or rustic, cold or hot, gently flavored with only the fresh overtones of celery, carrots, and onions, or fiery and heady with ginger, chilies, coriander, and lemongrass, or frumpily reassuring with earthy root vegetables like parsnips, parsley root, knob celery, turnips, and even the pungent horseradish.

The recipes for this book were gathered from many sources. Most are my own versions arrived at by combining elements of recipes in many ethnic cookbooks, old and new. Others were gathered during years of travel and conversations with the cooks who prepared them. There also are a few that I adapted from soups not traditionally made with chicken but with vegetables (Green Minestrone with Chicken and Pesto, page 129) or other meats (Goulash Soup, page 146), but always in the spirit of the original. Some, such as Chicken Bouillabaisse (page 106) and Chicken Bourride (page 102), are authentically based on fish, but have been reinvented by nouvelle cuisine chefs who have already made them modern classics. Last, and certainly among the best, are a few recipes from talented chefs and restaurateurs in New York.

For the most part, the soups in this book are grouped geographically. However, because culinary geography often ignores politics, history, and religion, some countries may not be where readers might expect to find them. Cases in point are Greece and Turkey, both a part of Europe geographically; Albania, Romania, and Bulgaria, which can be classified as European, Near Eastern, or Balkan; and Armenia. These are included in Chapter 9, covering the Middle East and North Africa. All of these countries share a similar cuisine, broadly considered Middle Eastern and based on pilaffs, kabobs, yogurt, stuffed vine leaves, and, more to the point, chicken soups enriched with eggs and lemon. Israel, although truly Middle Eastern, does not appear here because the chicken soups served there are either of Eastern European Jewish origin, as in Chapter 4, or they originated in other countries from which Jews emigrated and so are covered elsewhere in this book. Unless otherwise indicated, all servings are first-course portions.

Although it is common enough to serve one chicken soup or another as a first or main course, it is rare indeed to be served an all–chicken soup dinner. Our late, great poet laureate of food, M. F. K. Fisher, describes "A Chicken Soup Supper" in her delicious cookbook *With Bold Knife and Fork*. She began by preparing a rich chicken broth that she served in hot pitchers. Pouring this into bowls, guests helped themselves from a buffet set with bowls of chopped chicken meat, hot rice or buckwheat kasha, chopped parsley, chives or scallions, cream perhaps mixed with curry powder, hard-cooked eggs, sautéed mushrooms, and ground pecans or almonds, all to be mixed and matched to individual tastes.

Intrigued by the great variety of ethnic soups, I planned a dinner in which every course was a different kind of chicken soup. I served each of six soups in the bowl or cup, and with the spoon, that seemed most appropriate to its strength and richness.

The meal began with drinks and hors d'oeuvres in the living room, and

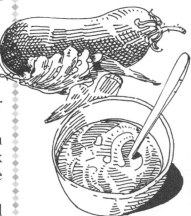

I utilized the by-product chicken livers by blending them into a mild, smooth, brandy-scented pâté. To add fish, a flavor element that would not be present in the rest of the meal, I also prepared canapés of buttered Danish pumpernickel topped with smoked salmon and red salmon caviar, accented by dill and lemon.

The first soup was Baked Chicken Custard, a cold, thick, ivory blend of strong broth, cream, and egg yolks, cooked and then chilled to attain the custard texture. I served it in small ramekins along with tiny, antique silver spoons that had vermeil bowls, the gold lining indicating that perhaps the spoons were meant to be used for soft-boiled eggs.

Drinks and Hors d'oeuvres
◆
Baked Chicken Custard (page 101)
◆
Yunnan Steamed Chicken Soup (page 207)
◆
Ezra Tull's Gizzard Soup (page 58)
◆
Sopa de Fideos (page 70)
◆
Poltava Borscht (page 156)
◆
Fried Chicken and Andouille Filé Gumbo (page 61)
◆
Assorted Breads
◆
Apple Tart
◆
Wine: Dolcetto d'Alba

The bracing Yunnan Steamed Chicken Soup, aromatic with ginger, scallions, and rice wine, also lent itself to small portions; and because it was clear, I ladled it into demitasse cups from which it could be sipped, requiring no spoons.

Ranging from light to heavy, both in texture and in flavor, we proceeded to Ezra Tull's Gizzard Soup, the Hungarian-via-Baltimore literary adaptation of Anne Tyler, for her memorable novel *Dinner at the Homesick*

Restaurant. I used small shallow bowls and regular teaspoons for this, realizing that the pungent overtones of garlic and the knowledge that gizzards were the basis for the soup might cause guests to partake cautiously. Several stopped at the first taste, saying politely they were pacing themselves; others downed every drop.

Next came Sopa de Fideos, the thin but piquant Mexican chicken soup enlivened with tomato, green chilies, garlic, avocado, coriander, and lacy golden-brown *fideos*, the noodles as fine as the threads they are named for. Dessert-size Japanese lotus bowls held the soup that was eaten from white porcelain Chinese spoons, a cross-cultural mix that proved practical.

Standard cream soup bowls and spoons worked for the Poltava Borscht, a rustic Ukrainian combination of chicken, beets, cabbage, and other vegetables, strewn with dill and sour cream and fleshed out with chewy dumplings.

The last course, served in big, wide soup plates with full-size tablespoons, was Fried Chicken and Andouille Filé Gumbo, a lusty and savory Cajun charmer, with a mound of steamed white rice as a foil for its tangy herbs and spices.

To restore palates between courses, there were sesame breadsticks, cheddar cheese twists, French baguettes, blue cornmeal taco chips, and Chinese fried noodles.

Dessert was a coolly sweet and light crustless apple tart. Wine posed a problem as my husband, whose department this is, preferred to stick to one for the sake of simplicity. His solution worked beautifully. He decided that since there would be drinks with the hors d'oeuvres and the first two soups were small and intense, we would serve no wine at all with those. After that, he poured Dolcetto d'Alba, a dry, sprightly red from Italy's Piedmont region, that complemented and stood up to the diverse and assertive seasonings of the final four soups. Suitable alternatives would be a California cabernet or, among French wines, a Beaune or a Côtes du Rhône.

Admittedly, that's a lot of chicken soup for one night, but then there are a lot of great chicken soups in the world, and only a limited time in which to enjoy them all, and I hope you do.

> *If you use "chicken soup" as a modifier—as in "chicken-soup philosophy," "chicken-soup treatment," or even "chicken-soup regimen," you are turning the phrase into a compound attributive noun, which requires a hyphen (and a well-parsed parsnip wouldn't hurt).*
>
> —WILLIAM SAFIRE, *NEW YORK TIMES* COLUMNIST AND LANGUAGE CRITIC

ODES TO CHICKEN SOUPS

·········◆·········

C hicken soup brings out the poet in many, including professionals such as Allen Ginsberg (page 44) and Maurice Sendak, the artist-writer whose miniature Nutshell Library delights children with its tiny volume *Chicken Soup and Rice*. It also inspires amateurs like Dr. Douglas Torre, a New Orleans native whose mother specialized in chicken gumbo, like those on pages 59 and 61. But in New York where he practices dermatology, Dr. Torre adopted the Jewish chicken soup mystique, and celebrated it in the following poem.

Chicken Soup

Mama had the secret recipe
For medicine to comfort me.
Not antibiotic by description,
Chicken soup was her prescription.
Feeling depressed and oh, so blue,
Chicken soup was right for you.
And for a newly broken heart,
Chicken soup could do its part.
If in bed with sniffle sneezes,
Fever, aches, or loud wheezes,
For nourishment at noon or night,
Chicken soup was always right.
But, for chicken soup to be expedient,
Love must be its main ingredient.

—DOUGLAS TORRE

Chapter 1

IS IT REALLY PENICILLIN?

The pros and cons of chicken soup as a curative •
Separating sentiment from science • Mother's myths and
medical experiments in Miami Beach

On the off chance that your mother never told you, chicken soup is good for just about everything that ails you. Could such a widely held belief be false? Did people ever believe that the earth was flat or that the sun revolved around it?

The universality of that belief is even more mysterious than chicken soup's ecumenical gustatory appeal. After all, many foods and flavor combinations are favorites in widely different cultures, among them chocolate, sweet desserts, rice with beans or chicken, and pastas-of-all-nations. But none of those share chicken soup's reputation as a strength-builder and a primary cure for colds and flu. Perhaps only bitter foods such as certain greens, roots, and onions are held in equally high and widespread repute as systemic purifiers, and it is probably their bitterness that suggests medicinal properties. Even Moses Maimonides, the twelfth-century philosopher and physician, wrote that chicken soup was excellent as both food and medicine. But then, of course, he was Jewish.

The actual physical benefits of chicken soup have been both refuted and upheld, and we might as well get the bad news over with first. Given the current fears of cholesterol, fat, and sodium, it is no surprise that some nutritionists and physicians have in recent years denounced this soup as a devil's brew, even though it has far less fat than soups based on beef or other red meats. Fat can be greatly if not totally banished (see Low-Fat Chicken Soup, page 31), but if it were possible to eliminate all fat and sodium, the result would be about as appealing as unsalted hot water in which vegetables and chicken had been summarily dunked.

Calculating a consistently accurate nutrient breakdown of homemade chicken soup is impossible, as it depends not only on a specific and uniform recipe but the fat and sodium content of the particular chicken and vegetables used. There is even the sodium in the water to be considered as well as evaporation and therefore the concentration of components in the final soup. Indeed, in this regard, canned or dehydrated soups allow for more consistent nutrient data as they are adjusted, one trusts, to match the breakdowns printed on their labels.

So let's admit that chicken soup as we know and love it may not be what every doctor orders. It has also been my experience that chicken soup is not the best thing to settle an upset stomach, although I have found it to be a restorative third step following the usual warm Coca-Cola (Classic, please), then dry toast and weak, lightly sweetened tea. After that, it's clear, strong chicken soup sipped from a cup, to be followed by a bowlful flecked with rice or pastina, those tiny asterisks of baby-fine pasta. As a complete cure, the delectable final stage for me is chicken soup not only with pastina but with an egg beaten into it to form soft curds that enfold gently melting grated Parmesan.

As a special promotion a few years ago, the Empire Poultry Company, purveyors of kosher poultry, offered a chicken soup recipe to anyone who sent in a box top from cough drops or other cold remedy.

As for the good news, there is first the simple, practical advantages of having something hot when you feel a chill. Also, the aroma and flavor whet the appetite, and with some added solids—bits of chicken, vegetables, pasta, or rice—the soup offers valuable nourishment. Because soup generally engenders thirst, it causes one to drink water, another aid in recovering from a cold or flu. Then there is the psychological lift gained from sipping something as warm, golden, and homey as a savory broth, especially if it is a lore-enriched, sentimental favorite connected to home, mother, a nurturing spouse, or—these days—a friendly delivery boy from a nearby Chinese restaurant. That in itself can boost one's sense of well-being and so inspire the positive thinking that leads to feeling "better."

Wondering if it is true what they say about chicken soup, three scientists at Mount Sinai Hospital in Miami Beach conducted an experiment and reported their findings in the professional journal for respiratory specialists. The results, as you might guess, proved chicken soup the winner, with hot water a close second. However, all nasal passages returned to their former clogged states thirty minutes after the treatment was stopped.

Other studies have reported the results of drinking hot tea similar to those for soup, and all indicate that the benefit is greater when the cup or bowl is not covered with a lid (as they were in experiments with straws), so that vapors rise into the nasal passages. One lesson, then, is not to sip chicken soup through a straw, especially if it contains matzoh balls.

I asked Dr. Marvin A. Sackner, one of the authors of the study done at Mount Sinai Hospital, why chicken soup did better than hot water and perhaps if the fat content had provided extra lubrication. He felt that aroma was the more decisive factor. Unfortunately, his team did not test beef broth against chicken, nor did he try one of my mother's favorite cold remedies—brandy, cloves, and butter stirred into tea, thereby adding aroma and fatty lubrication.

During severe head colds, I feel extra relief from a mug of chicken broth laced with an ounce of warmed vodka, a shot or two of lemon juice, or a half-and-half blend with hot clam juice. My most dependable chicken soup cure for a really stubborn, clogging head cold is Chinese Hot and Sour Soup (page 204). In that bewitching brew, the hot pepper and pungent vinegar cause cascades of water to flow from nose and eyes, clearing the passages so one can really taste and smell the soothing sesame oil, the fragrant ginger, and earthy dried mushrooms, and then regain strength from the protein boost of bean curd, egg drops, and chicken. You don't need a fortune cookie to predict the effectiveness of this cold remedy.

Chapter 2

IN THE SOUP

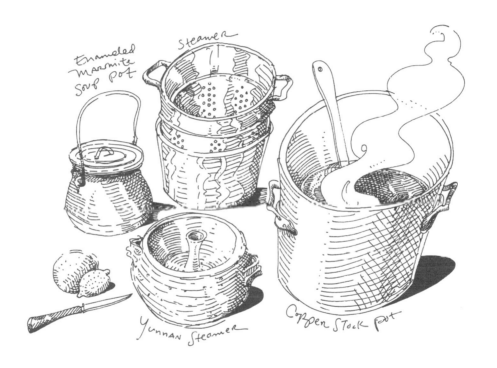

Choosing the right chicken and preparing it • Basic ingredients and instructions on cooking, finishing, storing, and serving

There is something magical about the soup-making process, as each ingredient gives up its essence for the good of the new and harmonious whole, as water is transformed into a nourishing elixir. Taste, color, and texture develop during the gentle simmering, as the cook nudges flavors into place with the gradual additions of salt, herbs, and spices—gradual because the intensity of the seasonings increases as the liquid evaporates, and so caution is wise at the earliest stages. I am most in awe of chicken soup in progress because of the tantalizing aromas and reassuring flavors that emanate from a broth as lustrously transparent as a yellow diamond.

As with almost everything that appears simple, the preparation of chicken soup requires great attention to detail and allows little margin for error. The most elemental requirements for this soup are a chicken, water, a pot, cooking fuel, and salt. A soup without salt is to me even more disappointing than an unsalted egg, although it is a deprivation that must be endured if a physician has so indicated. (My solution to that verdict would be to find another doctor who is more relenting.)

All of which leaves the following considerations.

IN THE BEGINNING, THERE IS CHICKEN

.... ◆ ....

A fowl, hen, or stewing chicken (the terms may be used interchangeably) is my favorite for soup. In the best of all possible worlds, it would be a 6-pound kosher bird that was raised truly free-range. It would also be freshly killed, whether from a live poultry market or a farm. Ideally, it should be a pullet, a young female that has not yet reached the egg-laying stage. In its strictest sense, "free-range" indicates a chicken that has walked around the barnyard eating worms, bugs, and other goodies instead of being cooped up with chemically hyped feed for its entire life. "Free-range" today often means a chicken that has walked around a lot, but lives on prepared feed that may or may not be organic and which, according to my tests

Chicken feet, highly prized for the flavor and viscosity they lend to soup, can only be had with freshly killed chickens, as it has been illegal to sell them separately. They must be scalded for about 5 minutes in boiling water, then rinsed in cold water so that the tough, scaly outer skin loosens and can be removed along with the toenails. The gizzard will also have to be scalded. It should be split and the contents of the stomach discarded. Boil for 5 minutes, rinse under cold water, and pull off the yellowish crinkled lining from the inside of the stomach.

with any size bird, provides so little flavor bonus for soup it is hardly worth the extra cost. I like a kosher chicken for soup because it has been thoroughly bled, resulting in a clearer broth with a quintessential pure chicken taste, and because of the strict dietary laws, it is most likely to be fresh.

For practicality, however, my choice from a high-quality butcher shop or supermarket would be the kosher *fowl* if possible. In many markets, fowls can be ordered if they are not stocked. Six pounds is the ideal size because the bird has grown enough to develop flavor and can be cooked in enough water (usually about 12 cups or 3 quarts) to provide a generous amount of rich soup. The meat of that bird will be edible if kept moist and served in the soup, or in a salad with an oil-based dressing such as mayonnaise or vinaigrette, or in chicken pie, or as a sandwich made with lettuce and butter or a dressing.

A SOUP CHICKEN OR FOWL—an older, larger, wrinkled-skin specimen with an unevenly shaped, stiff-boned breast and at the end of her egg-laying days—makes good soup, but the meat will be dry and stringy. This type of bird is useful, however, if the soup or stock is all you are after.

A ROOSTER OR COCK (as in Cock-a-Leekie, page 88) is a nearly comparable, if rarely marketed bird, weighing about 7 pounds. The meat will be only marginally edible, but the soup will be fine.

A ROASTER is the 5- to 7-pound chicken commonly found in our markets. I think it is excessively fatty and cooks too rapidly to produce a well-flavored soup.

BROILERS of 3½ to 4½ pounds are better choices than the roaster, although it might be necessary to buy two, or one and a half to equal the weight of a fowl called for in a recipe. The largest of these broilers are preferable; anything under 3½ pounds will be immature and flavorless. When

BUYING AND CLEANING LIVE POULTRY

◆◆◆

Live poultry markets can still be found in large cities, usually in Chinese, Hispanic, Italian, Eastern European, Islamic, and Jewish neighborhoods, and in some rural areas there are chicken farms selling to the public. In most such places, chickens can be slaughtered kosher style, without the religious ritual but by cutting the jugular vein so that all the blood drains out. When selecting a live chicken, look for a supple breastbone and a light yellow layer of fat seen under the smooth skin when the feathers are blown. Freshly killed chickens must be even more thoroughly cleaned, then lightly salted or sprinkled with lemon juice inside and out, covered with waxed paper or plastic wrap, and kept under refrigeration for between 24 and 48 hours before being cooked; if rigor mortis has not subsided, the meat will be tough. Singe no more than 5 or 6 hours before cooking (see page 17).

using broilers instead of fowl, it is a good idea to use 25 percent more chicken or less water, and to add a veal knuckle for extra body.

CAPONS, the most expensive of chickens, are castrated males weighing 6 to 9 pounds and are primarily used for roasting. They are also luscious when poached, and produce a luxurious yet delicate soup much favored in Italy (see Capon Broth, page 122). As they are quite fat, the soup will need diligent skimming.

FROZEN CHICKEN is not desirable for soup, but if it is the only option, increase the weight called for by half and add some decent canned chicken broth (see page 30) to the cooking water for extra body. Never refreeze thawed frozen poultry. It can be dangerous, and at best provides stringy, tasteless meat.

Chicken Trimmings

Raw carcasses (much favored for soup in Asia; see Basic Asian Chicken Soup, page 192), necks, backbones, wing tips, and all giblets except livers can be added to chicken or used alone to make stock or a soup that calls for no chicken meat. Use the same amount, by weight, called for in a recipe for fowl, but know that the flavor will be thinner. Theoretically this is an economical practice, but such parts are difficult to find now that so many markets buy poultry already cut up, and so have few of the trimmings. Most markets sell chicken wings and drumsticks that can be used for soup, and in some neighborhoods, other trimmings might be available, but sniff them carefully for freshness, as described below.

Buying, Cleaning, and Storing

When buying chicken, I always smell it for freshness, even if that means lifting or poking a small hole in the plastic wrap around supermarket packages. There should be no hint of ammonia, chemicals, sourness or ripeness—just a fresh, meaty scent. Avoid any packaged chicken that contains a lot of pink liquid, or any chicken with skin or meat that looks bruised, dark, and dry, or shows blood spots. The skin should feel firm, not slippery, and no brown blood coagulation should show at cut joints.

In a supermarket, it is better to buy whole chickens than those cut into parts, even if you want the chicken cut up for cooking. At a butcher shop, it is fine to have the whole chicken cut up when you order it. An intact chicken is more likely to remain fresh and retain its juices.

Once home, unwrap the chicken immediately, whether it is in butcher's

> *The rooster and the chicken had a fight,*
>
> *The chicken knocked the rooster out of sight,*
>
> *The rooster told the chicken, That's all right,*
>
> *I'll meet you in the gumbo tomorrow night.*
>
> —"THE ROOSTER AND THE CHICKEN," AN OLD LOUISIANA NURSERY RHYME

paper or a supermarket package. Rinse it under running cold water and trim off excess fat, especially around cavity and neck, and any bits of tubes, raggedy innards, excess skin such as the crop, and livery globs along the inside backbone that will turn bitter during cooking. Pat the chicken dry. To get rid of the excessive chickeny odor (the Chinese achieve this by blanching—see Basic Asian Chicken Soup, page 192), sprinkle the chicken inside and out with salt (preferably coarse), lemon juice, or a little brandy, depending on the particular dish to be prepared. Then loosely wrap the bird in waxed paper or plastic wrap and store it in the meat drawer or in the lowest (coldest) part of the refrigerator until cooking time. Rinse before cooking. After 24 hours, rerinse chicken and either cook it or rewrap and store in the refrigerator for no more than two additional days.

Singeing

Commercial chickens usually are free of feathers, but examine them anyway, especially if you buy a fowl and certainly if you buy a free-range or fresh-killed chicken. Using fingers or tweezers, pluck out any feathery vestiges or stubby pinfeathers and check carefully around wings, drumsticks, and along the back for the fine hairs that must be singed. To singe a chicken, hold it above a moderate flame or coil of a stove burner and rotate it, letting the wings or legs hang lower if necessary. It is unwise to singe a chicken more than 5 or 6 hours before it will be cooked. The heat tends to melt the fat in the skin, and when that fat has broken down, the meat spoils more rapidly. A chicken that is to be frozen or stored for more than 5 or 6 hours should be singed just before it is cooked.

PREPARING THE CHICKEN FOR SOUP: TO CUT OR NOT TO CUT

Cooking a chicken whole produces a clearer, stronger soup because the chicken takes longer to cook than one that is cut up. However, it usually requires more water to cover the chicken. To section a chicken for soup, I prefer not to cut through too many bones, thereby exposing the bloody sort of marrow that can cloud the soup. (In many old cookbooks, the recipes for chicken soup for convalescents advise cracking the bones as an extra source of nutrients.) I disjoint the chicken instead of cutting it into com-

Although President Herbert Hoover usually gets credit for the campaign promise of "a chicken in every pot," according to William Safire, in his New Political Dictionary, Hoover never uttered the phrase. Rather, its origin goes back to Henri IV of France (1553–1610), who said, "I wish there would not be a peasant so poor in all my realm who would not have a chicken in his pot every Sunday." (See page 110 for Henri's favorite poule-au-pot.)

plete quarters. To do that, cut skin around the hindquarters and pull back from carcass until disjointed. Cut skin and flesh free of backbone. Break off lower half of backbone. Whole breast with wings and upper backbone are in one piece, for a total of four pieces. (See diagram.) It requires no more water to be covered and results in moister, more flavorful breast meat.

Some recipes call for trussing the chicken when preparing soup. I find that this does less for the soup than for the chicken by enabling it to cook evenly.

Bones

B ones add a gelatinous richness, extra nutrients, and flavor to chicken soup. They also cause the soup to gel when cold, an advantage when making Jellied Consommé (page 84), although powdered gelatin easily performs that function.

A calf's foot is the most flavorful addition for gelling, and usually any butcher selling it will have it already cleaned and scalded and, probably, frozen. Have him split it for you. It is not necessary to thaw before adding it to the soup pot.

Veal knuckles or long beef marrow bones are more readily available and fine for flavor, but you will need one or two pieces to make soup truly gel. They will add fat to the soup, but they provide a rich bonus for those who eat the poached marrow, either spread on toast or diced and put back into the soup. Bones add minerals to the soup, too, most especially calcium, which is extracted most efficiently if the bones are soaked in a little vinegar or lemon juice for about 20 minutes before being patted dry and added to the soup; the acid helps leach out the calcium. At least this was the advice of Adelle Davis, the health-food guru of the 1950s, which was corroborated by Harold McGee, the author of *On Food and Cooking*: *The Science and Lore of the Kitchen*, who felt that the suggestion made sense.

Pot Vegetables and Herbs

U sed as flavorings, pot vegetables, or soup greens, as they are known—carrots, celery, onions, leeks, various roots, and parsley— must be fresh. Such combinations are often sold packaged in produce departments of supermarkets. Corn and other vegetables intended as garnishes—peas and lima beans, for example—may be frozen but should be added to soup unthawed for the last 10 or 15 minutes of cooking or reheating.

It is often suggested that pot vegetables along with parsley, thyme, bay leaf, and such be added to soup in the form of a bouquet garni—tied in a bunch with kitchen string—so they can easily be extricated. I have found this step usually pointless, since the vegetables slip out of the bundle as they soften in cooking. Furthermore, all soups are strained one way or another, and so the vegetables and herbs are easily eliminated.

Water

In most parts of the country, cold (never hot) tap water is fine for soup. However, if you live in an area where the water tastes heavily of chlorine or has otherwise peculiar flavors, those will affect your soup, just as they do your coffee. If that bothers you, it is best to prepare soup from the relatively inexpensive uncarbonated spring water sold in big plastic bottles in supermarkets. It would be a ridiculous waste to buy imported water.

Salt

Sea salt is lovely and mild for table use, but an unnecessary expense for soup. However, I do not use iodized salt for any cooking, as it imparts chemical overtones. Kosher coarse salt, available in most supermarkets, is preferable for all cooking, as is sea salt at the table.

A CHICKEN IN EVERY POT, BUT WHICH POT?

If you study the shape of the pots illustrated here, you will see that they are all taller than they are wide, relatively narrow, and straight-sided. Some also taper toward the top. That shape enables you to cover the chicken and other solids with a minimum of water if the chicken and other ingredients are placed in the closest-fitting size. The tapering soup kettle also allows for easy skimming of fat and foamy solids.

The material of the pot matters, too. I prefer enameled cast-iron marmites or kettles for soups because they are well insulated and the surface is virtually nonreactive—unless the enamel is chipped, in which case the iron leaches out. Enameled steel is a less expensive, lighter-weight second choice, but it offers poor insulation, so the liquid evaporates more rapidly as the soup takes longer to cook. Also, enameled steel chips easily, so it must be used carefully. My third choice would be a stainless-steel pot with a clad (aluminum or copper) bottom to distribute heat evenly. I do not like to cook soup in aluminum, for, as Harold McGee states in *On Food and Cooking: The Science and Lore of the Kitchen*, the unanodized aluminum develops a thin oxide layer (darkens) when in contact with acids, alkalis, and anything sulphurous, such as eggs, and so turns the contents gray or black, a disadvantage with anything so light colored as chicken soup. McGee also notes that such aluminum intensifies the odor of cabbage, used in many of the soups in this book, and I find it does the same with turnips and other strong-flavored roots. If soup is cooked in aluminum, it should be stored in a glass, ceramic, or other nonreactive vessel.

All of my considerations here are either esthetic or relate to cooking efficiency, although there are lingering health questions about aluminum. In his book, McGee states that there is no toxic effect on humans from aluminum, and that most of the concern about its causing Alzheimer's disease has been refuted. There still seem to be some questions, however, about its effect on nutrients. I use restaurant-weight anodized aluminum pots only for things boiled in a great deal of water for a short time (pasta, lobster, shrimp, corn-on-the-cob), because such pots tend to be huge and other materials are expensive and heavy to handle.

Classic French copper stockpots or marmites lined in tin are wonderful as long as the tin is smooth and intact, but such pots need relining if the copper begins to show through. Also excellent is copper lined with stainless steel, which never needs relining. However, copper is extremely heavy and difficult to handle in large sizes and is also very expensive.

> *A really wonderful homemade chicken soup is enriched with self-satisfaction, an incomparable seasoning for which there is no ready substitute.*

COOKING THE SOUP

·········· ◆ ··········

I f the quality of the finished chicken is more important than the broth, start cooking it in boiling water that seals in juices and results in a slightly less flavorful broth. If the soup's the thing, as it surely is in this book, place the chicken, giblets, and bones in the pot with cold water. Cover the pot, bring the water to a boil, reduce to a simmer, and using a large tablespoon or a small, unslotted, metal cooking spoon, begin to skim off foamy solids and scum that rise to the surface. This is standard advice intended to produce a clear soup without floating fragments, but many old ethnic cookbooks advise against skimming foam for the sake of added nutrition. Its flavor is pleasant and much like that of marrow.

When the foam has subsided and the soup is clear and simmering, add vegetables and seasonings as described in the recipe for Basic Chicken Soup (page 28). Be sure the soup cooks steadily and, most ideally, at the low simmer known as a smile—a sort of twinkling, trembly, faint rippling just below the surface. Cooked too rapidly, soup becomes cloudy and the chicken meat will toughen, as will all protein cooked at high heat.

Recommending the smile as the proper rate for cooking soup or bouillon, the eighteenth-century French literary gastronome Jean Anthelme Brillat-Savarin, in his classic work, *The Physiology of Taste* (best is the M. F. K. Fisher translation published by Knopf), says that is the only way to husband the substance in meats known as osmazome. This he describes as "the preeminently sapid part of meat which is soluble in cold water, and which differs completely from the extractive part of the meat, which is soluble only in water that is boiling." He points out that it is osmazome that gives the value to soups and that it is present only in truly red meat (not lamb or pork, for example) and the dark flesh of poultry. A soup made with only the white meat of chicken, then, would be lacking in hefty flavor.

Referring to the osmazome theory in his invaluable book on the science of cooking, Harold McGee states that we now know the problem of flavor is much more complicated, but that Brillat-Savarin and his confrères were not entirely wrong. Too rapid heating, McGee told me, causes meat to tense up and therefore not release flavor molecules efficiently to create a soup—technically an extract, if not quite an infusion.

FINISHING THE SOUP

I ndividual recipes throughout this book indicate when the chicken and solids should be removed from the soup and how they should be handled. All clear chicken soups should be strained to catch stray solids, bits of bone, and so on. Unless the soup is to be very refined, I use a regular kitchen strainer set over a bowl or, if I am in a hurry and all solids are to be removed together, I use a Chinese skimmer—a large, round, slightly concave wire strainer at the end of a long bamboo handle that reaches to the bottom of large soup pots. For especially clear soup, use the fine-meshed conical sieve known as a chinois. For the clearest, most elegant soup, use a double thickness of unused, dampened cheesecloth as a lining for either a regular strainer or a chinois.

Skimming the Soup

Skimming fat from soup with a stainless-steel spoon can be done at several points. Some can be skimmed off as it appears during cooking. Or, if you prefer, it can be done after cooking. Adding a couple ice cubes to hot soup will aid the process. First skim with a spoon, tipping the pot to remove as much fat as possible. Then use sheets of clean, dry paper towels as blotters; lay them gently, one at a time, over the surface of the soup. As each sheet absorbs fat, remove it carefully and replace with a clean piece of towel.

The cooler the soup, the easier it will be to degrease. Easiest of all is the skimming of soup that has been chilled, as the coagulated fat virtually lifts off. However, if soup is to be stored for one to three days in the refrigerator, it is best to remove the fat just before cooking, as it is a protective layer that keeps air away from the broth. Similarly, if you freeze chicken soup, scrape off the fat just before thawing; if it has been frozen for more than a week, be sure to remove and discard fat completely before heating, because it never totally freezes and can impart a musty flavor to the soup. It is neither possible nor desirable to remove all fat from chicken soup. Not to worry, as it adds much of the flavor.

Reducing the Soup

Consommé is reduced, clarified meat or poultry broth. It may be garnished with various solids (see Garnished Consommé, page 100).

The water content of soup can be greatly reduced by very long, slow cooking—say, 3 to 4 hours for a soup that began with 12 to 14 cups—partly covered and with all of the chicken and vegetables in it, although they will be virtually inedible by that time. (Meat and bone soups are more generally prepared that way than those with poultry.) If you want to serve the chicken, remove it when it is done, about 1½ hours, along with all other solids. Then gently reduce the soup by simmering it steadily, uncovered, until you have the desired amount. Double consommé means that the cooked broth has been reduced by half, and triple consommé means it has been reduced to one third of its original volume, by which time it will be dark in color and strong in flavor.

Chicken Soup for the Soul *was understandably the title chosen by Jack Canfield and Mark Victor Hansen for their bestselling collection of "101 stories to open the heart and rekindle the spirits."*

Clarifying

I feel it is necessary only to truly clarify soup beyond straining it through cheesecloth if it is to be served cold, when coagulated fat globules are unpleasant. This is because clarification subtracts flavor. To clarify chicken broth, remove all solids, strain, cool, and skim the fat from the surface. Prepare a strainer lined with a triple thickness of unused, dampened cheesecloth and set it over a bowl large enough to hold the soup. For 2 quarts of clear soup, lightly crush the uncooked shells of 2 raw eggs and add them to the cold broth along with their lightly beaten whites, stirring gently until the stock simmers, at which point you should stop stirring. Reduce the heat to an almost imperceptible simmer until a thick, rather firm cap of white foam forms, about 5 to 8 minutes. Let cool for 10 minutes, then pour the soup gently through the lined sieve, trying not to break the foam; let foam drain through the cloth for 7 or 8 minutes. All solids should have been collected by the egg white, or albumen. Add salt to taste when you reheat the clarified soup.

STORING CHICKEN SOUP

There are many thick soups in this book that improve in flavor when kept chilled for a day or two, and, of course, chicken soup that is to be served clear can certainly be covered and stored for up to three days in the coldest part of the refrigerator. If it is to be held after three days, re-simmer it for 15 minutes, cool, cover, and refrigerate for up to two days more. However, I think that clear chicken soup tastes best fresh and takes on a flat, stale flavor with each day of storage and each reheating. The same is true of the chicken, which should be stored in the refrigerator, out of the soup, and wrapped in waxed paper or plastic wrap. If you are freezing leftovers, however, put the chicken in the soup.

Soup should be thoroughly cooled, *uncovered*, before being covered and stored in the freezer or refrigerator. Covering warm soup can cause it to ferment. It is safest to chill the soup rapidly, either by dropping a couple ice cubes into it or by setting it in a sinkful of ice water and stirring several times.

Chicken soup keeps if solidly frozen for three months, but I find two months a better limit for the sake of flavor.

Do not season chicken soup while it is cold, as you are sure to oversalt it. Heat before adjusting the flavor. You are also likely to oversalt anything you cook if you taste it from a wooden spoon. Use an ordinary stainless-steel tablespoon or, if you like specialized equipment, a porcelain tasting spoon. A sterling or silver-plated spoon is not a good idea for tasting and skimming because the metal tarnishes.

SERVING SOUP

........◆........

Cold soups should be served very cold; hot soups, steamingly hot. Bowls should be of porcelain or earthenware, with glass reserved for cold soups only. Chill the bowls for cold soups. For hot soups, place the bowls on a warm spot near the stove or in a 250° F. oven for about 5 minutes, or fill them with boiling water and dry them before adding soup. Or for a large number, place the bowls in the dishwasher set on the dry stage. Plates that go under soup bowls need not be heated or chilled, as they protect wood tabletops from temperature extremes.

Given the normal limitations of storage space and budgets, a wardrobe of soup bowls and spoons in many shapes and sizes is impractical. Still, there are some attractive, moderately priced, sturdy basic variations that greatly add to the enjoyment of soup.

As a general rule, you will want smaller bowls with spoons to fit them for very rich or intense soups, especially those that are creamed. The so-called cream soup bowl, traditionally with two ears and a matching plate, is attractive for consommé and first-course portions of thick soups such as chowders. Cereal bowls are good substitutes. The cream soup bowl holds between 1 1/2 and 2 cups of soup. The cream soup spoon to fit this should have a round bowl, but an oval medium-size tablespoon or dessert spoon will do. It is similar to but smaller than a round bouillon spoon.

Main-course soups that usually contain meat and vegetables, some of which may have to be eaten with a fork and perhaps even a knife, should be served in the large, wide bowls that used to be known as soup plates and that now double for serving pasta. Because such soups are served in large quantities, it is best to use large oval tablespoons that enable one to eat the soup more rapidly than with a small spoon.

Those are the two most basic types of bowls, but for smaller portions of clear consommé and cream soups, especially those without solids that can be sipped, use either a standard tea or coffee cup that is round-bowled rather than deep and straight-sided.

Inexpensive and attractive small porcelain Asian soup bowls that may

Chicken soup was the traditional Sunday-night supper at my grandmother's house in Chicago. It was made by her Swedish cook, Anna, and was thick and yellow because she used a big, fat fowl. There were fluffy baking powder drop dumplings and shredded chicken breast meat floating in it, and it was ladled out of a big white ironstone salad bowl. It was the meal we most looked forward to as children.

—JOHN LORING, DESIGN DIRECTOR, TIFFANY & CO.

have covers are also pleasant to use, especially if you add traditional porcelain spoons, available from $1 and up in Chinese and Japanese shops. These bowls and spoons are also available in lacquer, but they cannot be put in a dishwasher and seem right only for the lightest, clearest of Japanese broths (see page 211).

For an idea on how to match soup to bowl, see my description of an all–chicken soup dinner party, pages 4–6.

Tureens can be stunning accessories on a table, but they should be large enough to hold the needed number of portions without being refilled. They should be used only when one can serve from them without making a mess. A tureen should be warmed for hot soup or chilled for cold soups.

To serve soup neatly from the pot, use a slotted kitchen spoon to remove equal portions of solids and place them in individual bowls. Then use a ladle to add liquid.

Chapter 3

BASIC SOUPMANSHIP

Soup plate

Cream Soup bowl & Spoon

Asian lotus Bowl

Asian Spoon

Ramekin

Asian Bowl

Rim Soup Bowl

*Recipes for basic soups, homemade and canned,
and for noodles, dumplings, egg drops, crepes, and
other classic garnishes*

There are a few basic recipes for chicken soups and garnishes that appear under various names throughout the world, with the exception of Asia. (Most Asian soups and garnishes are very different, and are described in the recipes for those countries.) Those generic recipes are described here for easy reference.

DEFINING TERMS

Soup, broth, stock, consommé, and bouillon *all have various meanings. Throughout this book, I have tended to use* soup *and* broth *interchangeably because so many of the preparations have clear soup or broth bases, and because I got tired of repeating the same word. For the record, here is what is meant by their use.*

SOUP *refers to the finished dish of* both liquid and solids, as in Cock-a-Leekie Soup, Baked Cottage Soup, or Corn and Chicken Soup. But I also use it for the liquid alone—that is, "skim and strain soup before adding matzoh balls."

BROTH *is the clear liquid to which solids may be added.*

STOCK, *used rarely in this book, is a mildly seasoned broth on which other soups (or, in general cooking, other* dishes such as sauces and stews) are based. True stock has to be finished to become a soup.

CONSOMMÉ *is the often misused, raised-pinkie euphemism for broth. Classically, it is broth or soup that is reduced and clarified and is served clear, hot or cold, with or without solid garnishes.*

BOUILLON *is a synonym for* stock *or* broth.

BASIC CHICKEN SOUP

The vegetables included here, as well as the optional ones listed, make up what are known as pot vegetables or soup greens.

FOR THE SOUP
One 5- to 6-pound fowl, or 7 to 8 pounds of broilers, with neck and
    all giblets except liver
10 to 12 cups water, as needed
2 medium carrots, scraped and quartered
2 or 3 celery stalks with leaves, whole or cut in half
1 medium yellow onion, whole or cut in half, peeled or unpeeled
3 parsley sprigs, preferably the flat Italian type
8 to 10 black peppercorns
2 to 3 teaspoons coarse salt, or 1 to 2 teaspoons table salt, or to taste

FOR THE OPTIONAL GARNISH
Chopped fresh parsley and/or dill

....

Clean, trim, and singe chicken as described on page 17. Quarter the chicken if necessary; see page 17. Place quartered chicken in a close-fitting 5-quart soup pot. A whole chicken should fit into a 6- to 7-quart pot. Add 10 cups water if you use broilers or 12 if you use a fowl. Water should cover chicken. Cover pot and bring to a boil. Reduce to a slow simmer and skim foam as it rises to the surface. Soup should cook at a smile (see page 21).

When foam subsides, add all remaining ingredients with only 1 teaspoonful of salt. Cook chicken until it is loosening from the bone. If chicken is quartered, allow about $1\frac{1}{4}$ hours for cooking broilers and $2\frac{1}{2}$ to 3 hours for a fowl. If you cook the chickens whole, allow an extra 15 minutes for broilers and 30 minutes for the fowl. Add more water during cooking if chicken is not seven-eighths covered. Turn chicken 2 or 3 times during cooking. Add salt gradually, tasting as the soup progresses.

Remove chicken, giblets, and bones and set aside. Pour soup through a sieve, rinse pot, and then return soup to pot if it is to be served immediately. Skim fat from surface of soup if it is to be served without being stored, following directions for skimming (on page 22).

Soup can be prepared in advance up to this point. If you are going to store the soup, strain it over a bowl but do not skim. Cool thoroughly, uncovered, then cover and place in refrigerator. Store wrapped chicken separately in the refrigerator. Discard (or nibble on) giblets, bones, and soup vegetables.

Chicken can be reheated in soup, either in quarters with bones and skins for a lusty dish, or trimmed of bones and skin and cut into smaller, easily spooned pieces.

Sprinklings of chopped parsley and/or dill are lovely garnishes. See "Classic Garnishes," page 33, for other possibilities.

....

YIELD: 6 TO 8 FIRST-COURSE SERVINGS; 4 TO 6 MAIN-COURSE SERVINGS

VARIATION

Optional Bones and Pot Vegetables

.........◆.........

Bones such as veal knuckles, beef marrow bones, or a calf's foot are washed and added to the pot and removed with the chicken.

Following are the most commonly added vegetables and herbs. The root vegetables are most common in Northern and Eastern Europe. Be careful when adding root vegetables, as they can make soup too sweet. If you use several, use only a small piece of each. Add with carrots, celery, and onions as described in the master recipe.

....

1 large or 2 small leeks, green and white portions, split and well
*   washed of sand*
1 medium white turnip, peeled and quartered
A 2- to 3-inch length of parsnip, peeled and cut in half lengthwise
1/2 small celery root (celeriac), peeled and cut up
1 small Italian parsley root (petrouchka), peeled and cut
*   lengthwise; or 1 to 2 inches additional parsnip*
2 fresh thyme sprigs, or 1/2 teaspoon dried leaf thyme
1 small bay leaf
5 or 6 whole cloves
1 large potato, peeled and quartered
1 or 2 fresh or canned peeled and seeded tomatoes
1 or more garlic cloves

IMPROVED CANNED CHICKEN BROTH

.... ◆ ....

B ecause of their saltiness, chicken bouillon cubes are generally undesirable. It is better to use canned chicken broth in emergencies. I use College Inn chicken broth or if available, Health Valley low-fat broth. You may have a local brand you prefer, but it should be clear (without noodles, etc.) and should not call for added water.

Fat in canned soup adds an overpowering flavor and is best removed. Therefore, store 2 or 3 cans in the refrigerator so fat coagulates at the top and practically comes off with the lid, or is easily lifted off. Combine the 13 3/4-ounce can of soup with 1/4 can of cold water and simmer it slowly for 10 or 15 minutes with a celery stalk with 4 or 5 leaves, a small piece of onion, and a piece of carrot, although it is the first two that are essential. A few parsley sprigs add freshness. Raw chicken trimmings or giblets (other than livers) add flavor, and if you have those you can then add a little more water. Do not salt until all cooking is finished, as most canned soup is inclined to be heavily salted. If possible buy reduced-sodium chicken broth, although it is rarely available in large cans. Strain before serving and garnish to taste. Canned

broth can also be substituted for some water when you are making soup with a small chicken. For a 3-pound chicken, use 4 cups each water and defatted canned chicken soup. In this instance, it is obviously unnecessary to simmer the soup first with vegetables.

LOW-FAT CHICKEN SOUP

In addition to the various skimming steps described on page 22, anyone on the strictest low-fat diet should remove all skin and every visible streak and clump of yellow fat from the raw chicken before cooking. Do not add veal or beef bones, or the chicken backbone, although the gizzard, heart, and neck are fine if all fat has been trimmed. There is no point in pretending that the soup will be as flavorful without the skin and fat, but adding extra vegetables and herbs—celery, onions, leeks, and carrot—will help somewhat. For the very leanest soup, use skinless white meat leaving the bones in, but do not expect a great soup. No osmazome! (see page 21).

BROWN CHICKEN STOCK OR SOUP

This is a very robust preparation, but not a personal favorite, except in recipes such as Christer's Chicken and Savoy Cabbage Soup (page 95). I prepare it as a base for complex soups such as borscht or as a stock for hearty dishes. For a milder version with a golden glow, brown only the pot vegetables, a preparation known in French as a *brunoise*. Browning the chicken and trimmings intensifies the flavor. Either way, the soup will have a greasier look and flavor than the standard light chicken soup.

For the lighter version, follow the recipe for Basic Chicken Soup (page 28), but chop the carrots, celery, and peeled onion, reserving its skin. Cook the vegetables slowly until golden brown (but not black) in 1½ tablespoons rendered chicken fat or butter. The health-conscious might prefer corn, canola, or safflower (not olive) oil or margarine. The vegetables can be browned by sautéing for about 10 minutes, or by being tossed with the cooking fat and placed in a single layer in a baking pan in the middle of a 400°F. oven for about 20 minutes. Stir once or twice to brown evenly and avoid blackening. Drain on paper towel and add vegetables to soup with the cooking chicken when foam has subsided. Add reserved onion skin and proceed as in Basic Chicken Soup recipe.

For a stronger flavor, brown chopped chicken pieces or chopped backbones, wing tips, and other trimmings with the vegetables, using no additional fat, or roast in the oven as described above, but with the temperature at 450° F. for about 40 minutes. Drain on paper towels, and cook chicken and vegetables in water, as called for above. Strain, discard chicken or trimmings and vegetables, and finish as called for in specific recipes or serve clear, as broth.

LEFTOVER
ROASTED CHICKEN SOUP
········◆········

The leftover carcass, with or without stuffing and gravy, makes a thrifty, hearty soup that is found throughout Europe and the United States. I adapted this recipe from one appearing in *Ola's Norwegian Cookbook*, published in 1946 and written by Lucie Keyser Frolich, an immigrant from Oslo who ran Ola's restaurant in Boston during the Depression.

Standard herbed bread stuffing with mushrooms or meat such as bacon, ham, giblets, or mild sausage would be fine for this soup, but do not use those made with cornbread, seafood such as oysters, or anything very pungent, such as hot sausage, capers, or anchovies, or sweets such as prunes or raisins. Remember that the herbs will affect the flavor, too. The carcass can be used alone if there is no stuffing or gravy.

··················

FOR THE SOUP
Carcass of a 5- to 7-pound roasted chicken
1 to 2 cups leftover herbed bread stuffing, as available
1 to 2 cups lightly thickened brown pan gravy, as available
2 medium onions, cut into quarters
1 medium carrot, sliced
2 celery stalks with 3 sprigs of leaves
7 to 8 cups water, as needed
3 tablespoons unsalted butter
4 tablespoons flour
2 to 3 tablespoons sherry or Madeira
1 cup half-and-half
Salt and black pepper, to taste

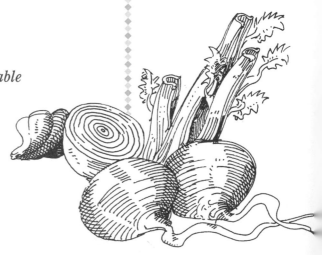

FOR THE OPTIONAL GARNISH
Cooked rice
¼ pound thinly sliced white mushrooms sautéed in butter
Chopped fresh parsley

....

Discard all leftover roasted skin as it will impart a greasy texture and stale flavor. Other meat on the carcass is fine. Break carcass into sections and place in a 5-quart soup pot with stuffing, gravy, onions, carrot, and celery, adding water to cover.

Simmer for about 1 hour, or until soup is golden and richly flavored. Discard bones and vegetables. Pour remaining contents through a strainer, rubbing through as much of the solids as possible. Discard residue in strainer.

In a 3-quart saucepan, melt butter and stir in flour, sautéing for about 5 minutes or until smooth and bright yellow. Pour in hot soup stock all at once, and stir constantly over moderate heat until soup is smooth and creamy.

If it is to be served within 3 or 4 hours, soup can be prepared in advance up to this point. Do not store longer, even if chilled, as it is already made of leftovers.

Ten minutes before serving, add the wine. Simmer for 5 minutes, then add half-and-half. Heat thoroughly but do not boil. Adjust seasonings. Serve with any of the suggested garnishes.

....

YIELD: ABOUT 6 SERVINGS

CLASSIC GARNISHES FOR CHICKEN SOUP

.........◆.........

These garnishes are found throughout Europe and the United States, and often give the soup its name.

Egg Noodles

.........◆.........

Cut into many shapes or used as wrappers for various fillings, basic egg noodle dough is a favorite in chicken soups. Recipes for Asian-style noodles and specific ethnic fillings, as for Jewish kreplach or Italian tortellini, appear in those sections of this book. All pasta to be served in soup should be dried until it is firm, or it will tend to melt in the soup. Packaged dried noodles and small pastas are especially good in soups.

....

About 3 cups unbleached all-purpose flour
3 eggs
1 teaspoon salt
2 tablespoons warm water, or as needed

....

Turn out flour onto a wooden board or countertop and make a well in the center. Drop unbeaten eggs into the well with salt, and stir slightly with a fork to break the yolks but not combine them completely with the whites. Working inward toward the well, gradually stir the flour into the egg mixture until you have a dough that is stiff but slightly elastic. Add more flour if the dough is too soft or sticky, or a few drops of water if it is too crumbly. Knead for about 10 minutes, or until dough is smooth and elastic.

Divide into halves or thirds, depending on how large a piece you can roll out at once. Keep the unrolled portions covered with plastic wrap so they do not dry. Sprinkle flour onto the board and with a heavy, even rolling pin, roll each section of dough to paper thinness, working from the center to the edges and rotating dough for evenness. The sheets of dough should be thin and clothlike. Drape on a towel hung over the back of a chair or a rack, and dry for 20 to 30 minutes, until dry but not brittle. The time will vary with the humidity of the air.

Roll each sheet snugly, jelly-roll style, being careful not to press down as you do so. With a thin, sharp knife, cut down making strips of the desired width—with ³/₄ inch about the widest for soup, down to the threadlike fineness of angel's hair pasta.

Unroll the cut strips and scatter in a single layer on a towel. For soup, you will want these to dry for about 3 hours, so do not cover. To dry completely for storing, keep on the towel overnight until completely brittle, then store in a covered jar or tin for up to 1 week.

Cook in 3 quarts boiling salted water for about 7 minutes. Drain and serve in soup.

....

YIELD: ABOUT 1¹/₄ POUNDS NOODLES; ENOUGH FOR 8 TO 10 SERVINGS WITH SOUP

To slightly intensify the golden color of the soup, prepare it with an unpeeled deep yellow-brown onion.

Filled Noodle Dough Dumplings

..........◆..........

For dough for kreplach, tortellini, and the like, follow recipe for Egg Noodles (page 33), but use 2 whole eggs plus 2 egg yolks instead of the 3 eggs called for. This is a soft, sticky dough and may require more flour on the board and rolling pin.

Prepare chosen filling first, then roll out dough so it will be fresh and moist. (In most cities, it is possible to buy high-quality prepared fresh pasta in sheets for wrappers that you fill, to say nothing of fresh frozen tortellini and similar dumplings.) The sheets of dough must be rolled within an hour or two of the time they are to be used, and kept covered to remain moist, otherwise dough will be dry and crumble when folded and edges will not seal. That last can be overcome somewhat by moistening edges of dough with water or beaten egg white, and then pinching them tightly, but you will not be able to fold the dumplings as for tortellini or kreplach. If you are satisfied with small-square ravioli, or half-moon agnolotti, that dough will work. These shapes should dry for 2 or 3 hours after being filled and formed.

Follow individual recipe instructions as to size, shape, and filling. The dough will dry after being filled.

Noodle Squares

..........◆..........

These are popular in Jewish cooking, where they are known as *farfel* (also used for the grated-dough dumplings below), and in Italy, where they are called *quadrucci* or *quadrettini*, "little squares." Follow the recipe for Egg Noodles (page 33), and cut the sheets of rolled dough into $^1\!/_2$-inch strips. Cut across these again horizontally to form $^1\!/_2$-inch squares.

Pinched Noodles
Riebele, Farfel, or Tarhonya

..........◆..........

Whether by their German name *Riebele*, or the Yiddish *farfel*, or Hungarian *tarhonya*, these pinched or grated flecks of dough have a nice, chewy texture and are really tiny dumplings.

Prepare the Egg Noodle (page 33) dough using only 2 eggs and no water. After kneading, gather the dough into a ball, cut in quarters, and let each piece dry, uncovered, for about 1 hour. When the dough is firm and powdery to the touch, either pinch off small pieces about the size of tiny green peas or rub through the fine side of a grater onto a platter or a sheet of waxed paper. Move the grater as you work to avoid clusters. Dry for 30 minutes. Drop into boiling salted water and cook gently but steadily, covered, for about 10 minutes, or until floating and tender. Drain and serve in hot soup.

These can be thoroughly dried overnight and stored in a covered tin or jar for several weeks.

....

YIELD: ABOUT 1 POUND DRIED; ENOUGH FOR 8 SERVINGS OF SOUP

Royal Custard
........◆........

T his diced custard has many names throughout Europe, usually signifying it as "royale" or kingly.

....

FOR THE CUSTARD
2 eggs
2 tablespoons whole milk or chicken broth
1/4 teaspoon salt

FOR THE OPTIONAL FLAVORINGS
Dash of grated nutmeg
2 teaspoons grated lemon rind
1 tablespoon grated Parmesan cheese
1 tablespoon minced fresh parsley, or 1/2 tablespoon minced fresh
*   herbs such as dill, chives, or chervil*

....

Using a fork, beat eggs with whichever liquid you are using, the salt, and any combination of the flavorings. Lightly grease a small glass or ceramic heat-proof baking dish (about 4 inches square or round) with butter, light vegetable oil, or rendered chicken fat. Pour egg mixture into dish to a depth of about 1 inch.

Cover dish snugly with foil and set in a large skillet. Pour hot, not boiling, water into skillet until it comes halfway up the sides of the dish. Keep water cooking at a steady simmer for 15 to 20 minutes, or until custard is set and a knife blade inserted in the center comes out clean.

Remove custard dish, uncover, and cool for about 10 minutes. Uncut, it

can stand at room temperature for 2 hours before serving. Unmold onto a flat plate and cut into dice. Set aside in a warm place. Add to soup just before serving.

....

YIELD: ENOUGH FOR 4 SERVINGS OF SOUP

VARIATION

Pink Royal Custard is a colorful addition to soup. Blend 1 teaspoon tomato puree into the eggs and liquid and proceed as for Royal Custard, adding herbs to taste but not cheese, lemon rind, or nutmeg.

Egg Flakes

This is a light, restorative garnish for convalescents or anyone who is just plain tired.

....

2 eggs
Pinch of salt
1 tablespoon grated Parmesan cheese (optional)
1 1/2 tablespoons flour, or more as needed
About 6 cups chicken broth

....

Beat eggs, salt, and cheese, if you use it, with a fork, then sift in flour and beat until mixture is smooth and the consistency of heavy cream. Add more flour if needed.

Bring broth to a simmer, and dribble egg mixture into it, pouring through a colander or a perforated spoon. It should run through in broken streams. Simmer 2 to 3 minutes, until droplets are set. Ladle them along with soup into individual bowls. Serve immediately.

....

YIELD: FOR 4 TO 6 SERVINGS OF SOUP

Egg Drops

These are as popular in China as they are throughout Europe. For very thin drops, add water.

....

2 eggs, well beaten with a fork until thin
Pinch of salt
2 teaspoons water (optional)
4 cups Basic Asian (page 192) or Basic Chicken Soup (page 28)

....

Stir beaten eggs with salt and water, in a glass measuring cup or other utensil from which it is easy to pour.

Bring soup to a simmer. Pour egg mixture in very slowly, in a trickle. It should run in a thin, broken stream. As egg begins to set in soup, stir gently with a fork to break up clumps. Serve immediately.

....

Yield: For 4 servings of soup

Soup Nuts or Puffs

This is the basic cooked dough known as cream puff pastry, or *pâte à choux*. It is used as a soup garnish in various forms. Pinched off and boiled, it becomes a kind of dumpling or gnocchi; deep-fried or baked, it becomes crisp and brown and is known, among other things, as soup nuts or *mandlen* (almonds) in Yiddish, in German as *Gebackene Erbsen* (baked peas), or *profiteroles* in French. Other specific ethnic names are given in individual recipes.

....

¼ cup (½ stick) unsalted butter or margarine
½ cup water
Pinch of salt
½ cup all-purpose flour
2 eggs
Oil, for frying (optional)

....

"Give my father a hearty chicken soup, a can of beer, and a bag of popcorn, and he is as close to heaven as he can get," says Nell Newman, daughter of Paul Newman. She cooks his favorite with the conventional vegetables (page 29), plus Spike, an herb and seaweed blend sold at health food stores. Perhaps that soup will become part of Newman's Own, the line of prepared foods Paul Newman produces with all of his profits going to charities.

Combine butter or margarine, water, and salt in a 2-quart saucepan. Bring to a boil and simmer slowly until fat is completely melted. Lower the heat and add all the flour at once, stirring rapidly until mixture pulls away from the sides of the pan in a mass.

Remove from the heat. Add one egg and beat in thoroughly until completely asborbed, then add and beat in the second. The mixture should be smooth and satiny.

Whatever final cooking method you use, the puffs should be about ½ inch in diameter.

For boiled dumplings, shape the dough with 2 teaspoons and drop into gently but steadily boiling lightly salted water. Cover and cook for about 4 minutes, or until dumplings float to the surface. Test one to see if it is thoroughly cooked and not doughy in the center. Remove from water with a slotted spoon and keep warm in a strainer or colander until ready to add to soup. Do not hold these for more than 2 hours before serving or they will become doughy.

If you are going to fry the dough, shape as described for boiling and drop into mild-flavored corn, safflower, or canola oil heated to 375° F. on a fat thermometer. Do not fry more than a dozen at a time. Cook uncovered for 2 or 3 minutes, or until puffs are evenly golden brown and float to the top. Drain on paper towels and continue frying until all of the dough is used. Keep in a warm spot until ready to serve. These can be prepared up to 4 hours before serving.

To bake the dough, shape as described for dumplings or squeeze it through a no. 7 tip of a pastry bag onto a lightly greased baking sheet. Or shape drops of dough with the tips of 2 teaspoons. Bake in a 375° F. oven for about 10 minutes. Using a needle or a skewer, prick a tiny hole in each puff and let it stand in the warm, but turned-off oven for about 10 minutes so puffs will retain their form without collapsing. Once cooled, these puffs will keep for a week or two in an airtight container in a cool room.

·················

YIELD: ABOUT 3 DOZEN PUFFS; ENOUGH FOR 6 TO 8 SERVINGS OF SOUP

Slivered Crepes

········◆········

This is a standard garnish throughout Europe and appears in many old American cookbooks as well. The thin pancakes, or crepes, are sliced to resemble noodles.

³/₄ cup all-purpose flour, or more as needed
Pinch each of salt and pepper
Pinch of grated nutmeg (optional)
2 eggs
³/₄ cup water, or more as needed
1¹/₂ tablespoons minced fresh chives or parsley (optional)
Unsalted butter, margarine, or corn oil, for frying

....

Sift flour, salt, pepper, and nutmeg into a mixing bowl. Beat eggs with water and add to flour. Beat (do not whip) with hand or electric rotary beater until batter is free of lumps and about the consistency of heavy cream. Add more water if it is too thick, or gradually sift in extra flour if it is too thin. Stir in herbs, if you use them. Let stand for 30 minutes before cooking.

Melt about 1 teaspoonful butter or oil in an 8-inch skillet or crepe pan. When bubbling, pour in about 2 tablespoons of batter. Raise pan above heat and quickly tip and rotate it so batter covers the bottom evenly. Let batter cook until golden brown on the underside, about 3 minutes, then flip over and brown second side. Place finished crepe on a towel to cool, and repeat frying with remaining batter, adding fat to the pan if crepes stick. If batter sets in ripples as soon as it touches the pan, the pan is too hot. Remove from heat to cool. This amount should make about 10 pancakes.

When all the crepes are made, roll each jelly-roll style and cut across in thin ¹/₄- to ¹/₃-inch slices, then unroll into strips. These can be made up to this point and kept uncovered at room temperature for about 2 hours, or covered with a towel in refrigerator for 2 days.

Divide slivers into individual soup bowls, and ladle soup over them.

....

YIELD: ENOUGH FOR ABOUT 10 SERVINGS OF SOUP

Rice and Small Dried Pastas

..........◆..........

Although rice is sometimes cooked right in the soup, it is better done separately in lightly salted water, because it must boil to cook properly and if boiled, the soup will become cloudy. The same is true of small dried pasta such as rice-shaped orzo, the seedlike semini, and the starry pastina. Cook, drain, and keep warm until placing them in individual servings of soup.

Barley

········◆·········

This grain is always cooked in the soup because it is intended to be a thickener.

Croutons and Toast Slices

········◆·········

Many soups are garnished with small toasted cubes of bread or toasted slices of the long, thin French-style baguettes. Both are what the French call *croûtons*, although we reserve that name for the cubes. They are available packaged, but those are almost always overseasoned, stale, and unpleasant. There are several simple ways of preparing them fresh, as follows.

The easiest way to prepare the cubes is to toast packaged white bread and cut it into ½-inch squares, eliminating the crusts. However, that is the least flavorful method and results in croutons that quickly become soggy. The better way is to cut the untoasted bread into squares, eliminating crusts, and fry them slowly in a little butter or olive oil (depending on the soup) in a small, heavy skillet, turning frequently so they brown evenly. It should take about 7 minutes to brown croutons from 6 slices of bread in a 10-inch skillet. If you want to season them with a little garlic, add a split clove to the pan, but remove before it browns.

Toasted slices of French bread about ½- to ¾-inch thick can also be fried as above, or they can be brushed on both sides with melted butter or oil and baked in a 450° F. oven for about 12 minutes. Turn once to brown both sides. They can be rubbed with a cut clove of garlic after they are toasted. To toast them without adding fat, place them under the broiler for about 7 minutes, turning once to brown both sides, then rub with garlic if you wish.

Cut French baguettes on the diagonal for longer slices if the loaf is very thin. If it is at least 3 inches around, cut straight across.

Allow ¾ slice of sandwich bread per person for cubes—two to four slices of toasted French bread, depending on the dish. It is best to serve both of these on the side so that they can be added to the soup during eating; otherwise they become mushy.

Chapter 4

THE MOTHER
of All
CHICKEN SOUPS

The lore, love, and language of
Jewish chicken soup •
along with the definitive recipe

T
he importance of chicken soup in Jewish lore is succinctly expressed in the opening line of Allen Ginsberg's poem on his identity. Say "chicken soup" in a word-association test and you will almost surely evoke an answer relating to Jewish home life. By their frequent use of this soup, and its almost mystical status, Jews have made it their own. Because they prepared basically the same soup wherever they settled, it transcends national boundaries, and so merits a special chapter.

Although we tend to think of this soup as being pan-Jewish, the typical version we know is of Eastern European origin, based on soup styles in Poland, Hungary, the Czech Republic, Romania, Russia, and Ukraine—the original homes of the Eastern or Ashkenazic Jews. As you will see further along, Jews from other parts of the world take an entirely different view of chicken soup—if, in fact, they take any notice at all. Just as I was at first surprised to meet Jews who did not speak Yiddish (Sephardim speak the Spanish-based Ladino), I felt a mild shock upon finding many who did not grow up with chicken soup, matzoh balls, or gefilte fish. There is a sort of international culinary alliance of Ashkenazic Jews in all countries, as I discovered when talking about family foods with a Danish-born Jewish friend whose mother followed the exact same recipes as my own. Funny, I thought. Those matzoh balls don't look Danish . . .

Long before the advent of antibiotics gave rise to the euphemisms of Jewish penicillin and Bubbamycin (a play on the Yiddish word *Bubbameises*, meaning a "grandmother's tale") for this supposed panacea, it was known as golden broth—*goldener yoich* (*gilderne* and *yoichl* in some dialects). It was a term I never heard as a child, as we used the word *zupp* for "soup."

Fortunately, I asked Dr. Mordkhe Schaechter, the linguist and lexicographer at the League for Yiddish in New York City. He assured me that *yoiche* was derived from the Old Polish word *jucha* and the later German word *Jauche*, both meaning "broth" and with the *j* pronounced as the *y* in yellow. "By now it's a Yiddish word, anyway," Dr. Schaechter insisted. "You consider *table* an English word even though it came from the French *table* and the Latin *tabula*. So *yoich* is Yiddish. Period!"

None of which explains the Ashkenazic obsession with chicken soup. Probably it has to do with that soup's universal visual, olfactory, and mythological appeal. It is worth noting that the Chinese are the world's leading consumers of chicken soup, which in part explains why their food has such great appeal to Jews, especially when garnished with rice, noodles, or the wontons (page 199) that resemble kreplach (page 51). Perhaps one of the lost tribes of Israel settled in China; but who gave chicken soup to whom may rival the mystery concerning the origin of pasta.

Neither the Mizrachic (Eastern) Jews of Persia nor the Sephardim of

I grew up in a small apartment house in the Williamsburg section of Brooklyn where most of the tenants were Jewish. Walking through the halls on Friday afternoons, you thought you had fallen into a soup pot. You could tell whose soup you were smelling by picking out the different ingredients each used. A whiff of garlic? That would be Mrs. Bernstein in 3C. Mrs. Moskowitz in 2B couldn't get enough onions into the pot, and my mother's contribution was dill.

One day I remember coming in and smelling chocolate and thinking that someone really had gone crazy. It turned out to be one of the few gentiles in the building making My-T-Fine pudding, maybe in self-defense.

You could get fat just by inhaling in those halls. You didn't have to eat anything!

—ALAN KING

Spain, Italy, Turkey, Greece, and the Middle East share that obsession, although they do eat chicken-based soups such as the egg-lemon soup on page 164; the Tunisian chicken, rice, and parsley chorba on page 165; and others of Middle Eastern origin. Because Israelis eat the chicken soups of the countries from which they emigrated, no soups in this book are classified as uniquely Israeli.

Few of the Sephardic Jews that I have asked claim they ever heard of chicken soup as a standard dish for Friday night or Passover before they came to this country. Gilda Angel, the wife of Rabbi Mark Angel, who officiates at Congregation Shearith Israel, New York's leading Sephardic synagogue, said that her husband's family, originally from Rhodes, resorts to chicken soup only for illness, when it is thickened with diced chicken, carrots, celery, onions, parsley, and lots of rice cooked in the soup.

Anyone fortunate enough to have eaten at Café Crocodile in New York, knows the savory Mediterranean–Middle Eastern dishes turned out by the chef, Andrée Abramoff, who owns this restaurant with her husband, Charles. An Egyptian-born Jew, Andrée does remember having chicken soup made with carrots, leeks, celery, onions, and parsley, and sometimes with vermicelli, but always with rice served on the side, as with almost all Egyptian dishes, and often on Friday night, although not for Passover.

"Chicken soup for Passover? Never!" said Ilana Amini, a Mizrachic Jew from Persia and a talented cook who with her husband, Albert, lives in Queens. "We prepared chicken soup often when we had large households— it was customary for all of the children to live in one house even after marriage, and so we had big potfuls of the soup made with potatoes, zucchini, carrots, onions, chickpeas, and meatballs" (page 172).

In his comprehensive and fascinating book *Sephardic Cooking*, Copeland Marks includes the food of non-Ashkenazic Jews (but not all technically Sephardim) in places such as India, Yemen, Ethiopia, Afghanistan, and Uzbekistan as well as more expected locales. For Passover, he describes a rather simple Kurdistan broth only of chicken, water, turmeric, and salt, but served with meat dumplings or Kibbeh (Bulgur meatballs) similar to those on page 174.

Similarly, Edda Servi Machlin, in her fine Tuscan-Jewish cookbook, *The Classic Cuisine of the Italian Jews*, writes that she grew up with a Passover chicken soup garnished with Italian-style chicken meatballs (page 134), unborn egg yolks (see box, page 49), and rice, a grain permitted to Sephardic and Mizrachic Jews during Passover but not to Ashkenazim.

MY FAVORITE CHICKEN SOUP

·········◆·········

Root vegetables are essential to this soup. If parsley root is unavailable, add an extra inch or two of parsnip. For a richer, heavier soup, use the veal knuckle. Tomato, white or sweet potato, and garlic are used in some Jewish homes, but not in mine. Try any or all if you like, but the result will then not be "My Favorite." Deviate, and you're on your own . . .

This soup usually is a first course, without chicken but with matzoh balls, kreplach, rice, or any of the noodle-based garnishes on pages 33 to 35.

To be truly "My Favorite Soup" this must be made with a fowl. Do the best you can.

···················

FOR THE SOUP
5- to 6-pound fowl, preferably fresh-killed, or 7 to 8 pounds broiling
 or frying chickens, with neck and all giblets except liver
Veal knuckle bone (optional)
10 to 12 cups water, or more as needed
2 large carrots, scraped and quartered
2 celery stalks with leaves, whole or cut up
1 medium onion
3 Italian parsley sprigs
1 small parsnip, scraped and cut in half
1/2 small celery root (celeriac), peeled
A 2- to 3-inch length of parsley root (petrouchka), scraped and cut
 in half
1 medium leek, green and white portions, split and well washed
Salt and white pepper, to taste
Pinch of sugar, if needed

FOR THE OPTIONAL GARNISH
Minced fresh parsley and/or dill
1 or 2 tablespoons cooked green peas per portion
1/4 cup cooked rice per portion
Matzoh Balls (page 49) or Kreplach (page 51)
Any of noodle forms or soup nuts (page 38)

···················

The chicken may be cooked whole, if pot is large enough, or quartered. Place in a close-fitting 6- to 7-quart enameled or stainless-steel soup pot along with giblets and veal knuckle, if you are using it. Cover with 10 cups of water if you use broilers, or 12 if you use a fowl. Cover and bring to a boil. Reduce to a simmer and skim foam as it rises to the surface. Soup should cook at a smile (see page 21).

When foam subsides, add all other ingredients except pepper and sugar, and with just 1 teaspoonful of salt. Let chicken simmer, partly covered, until very tender and just loosening from the bone, about 1¼ hours for broilers or 2½ to 3 hours for a fowl. Add more water during cooking if chicken is not seven-eighths covered. Turn chicken 2 or 3 times during cooking. Add salt gradually, tasting as cooking progresses.

Remove chicken, giblets, and bones and set aside. Pour soup through a sieve. Rinse pot and return soup to pot if it is to be served immediately or within 2 or 3 hours. Discard vegetables. Bones can be discarded or nibbled on. Chicken will be good only to be added in small spoon-size pieces to soup, or for chicken salad or pie.

The soup can be made ahead up to this point and stored in a ceramic or glass bowl. Cool thoroughly, uncovered, then cover and store in refrigerator for up to 2 days. Skim off solidified fat just before reheating. Add pepper and sugar when reheating. Store chicken separately, covered, in a bowl.

Serve soup very hot, with any of the suggested garnishes.

YIELD: 6 TO 8 SERVINGS

CHICKEN IN THE POT

This is a standard one-dish meal in Jewish restaurants that serve meat, especially in New York-style delicatessens. Follow the recipe for My Favorite Chicken Soup (page 46), serving quartered or jointed chicken pieces on the bone, with or without skin, and the soup in large, deep, heated bowls. Fifteen minutes before serving you can add 2 or 3 fresh, cut-up carrots and celery stalks and 1½ cups fresh or one 10-ounce package unthawed frozen green peas to the soup, and simmer. Garnish each portion with the vegetables, minced parsley, 1 or 2 matzoh balls and about ⅔ to 1 cup very fine cooked egg noodles. In restaurants, this is usually served in small, individual tureens or cocottes to be ladled out gradually.

YIELD: 4 FIRST- AND MAIN-COURSE SERVINGS

MUSHROOM AND BARLEY SOUP

·········◆·········

Second only to chicken soup in popularity among Jews, this soup is usually made with beef and is a variation of the Polish barley soup *krupnik*. Chicken produces a delicate, lower-fat variation.

··················

FOR THE SOUP
1 recipe My Favorite Chicken Soup (page 46), made with root
vegetables and veal knuckle
3 large or 4 small dried black mushroom caps, preferably Polish or
Russian, or any dried cèpes
¹/₂ cup very hot water
¹/₃ cup medium pearl barley
2 small carrots, diced
2 celery stalks, diced

FOR THE OPTIONAL GARNISH
Minced fresh dill
4 to 6 medium potatoes, peeled and boiled

··················

While chicken soup cooks, soak mushroom caps in very hot water for 30 minutes. Remove and let sediment in water settle. Cut mushroom caps into small pieces. Reserve mushrooms and their liquid.

Wash barley in one or two changes of cold water until water is clear.

When the chicken soup is half-cooked, add the mushrooms, their soaking water carefully poured in so that sediment is not added, and the barley. Continue with recipe. Barley and mushrooms should remain in the finished soup after the chicken and vegetables are removed. Skin and bone the chicken.

Add diced fresh carrots and celery to the soup and simmer for 20 minutes or until tender. Serve soup with vegetables and pieces of chicken. If desired, top with a sprinkling of dill. A boiled potato may be added to each portion if this is served as a main course.

The soup may be stored, covered, in the refrigerator for 3 days.

··················

YIELD: 6 TO 8 FIRST-COURSE SERVINGS; 4 TO 6 MAIN-COURSE SERVINGS

YOLKS OF UNBORN EGGS

One of the delights of chicken soup when I was growing up were the small yolks of unborn eggs (yolk sacs before the whites and shells had formed), found in fresh-killed fowls. They were cooked in the soup to become much like hard-cooked egg yolks, and because each chicken had only a few, they were much fought over by children. The yolks were considered good omens at Passover, when they were accompanied by matzoh balls. I have seen these eggs in chickens from Hispanic markets and from live poultry markets and farms. Because they are hard to find, I substitute hard-cooked egg yolks.

CHICKEN SOUP GARNISHES

.... ◆ ....

Some of the classic garnishes for Jewish chicken soup are Egg Noodles, in any width (page 33), Egg Flakes (page 37), Noodle Squares (page 35), Pinched Noodles (page 35), and Royal Custard (page 36) made with broth instead of milk and with oil or chicken fat to grease the baking dish instead of butter. Soup Nuts (page 38) are made with margarine instead of butter. You can also serve rice or small dried pasta such as egg barley.

Matzoh Balls
Knaidlach

.... ◆ ....

Related linguistically and gastronomically to the German *Knödel* and the Italian *gnocchi*— dumplings, all—this is the traditional garnish for the Passover chicken soup of the Ashkenazim, but it is popular throughout the year.

....

3 eggs
6 tablespoons cold water
3 heaping tablespoons rendered chicken fat (see page 50)
*   or softened margarine*
Salt
Pinch of ground white pepper
1 tablespoon finely minced fresh parsley (optional)
²/₃ to ³/₄ cup matzoh meal
2 ¹/₂ to 3 quarts water

....

Using a fork, beat the eggs lightly with the cold water. Add the chicken fat or margarine and stir until it dissolves. Add ¹/₂ teaspoon salt, the pepper, and the parsley, if you use it.

Gradually beat in matzoh meal, 2 tablespoons at a time, being very careful after ²/₃ cup has been added so that mixture does not suddenly become too thick. The mixture should be the consistency of soft mashed potatoes and a bit spongy. Cover bowl with plastic wrap or foil and chill for 5 to 7 hours.

Thirty minutes before serving, bring 2¹/₂ to 3 quarts of water to a rolling boil and add a handful of salt.

With wet hands, or 2 tablespoons dipped into cold water, shape the mixture into balls about 1 inch in diameter. Drop gently into boiling water, cover the pot loosely, and let boil at a moderately brisk pace for about 25 minutes or until they puff up and float to the surface.

Cut one matzoh ball to see if it is thoroughly cooked and not dark or wet in the center. Allow more cooking time for remaining batch if necessary. Remove all with a slotted spoon and drain. Serve in hot chicken soup.

RENDERED CHICKEN FAT (SCHMALTZ)

In German, Schmaltz *refers to any animal fat, including butter, that has been melted, separated from solids, and solidified by chilling. In Jewish cooking, it refers to the rendered fat of poultry—chicken, duck, and goose.*

Some recipes call for salt or even onions in preparing chicken fat, but that limits its use. The taste of browned onions in matzoh balls, for example, would be hideous.

For each tablespoonful of rendered fat called for, allow about 1¹/₂ tablespoons of raw fat. Use the thick yellow fat found inside the flaps of skin at the chicken's cavity and from around the neck. Pull it from the chicken and cut it into small chunks. To have cracklings that may be used in other dishes, cut off a few pieces of extra-loose skin, such as the crop, and cut into small pieces. (It is not necessary to use the skin if you do not want cracklings.)

Place the chunks of fat and skin in a small heavy-bottomed saucepan with just enough cold water to barely cover the fat. Bring to a boil, reduce *to a low simmer, and cook, half-covered, very slowly until the water has evaporated, the cracklings are crisp and golden brown, and the fat is clear and golden. Rendering ¹/₂ cup fat should take about 20 minutes. This can burn quickly, so watch carefully. If you do not have a heavy-bottomed saucepan, set pot over an asbestos mat or on a metal heat insulator.*

Remove any cracklings with a slotted spoon and drain, if you are using them, or discard. Cool remaining fat for 5 or 10 minutes in the pan so the small solids can sink to the bottom. Carefully pour off the clear fat into a heat-proof cup, jar, or glass. Cool, cover, and chill in the refrigerator. It will take 5 or 6 hours for fat to solidify to the consistency of soft butter. The rendered fat will keep, covered, in the refrigerator for about 10 days, but it can take on an off-flavor after 1 week. If frozen, it generally can be kept for 4 weeks, but taste before adding to other foods to be sure it has not become musty. Some fine brown sediment may col- *lect at the bottom of the solidified fat; it may be scooped up with the fat for added flavor.*

NOTE: *Rendered chicken fat may be purchased at some markets, but is desirable only if unseasoned and made without onions. The next best substitute for rendered chicken fat is softened margarine. Butter would be out of character in a Jewish dish, even if the food were not prepared according to kosher laws.*

An easy way to approximate rendered chicken fat is to skim the solidified fat from the top of a well-chilled chicken soup. Spoon it off carefully before it softens and drain on paper towels if necessary to remove droplets of soup you may have picked up. Because this fat is softer and contains more moisture than the true rendered version, you will need about one-quarter to one-third more in each recipe. For example, use 4 heaping tablespoons instead of 3 for Matzoh Balls (page 49) and about 2¹/₂ tablespoons for Kreplach (page 51).

Cooked matzoh balls can be drained and kept in a warm spot for several hours before serving, and then reheated for a few minutes in the soup. However, they taste best freshly made.

Leftover cooked matzoh balls can be kept in the refrigerator for up to 2 days, but they will have to be reheated in soup or water and will not have the best texture or flavor. They are delicious sliced and fried in butter, and served for breakfast or with meat such as pot roast.

YIELD: 10 TO 12 LARGE MATZOH BALLS; ALLOW 1 OR 2 TO A PORTION

Kreplach

Close to wontons in style and flavor, kreplach are considered one more reason why Jews are so partial to Chinese food. If you buy sheets of prepared dough to fill, be sure it is very fresh; if it has dried, the edges will not stick securely.

³/₄ pound beef flanken or lean chuck, in a single piece
1 small carrot, cut up
2 small onions, cut up
1 celery stalk with leaves
2 parsley sprigs
Salt
Freshly ground black pepper, to taste
2 tablespoons rendered chicken fat (see page 50)
    or margarine
1 tablespoon minced fresh parsley, plus more as needed
1 egg white
¹/₂ recipe Egg Noodles (page 33),
    or ³/₄ pound very fresh noodle dough in sheets
2 quarts well-salted water

Boil beef in water to cover along with carrot, 1 onion, celery, parsley, a pinch of salt, and a few grindings of pepper. Simmer for about 30 minutes or until half-tender. Drain the meat and reserve broth for other purposes. Cool the meat and chop or grind very fine (but not in a food processor). This can be done a day in advance of preparing the kreplach.

Chop the remaining onion. Melt the fat and add onion. Sauté the onion until it is soft and yellow but not brown. Add the sautéed onion and the fat remaining in the pan to the chopped beef. Season with salt, pepper, and more parsley. Stir in egg white. Set aside in a cool place, although not necessarily the refrigerator, while you prepare noodle dough.

Prepare the dough but do not dry out the sheets after rolling. Roll out to a little less than 1/4 inch thickness, then cut into 2½-inch squares. (Or buy sheets of fresh noodle dough and keep wrapped or covered until ready to fill. Cut just before filling.)

To fill the dough, turn a point of each square toward you to form a diamond shape. Place a generous teaspoon of filling on one side, then fold the square in half to form a triangle, pressing the top points firmly in place. Then pinch sides tightly closed. If the dough is moist, the seams will stick; if it has dried, moisten edges with cold water, then pinch closed.

Bring together the 2 outer points of each triangle to form a ring and press closed firmly. Let the kreplach stand at room temperature for about 20 minutes before cooking. These can be made 8 hours ahead up to this point and stored between towels in the refrigerator.

Bring the 2 quarts of water to a rapid boil and add a small handful of salt. Add the kreplach, about a dozen at a time, and cook, partly covered, for about 20 minutes, or until the dough of a test kreplach is tender.

Drain well, keep warm, and add to chicken soup when serving.

....

YIELD: ABOUT 36 KREPLACH; FOR ABOUT 12 SERVINGS OF SOUP

VARIATION

If you do not want to bother with boiling the beef, substitute ¾ pound lean ground round and sauté it with the onion only until it loses its red color; do not brown. Drain on paper towels and continue with recipe as above. The results are not quite as delicious, but wholly acceptable.

Chapter 5

UNITED STATES

*The Northeast, The Southeast,
The Midwest,
The West, The Southwest*

NEW ENGLAND CHICKEN AND CORN CHOWDER

·········◆·········

Chowder is a word that originated as the French *chaudeau*, literally meaning "hot water" but broadly applied to a hot beverage or soup. *Chaudeau* along France's Atlantic coast is a clear fish soup made with white wine and butter. As such, it is a close relative to New England clam chowder. This adaptation with chicken becomes all-American with the addition of corn. Fresh corn is preferable to frozen when available, but canned is too soft and sweet.

···················

6 cups Basic Chicken Soup (page 28)
2 pounds skinless and boneless chicken breast; or one 3¹/₂- to
   4-pound chicken, quartered
4 cups fresh or frozen corn kernels; 2 cups pureed in a blender or
   food processor and rest left whole
3 ounces lean, streaky salt pork without rind, well rinsed and diced
1 large onion, finely chopped
3 tender celery stalks, diced
3 medium boiling potatoes, peeled and diced
Salt and black pepper, to taste
1 cup half-and-half
¹/₂ cup heavy cream, or to taste
Unsalted butter, for garnish
Sweet or hot paprika
Pilot crackers or ships' biscuits

···················

If you have the soup prepared, simmer it with the chicken breast for about 8 minutes or until chicken is firm and white but not quite thoroughly cooked. Skim and reserve broth; cube and reserve chicken.

If you do not have the soup, prepare it with the quartered chicken according to the recipe on page 28. Degrease soup, strain and discard vegetables, and measure 6 cups of soup into a 2¹/₂- to 3-quart saucepan. Remove chicken meat from bones and skin. Cut breast and thigh meat into cubes and add to soup, along with the pureed and whole corn kernels. If using a whole chicken, reserve wings and drumsticks for nibbling.

Fry salt pork slowly in a small skillet until it is golden brown. Remove from pan, drain on paper towels, and reserve for garnish if you like, or discard. Sauté onion and celery in rendered pork fat until they are light golden brown. Add to soup along with potatoes. Simmer gently but steadily, partly covered, for about 10 minutes, or until potatoes are almost soft. Season with salt and pepper.

The soup can be prepared in advance up to this point and stored, covered, in the refrigerator, for 2 days. Return to room temperature before proceeding with recipe.

Stir in half-and-half and simmer 10 minutes. Just before serving, stir in cream and heat thoroughly. Serve in warm cups or bowls, garnished with a dab of butter and sprinklings of sweet or hot paprika. Top with reserved pork cracklings. Pass crackers or biscuits.

Leftovers can be stored, covered, in the refrigerator for 1 day, although this soup tastes best freshly made.

YIELD: 8 TO 10 SERVINGS

LANCASTER CHICKEN-CORN SOUP

This succulently thick and rich soup makes a sustaining main course. *Rivels*, as the little dumplings cooked in this soup are called in Pennsylvania Dutch dialect, derive from the German *Riebele* (see page 35), meaning "rubbed" or "grated," which is how the dough is prepared before being cooked. The packaged dried pasta or egg barley is a fine and easy substitute. This can be served as a first course, but only the lightest fish or vegetable dish need follow. As a substantial main-course soup, it needs only a green salad and a fruit dessert to round it out.

One 4- to 5-pound chicken, cut into 8 pieces
2 ¹/₂ to 3 quarts water, or as needed
1 large onion
8 to 10 black peppercorns
2 teaspoons salt, or to taste
8 to 10 threads of saffron, or ¹/₄ teaspoon crushed saffron (optional)
10 ears of corn, or 4 cups frozen corn kernels
3 celery stalks, diced with leaves
6 ounces wide egg noodles, packaged egg barley, or Rivels (recipe follows)
Freshly ground white pepper
²/₃ cup finely chopped fresh parsley
2 hard-cooked eggs, chopped

As with so many other dishes that we consider American, most of our popular chicken soups are foreign imports, and so appear under their countries of origin. Others, however, were modified by regional American products or evolved into ethnic recombinations to become, in a sense, the American soups included in this chapter.

Place chicken in soup pot with enough water to cover. Bring to a boil, reduce heat, and skim foam as it rises to the surface. When it has subsided, add onion, peppercorns, salt, and saffron. Simmer gently but steadily, partly covered, for about 1½ hours or until tender.

Remove chicken. Trim and discard bones and skin, and onion. Let soup cool, then skim fat from surface. Tear meat into spoonable pieces and return to soup.

Cut kernels from 4 ears of corn, then grate kernels from remaining 6 ears, catching all milk and pulp on foil or waxed paper. If using frozen kernels, puree half in a food processor or blender, adding a little soup if liquid is needed. Add whole kernels and grated or pureed corn to soup along with celery and noodles, barley, or rivels. Simmer gently until corn and noodles or rivels are cooked. Add salt and white pepper to taste. Stir in parsley and serve, garnishing each portion with chopped egg.

This soup freezes well, but do that before adding the noodles, barley, or dumplings. Prepare those when reheating soup. To prevent scorching during reheating, place the pot over an asbestos mat or on other insulating plate.

YIELD: 8 TO 10 FIRST-COURSE SERVINGS; 4 TO 6 MAIN-COURSE SERVINGS

Rivels

········◆········

½ teaspoon salt
Pinch of ground white pepper
1 large egg, beaten
¾ to 1 cup all-purpose flour, as needed

····················

Stir salt and pepper into egg and add ⅔ cup flour and beat. Keep adding and beating in flour until mixture is crumbly but a bit sticky. Rub between hands or pinch off pea-size pieces and drop them into simmering soup. Cover loosely and let cook for about 15 minutes or until rivels solidify. To make the rivels ahead of time, cook them in lightly salted boiling water or some extra soup stock and then drain and reserve them to be reheated in the soup just before it is served.

CRÈME SENEGALESE

·········◆·········

P ossibly a result of the French colonization of West Africa with its exotic spices, this soup is in the turn-of-the-century culinary style. Although it perhaps should be included under France or even Senegal, old cookbooks from various parts of the United States credit New York with this version, at both the "21" Club and the erstwhile Delmonico's. Michael Lamanaca, who is the chef at "21" as I write, still has this on the menu, prepared almost as the recipe below indicates. Current exceptions are his additions of chopped carrots and leeks to the vegetable mixture, and chopped, peeled tomato and a little coconut milk (a standard West African ingredient) to the broth. The soup may be served hot, but it is more subtle cold.

····················

FOR THE SOUP
3 tablespoons unsalted butter
2 medium Granny Smith or other tart apples, peeled and chopped
2 celery stalks, diced
1 medium onion, chopped
1/3 cup good curry powder
1/2 teaspoon turmeric, or to taste
1/2 teaspoon ground coriander, or to taste
Pinch of cayenne, or to taste
3 tablespoons flour
8 cups hot, degreased Basic Chicken Soup (page 28)
1 cup half-and-half, or 1/2 cup half-and-half and 1/2 cup canned
  coconut milk
2 cups finely chopped, skinless cooked chicken breast
1/2 to 1 cup heavy cream

FOR THE GARNISH
1 cup lightly salted whipped cream
Chopped pistachio nuts, chives, or toasted, grated coconut

····················

Melt butter in a 3-quart enameled soup pot and add apples, celery, and onion. Sauté until light golden brown. Add curry powder and spices and sauté gently, stirring constantly, for 10 minutes. Sprinkle on flour and sauté, stirring, for another 5 minutes, until blended.

Pour in hot soup and half-and-half with or without the coconut milk, stirring to blend. Simmer, partly covered, for 30 minutes. Strain through a fine sieve and chill thoroughly, for 8 to 24 hours.

Strain again through a fine sieve to remove all coagulated fat, then stir in chopped chicken and heavy cream. Adjust seasonings and pour into well-chilled soup cups.

Top each portion with a swirl of whipped cream if desired, and sprinkle on pistachio nuts, chives, or coconut.

....

YIELD: 10 TO 12 SERVINGS

EZRA TULL'S GIZZARD SOUP

.........◆.........

T ry our gizzard soup. It's really hot and garlicky and it's made with love," a waitress suggests to a customer in Anne Tyler's delicious novel *Dinner at the Homesick Restaurant*. Created by the book's cook-hero, Ezra Tull, this soup was said to be prepared with twenty cloves of garlic and lots of black pepper.

Anne Tyler generously obliged with this recipe. She also included the source from which Ezra adapted the recipe: *The Impoverished Students' Book of Cookery, Drinkery, & Housekeepery*, by Dr. Jay F. Rosenberg, who calls it *bechinalt* and identifies it as Hungarian. In George Lang's *Cuisine of Hungary*, the author uses the term "becsinált" for a quail soup and a beef stew. The term seems to indicate a sort of ragout, which this soup virtually is. Maryland gets the credit here, nonetheless, because Baltimore is the author's home and the setting for the novel.

Anne Tyler suggested that perhaps Ezra used twenty cloves of garlic in making large batches of this soup for his restaurant, but that three would suffice for the amount here, as they certainly do.

This soup is really meant to be served by itself, as a curative, with chunks of bread. It might be followed by a baked apple or perhaps by some cheese and fresh fruit.

....

FOR THE SOUP
1 pound chicken gizzards, well cleaned
1 teaspoon salt
$^1/_2$ teaspoon freshly ground black pepper
3 to 4 cups water, as needed
3 tablespoons butter
3 garlic cloves
2 tablespoons flour

"It does have a comforting effect," Ms. Tyler said. "You just sit drinking it and sniffling and weeping and you feel better in no time." All of which proved true.

FOR THE GARNISH
Crisp-crusted French or Italian bread

....

Cook gizzards with salt and pepper in 3 cups water, covered, for 1 hour, or until thoroughly tender, adding a little water if gizzards are not covered. Remove gizzards and chop by hand into small pieces and return to the pan. (I eliminate the tougher sinewy portions of the gizzards, but I am not sure that Ezra Tull does. Ms. Tyler notes that he might not return the gizzards to the broth at all, when serving finicky people such as children.)

Melt butter in a small saucepan and crush garlic through a press into it. Add flour and, over low heat, stir to a smooth paste. Remove from heat and carefully pour in about 1 cupful of hot broth, stirring constantly. When smooth, stir back into remaining broth and simmer, covered, for 15 minutes, adding a little extra water if mixture has become too thick. Adjust seasonings and serve in warm bowls with crusty bread for dunking.

....

YIELD: 2 MAIN-COURSE SERVINGS

CREOLE CHICKEN AND OKRA GUMBO

.........◆.........

Gumbo, the West African word for okra, gave this pungently complex soup its name, and that gelatinous pod lends viscosity to the soup and binds its flavors. (See page 184 for more on its origins.) Filé gumbo is made without okra, and represents one of the earliest examples of cross-cultural cooking in our country. Louisiana's Choctaw Indians used filé powder, which is ground from the dried leaves of the sassafras tree, and it became an alternative to okra as a thickener. Traditionally, okra and filé are not used together.

....

FOR THE STOCK
One 5-pound fowl, cleaned and cut into 8 pieces, with all giblets
*   except liver*
10 cups water, or as needed
2 medium carrots, scraped and cut in half
1 large or 2 medium onions, quartered
4 celery stalks with leaves
4 parsley sprigs
2 teaspoons salt

FOR THE SOUP
¹/₂ cup vegetable oil
¹/₂ cup all-purpose flour
1 pound fresh okra, or a 10-ounce package frozen okra,
    preferably whole
1 medium onion, chopped
3 celery stalks without leaves, chopped
¹/₄ pound cooked ham
One 16-ounce can whole tomatoes, chopped and with juice
¹/₃ cup chopped green and white portions of scallions
3 garlic cloves, finely minced
2 bay leaves
1 teaspoon dried thyme, or 3 fresh thyme sprigs
¹/₂ teaspoon dried marjoram
Salt and black pepper, to taste
Cayenne pepper or Tabasco sauce, to taste
5 cups cooked white rice

....

Place chicken and giblets in a 4- or 5-quart soup pot and add water to cover. Bring to a boil, then simmer, removing scum as it rises to the surface. When soup is clear, add carrots, onion, celery, parsley, and salt. Simmer gently for 1 to 1¹/₂ hours or until chicken is completely cooked and falling from the bones.

Remove chicken to a platter and strain soup, discarding vegetables. Simmer soup slowly, uncovered, for another 30 minutes, until reduced by one fourth to one third. Meanwhile, remove skin and bones from chicken and pull meat into generous but convenient spoon-size pieces and set aside.

To make a roux, heat oil in a large heavy 10-inch skillet and gradually add flour, stirring constantly over low heat. Continue to cook until roux turns a medium brown color. Add okra, onion, celery, and ham and keep stirring over moderate heat until okra stops stringing (emitting sticky threads). Stir in tomatoes and their juice and simmer, stirring to incorporate into the roux.

Stir vegetable mixture into slowly simmering chicken stock. Add scallions, garlic, bay leaves, thyme, marjoram, and chicken pieces. Gradually add salt, pepper, and cayenne or Tabasco sauce to taste, remembering that flavors will become stronger as soup cooks. Simmer, partly covered, for 40 minutes. Adjust seasonings and serve with a mound of white rice in the middle of each portion.

....

YIELD: 8 TO 10 FIRST-COURSE SERVINGS; 4 TO 6 MAIN-COURSE SERVINGS

FRIED CHICKEN AND ANDOUILLE FILÉ GUMBO

This is a main-course soup that can be preceded by a seafood or vegetable salad or a cooked hot or cold artichoke and followed by a slice of pecan pie or a fresh fruit salad.

....

¹/₂ to ²/₃ cup vegetable oil
One 4- to 4¹/₂-pound chicken,
    cut up and at room temperature
¹/₂ cup all-purpose flour
³/₄ pound spicy andouille or chorizo sausage, cut into ¹/₂-inch slices
¹/₄ pound tasso ham, with or without spicy rind, or plain cooked
    ham, diced
1 large onion, chopped
1 green bell pepper, seeded and chopped
3 celery stalks, diced
6 or 7 scallions, green and white portions, sliced
3 garlic cloves, minced
²/₃ cup chopped fresh parsley
2 teaspoons dried thyme
2 large bay leaves
1¹/₂ to 2 quarts water
Salt, to taste
Black pepper, to taste
Cayenne pepper or Tabasco sauce, to taste
2 to 2¹/₂ tablespoons filé powder
2 cups cooked white rice

....

Heat ¹/₂ cup oil in a heavy 5-quart pot or Dutch oven and brown chicken on all sides over moderate heat, turning so pieces brown evenly. Remove chicken and set aside.

Make a roux by blending flour into the remaining oil in the same pot and stirring constantly over moderate heat until roux is a deep coffee brown, adding a little more oil if mixture is dry. Add sausage slices, diced ham, onion, green pepper, and celery. Sauté, stirring, for about 10 minutes. Add browned chicken pieces, scallions, garlic, parsley, thyme, bay leaves, and water to cover, stirring to incorporate the roux into the liquid.

Add salt and black pepper and simmer soup, partly covered, for about 1

I know the chicken gumbo is perfect if all I can say after [tasting] it is "Ya-Ya! Yaya!! Ya!"

—GEOFFREY BEENE, FASHION DESIGNER, REFERRING TO THE CLASSIC BOOK ON LOUISIANA FOLKLORE *GUMBO YA-YA*, A TITLE DERIVED FROM THE SOUND OF MANY PEOPLE TALKING AT ONCE

hour or until chicken is tender. Remove chicken, trim off skin and bones, and return chicken in large pieces to the soup. If you are using the very spicy rind of the tasso ham, you will probably not need cayenne or Tabasco. Otherwise, add either toward the end of cooking and adjust other seasonings. This soup can be prepared in advance up to this point and stored, covered, in the refrigerator for 2 days.

Bring soup to a simmer. Five minutes before serving, remove from heat and stir in filé powder. Cover and let stand for about 5 minutes, but do not simmer or the filé will make the soup too thick. (If you prepare more of this gumbo than you need for one meal, remove the portion to be served and add a proportionate amount of filé to that. It is better not to boil soup once the filé has been added.) Ladle into wide soup plates with a mound of rice and pieces of chicken.

....

YIELD: 6 TO 8 FIRST-COURSE SERVINGS; 4 TO 5 MAIN-COURSE SERVINGS

NOTE: Tasso is a very spicy, peppery Cajun cure for ham and is perfect for a highly seasoned soup. For a milder soup, plain cooked ham or tasso without its rind is preferable. To control spiciness, add tasso ham to soup without rind, then add small pieces of rind gradually.

WISCONSIN CHICKEN BOUYAH

.... ◆ ....

French and Belgian settlers in the Green Bay area originally prepared this soup with game or turtle meat. Chicken is now the accepted substitute and makes for a light broth, with chunky vegetables adding a homey goodness. *Bouyah* or *booyah* (pronounced *BOO. yah*) is said to have been derived from *bouillon*. The choice of vegetables varies with the season, but strong runny beets and spinach are not desirable, nor are green and yellow squash that tend to disintegrate. Coarsely chopped, tender green spring cabbage would be fine.

....

FOR THE SOUP
One 4- to 4½-pound fowl
1 large leek, green and white portion split and washed
2 bay leaves
8 to 10 black peppercorns

Salt, to taste
2¹/₂ to 3 quarts water, as needed
4 medium boiling potatoes, peeled and cubed
4 celery stalks, cut into chunks
1 large onion, cut into chunks
3 large carrots, cut into chunks
1 cup sliced green beans, in 1-inch lengths
1 cup sliced yellow wax beans, in 1-inch lengths
1 cup green peas, fresh or frozen
1¹/₂ cups short, wide egg noodles (optional)

FOR THE GARNISH
Chopped fresh parsley, chives, and chervil

....

Simmer fowl with leek, bay leaves, peppercorns, and 2 teaspoons salt in a soup pot with water to cover. Simmer, partly covered, for 2 hours or until chicken is completely tender.

Remove chicken and skim fat from soup. Discard leek, bay leaves, and peppercorns. Trim skin and bones from chicken and cut meat into large but spoonable pieces. Set aside. This soup can be prepared up to this point and stored, covered, in the refrigerator for 2 days.

Degrease soup again if necessary and bring to a simmer. Add potatoes, celery, onion, carrots, and beans and cook until vegetables are tender. About 15 minutes before serving, add reserved chicken, peas, and noodles and simmer, partly covered, until tender.

Ladle into heated soup bowls and sprinkle with herbs.

....

YIELD: 6 TO 8 MAIN-COURSE SERVINGS

CHILLED CHICKEN AND AVOCADO BISQUE

........◆........

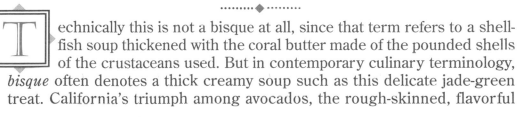

Technically this is not a bisque at all, since that term refers to a shellfish soup thickened with the coral butter made of the pounded shells of the crustaceans used. But in contemporary culinary terminology, *bisque* often denotes a thick creamy soup such as this delicate jade-green treat. California's triumph among avocados, the rough-skinned, flavorful

Haas, is the one to look for. This is a very rich soup, best appreciated in cup-size portions. To add a modern, Southwest-inspired zing, season with cayenne pepper, minced fresh chili peppers, or Tabasco sauce.

....

FOR THE SOUP
3 cups cold, thoroughly degreased Basic Chicken Soup (page 28)
1 very ripe medium avocado
1 cup crème fraîche or sour cream
Salt, to taste
Freshly ground black pepper
Pinch of cayenne pepper or a few drops Tabasco sauce,
*   to taste*
2 tablespoons finely minced chives

FOR THE GARNISH
1 cooked chicken breast, trimmed of skin and bones
1 tablespoon minced hot green or red chili pepper, or 2 tablespoons
*   peeled roasted red bell pepper or pimiento*
Breadsticks or cheese twists

....

Using a stainless-steel knife, peel and pit avocado and cut into chunks. Puree in a food processor or by rubbing through a sieve with a wooden spoon. Blend in chicken broth, using blender, food processor, or wire whisk. Beat in two-thirds cup crème fraîche or sour cream until smooth and frothy. Season with salt and peppers or Tabasco, and 1 tablespoon chives. Place in refrigerator to chill and thicken for 2 to 3 hours.

While soup chills, prepare garnishes. Chill 4 soup cups in the refrigerator. Chicken breast should be room temperature, so remove from refrigerator 30 minutes before serving. Cut into fine dice or, better yet, shred. Whether you use sweet or hot peppers, seeds and filaments should be discarded. Dice either or a combination of both.

To serve, divide chicken meat among 4 cups. Stir soup gently and adjust seasonings, then ladle into cups. Using a fork, beat remaining crème fraîche or sour cream until it is thin. Carefully let a little dribble from the fork onto the top of each portion of soup, preferably forming a spiral. Sprinkle on peppers; use twice as much sweet pepper as hot. Finally, sprinkle soup with remaining minced chives and serve with sesame breadsticks or cheddar cheese twists.

....

YIELD: 4 SERVINGS

GREEN CHILI CHICKEN
AND POSOLE SOUP

·········◆·········

T he plump and snowy, huskless white corn kernels known as posole or hominy are a Native American legacy, most popular in the Southwest. Usually it is cooked into a thick stew with green chilies and pork, but Bobby Flay, the creative and skillful chef-partner at the Mesa Grill restaurant in New York and the author of *Bobby Flay's Bold American Food*, generously developed this colorfully festive soup for me and put it on his winter menu. It is at once sophisticated and reassuringly rustic, and is based on canned cooked posole, or hominy. (The dried posole requires such long cooking that it produces an overpoweringly starchy soup.)

This soup looks especially appealing served in deep, terra-cotta bowls much like those used for chili or French onion soup. It can be a first course if served in cups, but is substantial enough to be a main course, followed by flan, sherbet, or a fresh fruit salad. Tostado chips with salsa and guacamole can precede it.

··················

FOR THE SOUP
20 unpeeled garlic cloves
Olive oil
3 poblano peppers
2 medium red bell peppers, roasted and peeled, fresh or jarred
1 large or 2 small canned chipotle peppers, rinsed and pureed
2 tablespoons (¹/₄ stick) unsalted butter
2 medium red onions, finely diced
2 cups dry white wine
4 large skinless and boneless chicken breasts, cut into ¹/₂-inch
*   pieces (about 2 cups)*
One 29-ounce can posole or hominy, rinsed under running cold water
10 to 12 cups Basic Chicken Soup (page 28) or Improved
*   Canned Chicken Broth (page 30), as needed*
1 to 3 tablespoons honey, to taste
2 to 3 teaspoons salt, to taste
Black pepper, to taste

FOR THE GARNISH
3 tablespoons minced chives
2 tablespoons finely chopped fresh cilantro (coriander)
1 cup grated Asiago or Parmesan cheese

··················

Preheat oven to 350°F. Rub each garlic clove with a little olive oil and place in a single layer in a shallow baking pan. Roast for about 30 minutes or until garlic is tender and skins are golden brown. When cool enough to handle, peel cloves. It does not matter if they remain whole or are broken up.

Grill poblano peppers by holding them over a flame (or a barbecue grill or in a hot iron skillet or stove-top griddle) on a long fork, turning so all sides char. Place in paper bag or foil wrap for 5 to 7 minutes to steam, then peel off skins and remove all sides and ribs. Chop finely.

Sweet red peppers can be grilled, peeled, and seeded in the same way as poblanos, or if using jarred roasted peppers, rinse under running cold water, drain on paper towels, and chop finely.

If canned chipotles are in adobo sauce or brine, rinse under running cold water, then puree through a sieve or with a hand blender.

All of the above steps can be prepared several hours before you make the soup, and held at room temperature.

In a large enameled or stainless-steel saucepan, melt butter over medium heat. Add garlic cloves and diced onions. Sauté gently, stirring frequently so onions soften but do not take on color, about 5 minutes. Add wine, raise heat, and boil, uncovered, until wine is almost completely evaporated, with only about $\frac{1}{8}$ to $\frac{1}{4}$ cup left. Add chicken, poblano and red peppers, posole or hominy, and 10 cups of chicken soup. Bring to a boil, reduce to a simmer, and cook, partly covered, for about 20 minutes or until chicken is completely tender. Add more soup if mixture becomes too thick.

Stir in a small amount of the pureed chipotle peppers and 1 tablespoon honey. Simmer for a few minutes, then adjust flavor with salt, pepper, more chipotle puree, and honey to taste. Serve very hot, sprinkling each portion with chives, cilantro, and about 1 tablespoon grated cheese.

This soup develops extra flavor if it is allowed to stand, uncovered, at room temperature for 1 hour before being reheated and served, but it is not a good idea to keep leftovers, as posole will become pasty.

....

YIELD: 8 TO 10 FIRST-COURSE SERVINGS; 4 TO 6 MAIN-COURSE SERVINGS

Chapter 6

LATIN AMERICA
and the
CARIBBEAN

Aruba, Brazil, Chile,
Colombia, Cuba, Ecuador,
Mexico, Venezuela

CARIBBEAN CHICKEN PEPPER POT SOUP

·········◆·········

This is quite possibly the origin of Crème Senegalese (page 57), descended from the spicy "Pepe" soups of Africa. Dried coconut is generally available in Middle Eastern and African food stores. Do not confuse it with the sweetened coconut flakes that are sold in supermarkets. Canned coconut milk is widely available in the gourmet packaged food section of many supermarkets.

··················

FOR THE SOUP
One 3- to 3 1/2-pound chicken, cut into 8 pieces
8 to 10 cups Basic Chicken Soup (page 28), or Improved Canned
*   Chicken Broth (page 30)*
6 whole cloves
1 bay leaf
2 thin slices peeled fresh ginger, or 5 or 6 pieces dried cracked
*   ginger, or 1 teaspoon powdered ginger*
2 tablespoons turmeric
1/2 to 1 teaspoon cayenne pepper, to taste
1 tablespoon good curry powder, or to taste
1/2 teaspoon black pepper, or to taste
1 cup grated, dried, unsweetened coconut; or 1 cup canned coconut
*   milk*
One 15-ounce can chickpeas, rinsed
4 tablespoons (1/2 stick) butter
2 garlic cloves, minced
4 tablespoons flour
1 cup heavy cream if using dried coconut; 1/2 cup if using coconut milk

FOR THE GARNISH
Lemon wedges
Fresh cilantro (coriander) or parsley leaves
Hot cooked white rice

··················

In a 5-quart enameled or stainless-steel soup pot, simmer chicken in enough soup to cover, adding cloves, bay leaf, ginger, turmeric, cayenne, curry powder, and pepper to vegetables in the chicken soup. Skim foam as it rises to the surface, then cover partly and simmer for about 1 hour or until chicken is tender and falling from the bones. Remove chicken and trim off

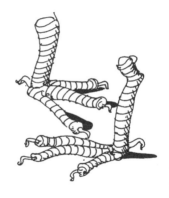

and discard skin and bones. Pull chicken meat into spoonable chunks and set aside. Skim and strain soup and return to rinsed pot.

If using dried coconut, puree with 1 to 2 cups of chicken soup (as needed) in a blender or food processor for a few minutes or until coconut is very fine. Let stand 20 minutes, then strain broth back into pot and discard coconut in strainer. (Do not add coconut milk at this point.)

Puree chickpeas in blender or food processor with 1 or 2 cups of soup as needed. Pour pureed chickpeas with their liquid back into soup and bring to a low simmer, partly covered.

Recipe can be prepared up to this point and stored, covered, in the refrigerator for 1 day.

About 30 minutes before serving, add chicken pieces to soup and bring to a simmer; add extra soup if liquid becomes too thick. Melt butter in a small skillet and when hot, sauté garlic for 3 or 4 minutes or until it just begins to take on color. Sprinkle in flour, stirring and sautéing for about 5 minutes, until it turns bright yellow. Beat into simmering soup with a whisk and cook 10 minutes.

Stir in coconut milk, if using, along with cream and simmer gently for about 5 minutes. Adjust seasonings, and then simmer for 5 minutes.

Serve in small bowls or cups garnished with a sprinkling of herbs and the lemon wedges. If serving as a main course, mound portions of rice on side plates.

YIELD: ABOUT 8 FIRST-COURSE SERVINGS; 4 TO 6 MAIN-COURSE SERVINGS

THE VIRTUES OF CHICKEN FEET

*M*any *Caribbeans and Africans demand the feet of chicken and make a fondly recalled soup,"* said Charles Ritzberg, *author of* Caribfrikan Portfolio, *now out of print. It was the source of the Caribbean Chicken Pepper Pot Soup (page 68), although I have altered it through the years. Savvy Europeans and Asians also prefer soup made with chicken feet. A history teacher who is also the author of* Classical Afrikan Cuisines *and the just-published* Little Gumbo/Calalu Book, *Mr. Ritzberg told me that chicken feet are considered especially nourishing for convalescents even though more prosperous African-Americans prefer choicer cuts.*

Chicken-feet soup is a specialty in Jamaica, Barbados, Haiti, Trinidad, and elsewhere. It is a rich, silky mix of chicken bits, the feet, and vegetables, usually with hot chilies, and is served with some form of fufu *(page 187). Thanks to proprietor* Lisa Gallimore, *a lovely one was prepared for me by Terry Wickes, the chef at Kwanzaa, a smart, convivial restaurant in New York City, named for the African-American harvest festival. Feet add a light gelatinous texture and are succulent to chew on, but are virtually impossible to get except from a live poultry market (especially in a Chinatown) or chicken farm or some supermarkets in Asia and Latin neighborhoods. (For more information see page 14.)*

MEXICAN CHICKEN NOODLE SOUP
Sopa de Fideos

........◆........

favorite in both Argentina and Mexico, this first-course soup gets a bright crackle from the pan-browned *fideos*, or threads. The saffron and chili powder are more typical in the Argentinian version.

....

FOR THE SOUP
2 medium onions, chopped
2 garlic cloves
8 fresh tomatoes, peeled and seeded; or 6 large canned tomatoes,
    drained
6 to 8 tablespoons melted lard or light olive oil, as needed
Pinch of powdered saffron (optional)
Pinch of chili powder (optional)
3 quarts Basic Chicken Soup (page 28) or Improved Canned
    Chicken Broth (page 30)
Salt and black pepper, to taste
1½ cups diced cooked chicken breast meat
¼ pound Mexican fideos, vermicelli, or cappellini, broken in 2-
    inch lengths

FOR THE GARNISH
Fresh cilantro (coriander)
Minced seeded hot green chilies
Diced avocado
Slivered Monterey jack and/or grated Parmesan cheese

....

Puree onions, garlic, and tomatoes in a food processor or in a blender, adding a little water if needed to puree. If you use a blender, pour contents through a strainer set over a bowl, then squeeze liquids out of pureed vegetables into the bowl; discard vegetables. If you use a food processor, that step is not necessary; the soup will be faintly pink instead of clear, but a bit more flavorful.

Heat 3 tablespoons of melted lard or oil in a 5-quart saucepan or soup pot and slowly pour in the vegetable liquid, being careful about splattering. Add saffron and chili powder, if using them. Simmer gently, partly covered, for 10 minutes. Add chicken soup and simmer gently, partly covered, for about 20 minutes. Season with salt and pepper and add chicken, keeping soup warm over very low heat.

A soup pot full of numerous culinary cultures is indeed an apt metaphor for this region with its strong African, European, and indigenous influences. Caribbean soups are essentially African, modified by European methodology and refinements. Latin and South American food strongly reflects Indian cookery, with mostly Spanish and Portuguese overlays.

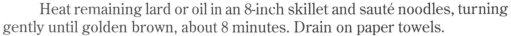
Heat remaining lard or oil in an 8-inch skillet and sauté noodles, turning gently until golden brown, about 8 minutes. Drain on paper towels.

Soup can be prepared to this point up to 30 minutes before finishing and serving.

Bring soup to a simmer, add noodles, and cook until tender, 7 or 8 minutes. Serve immediately, garnishing each portion with a sprig of cilantro. Pass other garnishes at the table.

....

YIELD: 10 TO 12 SERVINGS

AZTEC TORTILLA SOUP
Sopa Azteca

........◆........

I have no evidence that the wise old Aztecs of Mexico considered this tantalizing soup a cure-all, but I do.

....

FOR THE SOUP
2 fresh medium tomatoes
½ cup light olive or other vegetable oil
3 large garlic cloves, minced
1 medium onion, finely chopped
1 fresh or drained canned jalapeño or other hot green chili pepper,
*   chopped*
8 cups Basic Chicken Soup (page 28) or Improved Canned
*   Chicken Broth (page 30), seasoned with bay leaf*
1½ cups diced cooked chicken breast meat
Eight 6-inch corn tortillas, cut into ¼-inch slivers
Salt and black pepper, to taste

FOR THE GARNISH
Tortilla strips
Grated Monterey jack or fairly dry mozzarella cheese
Minced hot green chili peppers
Diced avocado
Fresh cilantro (coriander) leaves
Sour cream
Lime wedges

....

To peel tomatoes easily and give them a slightly smoky flavor, hold one at a time over the flame of a burner, using a long wood-handled carving fork; alternatively, cut in half and place cut side down on foil under broiler. Either way, skin will brown and crack and be easily pulled off. Squeeze seeds and juices from peeled tomatoes and chop.

Heat all but 3 tablespoons oil in a small skillet and sauté garlic, onion, and chilies until wilted and just beginning to turn light golden, about 8 minutes. Add tomatoes and sauté and stir until juice evaporates and mixture thickens a bit. Add to chicken soup in a 3-quart saucepan.

Simmer soup with chicken for 15 minutes before serving and adjust seasonings.

Meanwhile, heat remaining 3 tablespoons oil in a heavy 10-inch skillet and brown the tortilla strips in batches, one layer at a time, turning frequently so strips turn an even golden brown. This will take about 3 minutes, but watch carefully as strips blacken suddenly. Drain on paper towel.

Divide tortilla strips among 6 or 8 soup bowls and ladle soup with solids over them. Add other garnishes or pass them at the table.

YIELD: 6 TO 8 PORTIONS

POBLANO CHILI SOUP WITH CHICKEN AND CORN
Sopa de Elote

T he Mexicans' beloved corn adds a cheerful color and texture to this first-course soup, but for a more coolly elegant result it can be eliminated. Poblano chilies are the subtle best for this soup, but if unavailable substitute the combination of green bell pepper and a little of any hot green chili pepper.

FOR THE SOUP
3 medium poblano chilies, or 2 green bell peppers and
*   1 jalapeño, or 2 long hot green chilies*
4 tablespoons (¹/₂ stick) unsalted butter
1 small onion, finely minced
1 garlic clove, minced

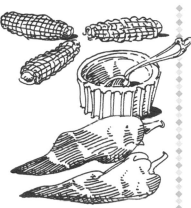

4 tablespoons flour
3 cups hot Basic Chicken Soup (page 28) or Improved Canned
*   Chicken Broth (page 30)*
1 cup diced cooked chicken white meat
1 ½ cups fresh or frozen corn kernels
⅔ cup half-and-half
Salt and black pepper, to taste

FOR THE GARNISH
Chopped fresh cilantro (coriander) or parsley

To peel either poblano chilies or green bell peppers, hold over the flame of the burner with a long wood-handled fork or grill under the broiler, turning frequently until skin is brown and blistered. Immediately wrap in foil or place in a paper bag. Close tightly and let steam for 5 to 10 minutes. Skin will loosen and can be easily rubbed or stripped off. Discard seeds and white ribs. Puree peeled, roasted peppers with unpeeled hot green chili peppers in a blender or food processor, adding a little broth if needed. (If you have a hand blender, just cut up peppers, add them to soup, and puree.)

Melt butter in a 2-quart saucepan and sauté onion and garlic until wilted but not taking on color, about 5 minutes. Blend in flour with a whisk over low heat, then add pureed chilies and soup. Simmer, partly covered, for about 5 minutes.

Add chicken, corn, and half-and-half to hot soup. Cook 10 minutes or until corn is plump and tender. Adjust seasonings and serve immediately in warm cups or small bowls.

YIELD: 4 TO 6 SERVINGS

BRAZILIAN CHICKEN, VEGETABLE, AND RICE SOUP
Canja

Bacon fat adds a lovely, smoky flavor but olive oil is lighter and also delicious. In parts of Brazil, the palm oil, *dende,* would be used, but as I discovered the hard way while in Bahia, it is pretty heavy going for the digestive track of the uninitiated.

FOR THE SOUP
²/₃ *cup rice*
8 to 10 cups strained Basic Chicken Soup (page 28) or Improved
    Canned Chicken Broth (page 30), heated
2 tablespoons rendered bacon fat or olive oil
2 tablespoons chopped cooked ham (optional)
3 medium carrots, chopped
1 large white turnip, chopped
1 garlic clove, minced
2 celery stalks, diced
2 medium onions, chopped
3 fresh or canned tomatoes, seeded and chopped
2 thin slices peeled, fresh ginger (optional)
4 or 5 parsley sprigs
1 small bay leaf
2 cups diced, cooked chicken breast meat
Salt and black pepper, to taste

FOR THE OPTIONAL GARNISH
Chopped fresh parsley
Lemon wedges

Rinse rice in a strainer by letting cold water run through it for a second or two. Add to 8 cups of hot soup and simmer, partly covered, for 10 minutes.

BRAZILIAN *CANJA*

◆◆◆

Using the same name as the Portuguese do for their egg-lemon version of this soup (see page 137), Brazilians simmer up quite a different result.

As explained in The South American Cook Book, *by Cora, Rose, and Bob Brown, canja trans-lates as "rice cream." According to the authors, Brazilians esteem it as highly as we do our ice cream and* say "E canja!" meaning "That's easy!" or "Pretty soft!"

They also tell us that when Theodore Roosevelt was in Brazil looking for the River of Doubt, he dubbed canja "the finest soup in the world." At least he had no doubt about that.

In her charming and highly original Iron Pots and Wooden Spoons, *a collection of African* recipes as they developed in the New World, Jessica Harris writes of the Brazilian reliance on canja: "The soup's reputed restorative powers makes it a cure-all for everything from colds to hangovers." And she warns that many who order it as a first course may wind up unable to finish the rest of the meal.

Meanwhile, heat oil in a heavy 10-inch skillet and sauté ham, carrots, turnip, garlic, celery, and onions until soft and very lightly browned, about 10 minutes. Stir into simmering soup along with tomatoes, ginger, parsley, and bay leaf. Cook for about 20 minutes, then add chicken and continue cooking for another 15 minutes or until vegetables and rice are very soft. Add soup as needed if soup becomes too thick. Add salt and pepper, and remove parsley and bay leaf.

To prepare this soup a day in advance, simmer vegetables and rice for only 15 minutes. Then store soup, covered, in the refrigerator for 1 day and finish cooking while reheating.

Sprinkle each portion with parsley and pass lemon wedges at the table. Serve with crusty, dense white bread such as Portuguese, Cuban, Sicilian, or French, preferable in that order.

....

YIELD: ABOUT 8 FIRST-COURSE SERVINGS;
4 TO 6 MAIN-COURSE SERVINGS

COLOMBIAN CHICKEN AND ROOT VEGETABLE SOUP
Ajiaco Colombiano

.........◆.........

This brilliant soup sparks the palate as it does the eye. The version here often appears on the winter menu at Patria in New York City— the stylish and intriguing *nueva Latino* restaurant presided over by the talented Douglas Rodriguez.

The root vegetables are available in Hispanic, West Indian, and Southeast Asian neighborhoods. They are rugged and starchy, are rich in minerals, and lend a rich, earthy flavor to the soup. If you cannot find yuca and/or malanga, substitute 3 large carrots cut into 1-inch-thick slices, 2 white turnips, or ½ pound yellow turnip (rutabaga), peeled and cubed. If you cannot find boniato (white sweet potato), substitute a large yam. The texture will a bit thinner, but the flavor and appearance will be fairly convincing.

....

FOR THE SOUP
10 cups Basic Chicken Soup (page 28), prepared with a 3¹/₂- to
*   4-pound chicken, 4 thyme sprigs, 2 garlic cloves, and 2 bay leaves*
2 tablespoons olive oil
1 small onion, diced
3 garlic cloves, minced
1 celery stalk, diced
1 tablespoon achiote seeds, pulverized with mortar and pestle or in
*   a spice grinder*
¹/₂ pound yuca root (cassava or manioc), peeled and diced
1 malanga (cocoyam), peeled and diced
1 boniato (white sweet potato) or large yam, peeled and diced
1¹/₂ pounds West Indian calabaza, pumpkin, or Hubbard or acorn
*   squash, peeled and cubed*
2 medium white boiling potatoes, unpeeled
2 ears of corn, cut into 1¹/₂-inch slices
Salt, to taste
1 fresh tomato, seeded and diced
3 scallions, green and white portions minced
2 tablespoons minced fresh chives
2 tablespoons minced fresh cilantro (coriander) leaves

FOR THE GARNISH
Cooked white rice
Avocado slices sprinkled with lime juice
Jalapeño Sauce (recipe follows)

....

Simmer soup over moderate heat, uncovered, until it reduces to 8 cups. Pick chicken meat from skin and bones, discarding the latter. Tear meat into large but still spoonable chunks and set aside.

Heat olive oil in a heavy 8-inch skillet and sauté onion, garlic, celery, and pulverized achiote until vegetables begin to soften and are translucent, about 7 minutes. Stir into soup.

Add root vegetables and squash and simmer for 35 minutes. Add potatoes and simmer 20 minutes, then add corn and cook 15 minutes more, or until all vegetables are very tender and beginning to disintegrate. (If you prefer firm corn, you can cook it for only the last few minutes, but it is more authentic when it has absorbed the soup's flavor and is quite soft.)

The soup can be prepared to this point, and stored, covered, in the refrigerator for 1 day.

Bring soup to a simmer, turn off heat, and season with salt, tomato, scal-

AJIACOS, CALDOS, CAZUELAS, COCIDOS, AND SANCOCHOS

All of these names are used in various countries throughout Latin and South America. They refer to lusty, colorful main-course soup-stews with a rainbow of root vegetables, squash, and assorted aromatics, and sometimes green plantains. There are alternatives among vegetables, but the mix of roots and squash is essential for color, texture, and flavor, to say nothing of vitamins and minerals. The recipes here are based on chicken, although other meats are often included.

Ajiaco seems to have two meanings, the most obvious being its reference to the fiery aji chili pepper used as a garnish. I have also seen it described as a chicken stew. However, many recipes for ajiacos *call for no hot peppers at all and include other meats or only vegetables.*

According to Linette Green, in her cookbook A Taste of Cuba, *ajiaco is from that country's native Taino Indians, and is a Creole dish because the Spaniards added the beef and*

sausages to the original vegetable and plantain stew.

Often these rustic soups are served with side dishes of rice, sliced or diced avocado, and Jalapeño Sauce (see below). All that is needed for dessert is a cool flan, sliced oranges and/or pineapple, a thin fruit tart, or cookies and sherbet.

lions, chives, and cilantro. Let stand for 5 minutes. Serve immediately in large bowls with a side dish of rice and sliced avocado for each portion. Pass Jalapeño Sauce at the table.

YIELD: 4 TO 6 MAIN-COURSE SERVINGS

Jalapeño Sauce

*6 jalapeño or other hot green chilies,
   preferably fresh
6 tablespoons lime juice
3 tablespoons olive oil
Pinch of salt*

Remove seeds from peppers and if they are fresh, the white ribs as well. Grind or chop peppers very finely, or chop for a second or two in a food processor but be careful they do not liquefy. By hand, mix in lime juice, oil, and salt. If mixture seems thick, add more lime juice and oil, but maintain the

2-to-1 proportion. Do not add juice and oil in food processor or result will be milky instead of bright green.

This sauce develops flavor if it is made an hour or two before it is served and kept covered, at cool room temperature. Allow $1/2$ to 1 teaspoon per portion, depending on individual palates.

VARIATIONS

Venezuelan and Ecuadorian *Sancocho*
········◆········

Follow master recipe, varying vegetables with availability and adding 2 peeled and diced green plantains (but not ripe plantains or conventional bananas). Substitute 2 to 3 tablespoons distilled white vinegar for the lime juice.

Aruba *Saucochi*
········◆········

Follow master recipe but do not add tomato and scallions. Finish hot soup with 1 seeded and minced hot green chili pepper, salt, black pepper, and 3 tablespoons minced chives. This is not served with rice and avocado on the side.

Mexican and Cuban *Cocido de Pollo*
········◆········

Follow master recipe using all vegetables except yuca and malanga, and add 3 small seeded and cubed zucchini to the mix. Soup may be garnished with a salsa of lime juice stirred into minced tomato, green bell pepper, jalapeño, and cilantro. Or serve with Jalapeño Sauce and hot corn tortillas.

CHILE'S "LITTLE POT"
Cazuela
········◆········

The enrichment of potato and egg yolk with the zap of vinegar adds an unusual texture and flavor to this very old recipe, adapted from one in the cookbook *Olla Podrida* by Elinor Burt.

The sautéed combination of butter, onion, red pepper, and cayenne is known as *colór*.

FOR THE SOUP
One 3¹/₂- to 4-pound chicken, cut into 8 pieces, with all giblets
    except liver
2 teaspoons salt
8 to 10 black peppercorns
8 to 10 cups water, or as needed
¹/₂ cup (1 stick) butter or vegetable oil
1 roasted and peeled red bell pepper or pimiento, finely minced
¹/₂ teaspoon cayenne pepper, or to taste
3 medium onions, chopped
2 small zucchini, cubed
1 pound Hubbard or acorn squash, peeled and cubed
¹/₂ pound green beans, cut into 1-inch lengths
1 large fennel bulb (about 1 pound), cut into slivers with tops
    reserved (optional)
1 teaspoon ground cumin
¹/₃ cup white rice
3 fennel or dill sprigs, or leaves from 2 mint sprigs
2 tablespoons minced fresh parsley
Kernels cut from 2 large ears of corn, or a 10-ounce package frozen
    corn kernels
1 cup fresh or frozen green peas
2 medium boiling potatoes, peeled
1 egg yolk, lightly beaten
2 tablespoons sherry, malt, or cider vinegar

FOR THE OPTIONAL GARNISH
Lime juice
Chopped fresh parsley

....

Place chicken, giblets, salt, and peppercorns in a 5-quart enameled or stainless-steel soup pot and add enough water to cover. Bring to a boil, reduce to a simmer, and skim foam as it rises to the surface. When foam subsides, simmer gently, partly covered, for about 1 hour or until chicken is falling from the bone. Add water to maintain original level. When chicken is tender, remove and trim meat from bones and skin, discarding the latter. Dice or shred meat and reserve.

To prepare *colór*, heat butter or oil in a small skillet and sauté the minced red pepper, cayenne, and 1 chopped onion. Sauté over low heat until onion and pepper are soft but not brown, about 7 minutes. Rub through a strainer into soup, pouring a little soup through the strainer to extract color and flavor. Or puree in a blender with a little soup as needed. Stir into soup.

Soup can be prepared to this point and stored, covered, in the refrigerator for 1 day.

Add zucchini, squash, beans, remaining chopped onion, fennel, cumin, rice, fennel or dill tops, and parsley. Cook, partly covered, for about 25 minutes or until all vegetables and rice are soft. Return chicken to soup and add corn and peas for last 10 minutes of cooking time. Adjust seasonings.

Meanwhile, boil potatoes in lightly salted water until soft. Mash, beating in egg yolk and vinegar to make a paste. To serve, place a dab of this paste in each bowl, then ladle in soup with chicken and vegetables. Garnish each with a dash of lime juice and a sprinkle of parsley.

....

YIELD: 4 TO 6 MAIN-COURSE SERVINGS

Chapter 7

EUROPE

Austria, Belgium, Denmark, England, France, Germany, Italy, Norway, Portugal, Scotland, Spain, Sweden, Switzerland

CONTINENTAL CREAM OF CHICKEN SOUP

·········◆·········

Whether thickened with egg yolks and cream or a béchamel (white) sauce made with butter, flour, and cream, or milk, creamed chicken soup is considered "royal" or "queenly" throughout Europe. Made with pureed chicken, it is *potage purée de volaille à la reine* in France, while the Swedes name it after their royal palace, Drottningholm, and in Germany it is dubbed *Konigin*, for "king," or *Kaisersuppe*, from the days of the Kaiser. According to the *Larousse Gastronomique*, the French version dates back to the sixteenth century, when it was served every Thursday to Queen Marguerite at the Court of Valois. More or less the same recipe is suggested for invalids (as well as gourmets) in many old American, English, and continental European cookbooks, as the pureed chicken adds nutrients yet is easy to chew and digest. The puree may be made of only white meat, but I find that dark meat adds flavor and a pleasant pink tint. Traditionally, the cooked chicken meat was pounded with a mortar and pestle, then rubbed through a sieve. A food processor purees more easily, though the finely ground meat should still be rubbed through a sieve for a really fine effect. If you do not have a food processor, use a blender, a grinder with the finest blade, or a mortar and pestle. The addition of extra celery cooked with the rice is not classic, but one I like for its delicate accent.

·················

FOR THE SOUP
6 cups degreased Basic Chicken Soup (page 28), prepared
*   with the optional leeks, thyme, and bay leaf*
2 celery stalks, diced (optional)
¹/₃ cup rice, drained and parboiled for 10 minutes
2 cooked chicken breasts; or 1 cooked breast and 1 cooked thigh
*   and leg, skinned and boned*
3 egg yolks, well beaten
1 cup heavy cream
1 to 2 tablespoons sherry or Madeira (optional)
Salt and white pepper, to taste

FOR THE GARNISH
Minced cooked chicken
Minced fresh parsley and/or chervil

·················

Simmer broth gently with celery and par-boiled rice in half-covered 2½- to 3-quart saucepan for about 25 minutes or until rice is soft. Remove and reserve celery and rice. Dice and set aside half a chicken breast for garnish. Puree the remaining chicken meat in a food processor for about 3 minutes or until it becomes a fine, grainy mass. Scrape down sides of bowl and add rice and celery and about 1 cup of broth, and puree until smooth, about 2 minutes. Place a sieve over the soup pot and, using a wooden spoon or spatula, rub chicken and rice mixture through the sieve into the soup.

The soup can be prepared up to this point and stored, covered, in the refrigerator overnight.

Just before serving, beat egg yolks with cream in a small bowl and slowly add half a ladle of hot soup, beating constantly with a wire whisk. Remove soup from stove. Slowly pour egg yolk mixture back into remaining soup, beating constantly. Stir in wine. Heat but do not boil. Serve in small cups or cream soup bowls, garnishing each portion with diced chicken breast and herbs.

YIELD: 4 TO 6 SERVINGS

VARIATIONS

Eggless Cream of Chicken Soup

This can be made by substituting a light béchamel sauce as the thickener. Prepare soup as described in the master recipe, adding the pureed chicken and rice to the soup. In a separate saucepan, melt 2 tablespoons butter, and when it is hot and bubbling, stir in 2 tablespoons flour. Stir and cook for 4 or 5 minutes over low heat, then pour in 1 cup hot light cream, half-and-half, or whole milk. Stir with a wire whisk until smooth and simmer for about 5 minutes or until thickened. Turn into soup and simmer for 10 minutes, stirring several times. Add wine to taste and adjust other seasonings. (To reduce starch when using flour, you can eliminate rice and puree only chicken and celery.)

Creamed Chicken Soup with Almonds

A European classic, this is an elegant starter to a formal dinner. Grind ¼ cup blanched almonds in the food processor for 2 or 3 minutes before adding chicken, rice, and broth. When smooth, rub through the sieve along with chicken and rice. Traditionally, 2 or 3 bitter almonds would be included, but

¹/₄ teaspoon almond extract, added with the wine, produces the same bracing effect. Adjust seasonings and garnish with herbs or slivers of toasted almonds.

JELLIED CONSOMMÉ
.........◆.........

Jellied consommé was a Roaring Twenties favorite at fancy dinners here as in France and elsewhere in Europe, and it is an old-time standard for convalescents. Because it melts rapidly, this soup classically is served in the dish known as a supreme, a small bowl set into a metal frame and suspended into a larger bowl filled with crushed ice. More practically, cups of the soup can be nested in larger bowls of crushed ice. It is even simpler, however, to spoon the jellied soup into small bowls that have been well chilled in the freezer and to serve immediately, as soon as diners are seated. It is a refreshing opener to a summer dinner, especially with a dash of lemon juice added at the table.

....

FOR THE SOUP
5 cups degreased, clarified Basic Chicken Soup (page 28),
  prepared with optional leeks, thyme, and bay leaf
2 envelopes (2 tablespoons) unflavored gelatin
¹/₂ cup dry white wine or water
Salt and pepper, to taste

FOR THE GARNISH
Minced chives, parsley, or chervil leaves, separately or in
  combination
Thin wedges of lemon

....

Be sure all traces of fat are gone from the broth or the final result will be unappealing. Sprinkle gelatin into white wine or water and let it stand for 5 minutes or until it has absorbed the liquid and softened.

Bring broth to a simmer. Add dissolved gelatin to simmering soup, stirring until gelatin is completely dissolved. Season with salt, pepper, and, if you like, another tablespoonful or two of white wine.

Pour into bowl and let cool, uncovered. Cover and chill for 5 to 7 hours.

Cut into spoon-size cubes and spoon into chilled, small soup bowls or cups and serve immediately. Sprinkle individual portions with herbs and serve with a lemon wedge.

....

YIELD: 4 SERVINGS

VARIATION

Jellied Consommé Made with Calf's Foot or Veal Knuckle Bones

This has much more flavor than consommé set with gelatin, but you have to start from scratch. Prepare the soup with a cleaned, scalded, and split calf's foot or 2 large cracked veal knuckle bones, along with the chicken as described in Basic Chicken Soup (page 28), using the optional leeks, thyme, and bay leaf. When chicken soup is done, discard foot or knuckle bones along with vegetables. Strain, reduce, and clarify soup as described on page 23. Adjust seasonings with salt, pepper, and a little white wine. Chill, covered, for at least 7 hours or until soup is set. Cut into spoon-size cubes and heap into chilled cups. Serve with herbs and lemon wedge.

ENGLAND
◆◆◆

BAKED COTTAGE SOUP

For this gently delicious soup I adapted a recipe from *The Encyclopedia of Practical Cookery*, a six-volume treasure published in England in the late nineteenth century which also became popular in the United States. The advantages of baking soup in the oven are a more intense flavor, little fuss, and less reduction of the liquid so it does not need replenishing. It was probably also economical in the days when wood- or coal-fired stoves burned constantly for warmth. The result is a sheer, restorative near-broth, only slightly thickened by the split peas, and with a very fresh vegetable and chicken flavor.

The recipe requires a 4- to 5-quart covered crock or bean pot.

....

FOR THE SOUP
One 3¹/₂- to 4-pound chicken, cut into 8 parts, with neck and all
    giblets except liver
2 medium onions, sliced
2 large carrots, cut into 1-inch-thick slices
2 large celery stalks, sliced
2 cups green split peas, washed and picked over
1 teaspoon salt
8 to 10 crushed black peppercorns
¹/₂ teaspoon dried leaf thyme, or 4 fresh thyme sprigs
2 quarts cold water

FOR THE GARNISH
Chopped fresh parsley
8 small oval slices of French bread, or 1¹/₂ cups croutons, browned
    in butter

....

Preheat the oven to 375° F.

Place chicken and giblets in the crock, then top with onions, carrots, celery, and split peas. Add salt, peppercorns, thyme, and water. Cover and bake for about 3 hours or until chicken and vegetables virtually disintegrate.

A 17TH-CENTURY CURE-ALL

*E*nglish chicken soups of the past seem more intriguing and varied than those of today, and they were accorded high status as health builders. In his historic cookbook The Closet of Sir Kenelme Digbie, Opened, *published in 1669, the author included several versions of* potage de santé, *literally "health soup," made with meat as well as fowl or capon. A variation on his oft-quoted recipe, "Portugal broth as made for the queen," is the greatly reduced, strongly aromatic eye-opener, "Queen's ordinary bouillon de Santé," meant to be drunk in* the morning and made as follows: "A hen, a handful of parsley, a sprig of thyme, three of spearmint, a little lemon balm, half a great onion, a little pepper and salt, and a clove, as much water as would cover the hen; and this boiled to less than a pint for one good porringer full."

Strain into a clean saucepan, rubbing through as much of the peas and vegetables as possible, but eliminating the giblets and shreds of chicken that by this time should be unpleasantly matted and flavorless. It may be necessary to pour strained soup back over the solids in the sieve to extract all the pea and vegetable puree. Skim off fat, of which there should be very little, reheat, and adjust seasonings.

Ladle soup into warm bowls, top with parsley, and pass croutons or bread slices.

This soup can be stored, covered, in the refrigerator for up to 2 days. It can be frozen for up to 3 months.

....

YIELD: 6 SERVINGS

GREEN PEA AND GIBLET SOUP

.........◆.........

Versions of this soup are in several early American cookbooks from the colony of Virginia, but the term "English peas" for dried green peas and the spicing of mace or red pepper point to its English origin. Although whole dried green peas were probably used, modern split peas requiring little if any presoaking streamline the recipe with no loss of flavor.

....

2 cups green split peas, or 3 cups whole dried green peas, washed and picked over
3 cups Basic Chicken Soup (page 28)
5 cups water, or as needed
Salt, to taste
1 pound chicken giblets that may include necks, gizzards, and hearts but not livers
12 to 14 whole cloves
Pinch of dried red pepper flakes; or 1 small fresh red chili pepper, seeded
Pinch of mace, or to taste
1/4 pound chicken livers, cleaned, trimmed, and diced

....

Boil peas in water to cover for 5 minutes. Drain and discard liquid. Rinse peas under running water and place in a 3-quart soup pot along with stock, water, a pinch of salt, and all remaining ingredients except chicken livers.

Bring to a boil, then simmer, partly covered, for about 1 hour or until peas are completely soft and giblets are tender. Stir during cooking and add water or stock if peas thicken too quickly. Discard cloves and fresh red pepper. Remove giblets and trim off all tender meat. Chop coarsely and return to soup.

Add diced chicken livers about 15 minutes before serving. Simmer until livers are cooked but not hard. Adjust seasonings and serve.

This soup can be stored, covered, in the refrigerator for 24 hours if chicken livers have been added or up to 48 hours if they have not. If livers have been added, soup should be reheated very gently and kept just below the boiling point.

....

YIELD: 6 SERVINGS

SCOTLAND

◆◆◆

COCK-A-LEEKIE

.........◆.........

Along with haggis and shortbread, cock-a-leekie is one of Scotland's best-known dishes. Probably because of the leeks, it seems especially efficacious for a head cold. Whether for that reason or simply because she liked it—or, perhaps, as a diplomatic gesture toward Scotland— Queen Victoria had it served at a royal dinner in Windsor Castle in 1892. Perhaps her chef followed the instructions of Mrs. Margaret Dods, author of *The Cook and Housewife's Manual,* published in Edinburgh in 1826, who advised, "The soup must be very thick of leeks, and the first part of them must be boiled down into the soup until it becomes a lubricous compound."

Strictly speaking, this soup should be made with an old rooster—a cock. In times past, that meant the losers of cockfights, who were thrown into pots and cooked as long as necessary to impart a rich flavor to the soup and to tenderize the meat. It is much easier to find a large hen or fowl that simmers long and slowly until the leeks and barley melt to a heady porridgelike, lubricous compound. If a hen is also unavailable, 2 large broilers and a veal knuckle bone should be substituted.

*Come me lords
and lieges, let us
all to dinner, for
the cocky-leeky is
a-cooling.*

—SIR WALTER SCOTT, *THE
FORTUNES OF NIGEL*

There are the inevitable pros and cons as to which ingredients are authentic. The most controversial seems to be prunes added toward the end of cooking time, a touch that sounded awful to me until I tasted the winy dimension they impart to the broth. I cared less for the flavor of the prune itself when eaten with the soup, and found it a mistake to store leftover soup with the fruit, as the broth then becomes too sweet. You can also get an argument as to whether the bird should be trussed, if it should be started in water or veal stock, if a veal bone should be added, and if the soup should include barley or herbs such as parsley, thyme, cloves, bay leaves, or mace.

The version below is the one I prefer.

....

One 5½- to 6-pound fowl or rooster, or two 3½- to 4-pound broilers, with all giblets except liver and 1 veal marrow bone
8 or 9 large leeks
1 fresh thyme sprig, or ½ teaspoon dried leaf thyme (optional)
10 black peppercorns
2 to 3 teaspoons salt, to taste
⅔ cup medium pearl barley, washed
4 to 5 quarts water, as needed
½ cup minced fresh parsley

....

Place fowl, giblets, and veal bone in a 10-quart soup pot, preferably of enameled cast-iron or other nonreactive material.

Use the white bulbs of the leeks plus about 1½ inches of the yellow-green tops. Separate layers and wash well under running cold water until all sand is removed. Wash a few of the larger but tender leaves and set them aside in a bowl of cold water. Slice leeks diagonally in thick ovals and add to chicken along with peppercorns, salt, and barley.

Pour in 3 quarts and bring to a boil slowly. Skim off scum as it rises. When the soup is clear, cover pot loosely and reduce heat to a very low but steady simmer. The cooking time should be about 3 hours or until the chicken practically falls off the bone and both leeks and barley are nearly mush. Add water sparingly, as needed, during cooking to keep chicken covered, and turn chicken several times.

Discard bone, removing any marrow to be diced and added to the soup. Discard giblets and thyme sprig. Remove chicken and trim off all skin and bones. Cut, or, better yet, pull chicken meat into spoon-size shreds and set aside. Skim all grease off top of soup, blotting with a paper towel to remove as much fat as possible. Slice reserved leek greens thinly and add to soup along with reserved chicken.

Bring soup to the boiling point, then reduce heat and simmer gently, partly covered, for 20 minutes or until greens are tender. Stir frequently to prevent barley from scorching. Add parsley and adjust salt. Simmer for another 5 minutes, then serve in large heated soup bowls.

Leftover Cock-a-Leekie keeps well for 24 hours in the refrigerator and freezes well for up to 2 weeks. But because it is starchy and scorches easily, it should be reheated gently in a heavy-bottomed pot, preferably over an asbestos pad or metal insulator, or in a double boiler.

....

YIELD: 10 FIRST-COURSE SERVINGS; 6 GENEROUS MAIN-COURSE SERVINGS

VARIATION

Cock-a-Leekie with Prunes

..........◆..........

Soak 10 unpitted, unsulphured prunes in cold water at room temperature for 5 hours. Add to the soup for the last 30 minutes of cooking time and serve 1 or 2 prunes per portion. (Do not use pitted prunes as their inside pulp will disintegrate and muddy the soup.)

FEATHER FOWLIE

..........◆..........

This is one of the many dishes said to have been a favorite of Mary Stuart, Queen of Scots. A version is also favored in Ireland, where the cooked chicken is covered with a parsley cream sauce and served as a separate course.

....

One 3½- to 4-pound chicken, disjointed (see page 17)
½ pound cooked ham, chopped
2 celery stalks, diced
1 medium onion, chopped
1 large carrot, scraped and diced
1 leek, split and washed
3 parsley sprigs
2 fresh thyme sprigs, or 1 teaspoon dried leaf thyme
8 to 10 cups water, as needed

Salt and pepper, to taste
$^1/_2$ teaspoon ground mace
3 egg yolks
$^1/_4$ cup heavy cream
Chopped fresh parsley

....

Place chicken in a close-fitting 5-quart soup pot along with ham, celery, onion, carrot, leek, parsley, and thyme. Cover with 8 to 10 cups water, then add salt, pepper, and mace.

Bring to a boil, reduce to a simmer, and skim off foam as it rises to the surface. When soup is clear, simmer gently, partly covered, for about 2 hours or until the meat is tender and falling from the bone. Remove chicken and trim off all skin and bones. Reserve dark meat for another use, and mince the white breast meat.

Strain soup and skim off grease. Pour soup into a clean 3-quart saucepan and simmer, uncovered, for about 15 minutes or until slightly reduced.

The soup can be prepared up to this point and stored, covered, in the refrigerator for 1 day. Skim before reheating.

Ten minutes before serving, heat soup to a simmer and adjust seasonings. Beat the egg yolks with the cream in a small bowl, then slowly add 2 cups of the soup, beating constantly. Pour warmed egg yolk mixture back into hot but not simmering soup, beating constantly. Stir in minced chicken meat and chopped parsley, adjust seasonings, and heat thoroughly but do not boil.

....

YIELD: 6 SERVINGS

DENMARK

◆■◆

CONFINEMENT SOUP
Barselsuppe
.... ◆ ....

Barsel means "confinement" in Danish, and until the early part of this century, this rich and clear reduced chicken soup was served as a strength builder to a new mother, so that she could be up and about her duties in nine days. Neighbors carried it in glazed stoneware *barselpots*, or confinement jars, that were tall and plump and had lids and handles. Jonna Dwinger, a friend and journalist who writes about food and other subjects for the Danish newspaper *Politiken*, said the dumplings and/or meatballs in Copenhagen Banquet Soup (page 93) might be included, but that generally confinement soup was served clear or only with the diced white meat of chicken. Reproductions of *barselpots* can be found in small shops around Denmark, but now they are used for flowers, alas.

....

Ingredients for Basic Chicken Soup (page 28), made with
*　　quartered chicken*
1 small parsnip, cut in half vertically
2 medium leeks, white and green sections
Salt and pepper, to taste
Chopped fresh parsley

....

Prepare soup according to ingredients on page 28, adding the parsnip and leeks. When chicken is done, remove from soup, trim off skin and bones, and dice breast meat to serve in soup or reserve with dark meat for other uses. Discard vegetables. Return soup to pot and boil rapidly, uncovered, for about 20 minutes or until it is reduced by about one third. Season with salt and pepper. Serve clear or with diced chicken. Sprinkle with chopped parsley.

....

YIELD: 6 TO 8 FIRST-COURSE SERVINGS;
4 MAIN-COURSE SERVINGS

COPENHAGEN BANQUET SOUP
Festsuppe
·········◆·········

s its name implies, this is an elegant and festive soup. It is traditionally a first course, in the style of Italian broth with tortellini, and is served in relatively small portions to be followed by a fish or meat main dish.

The soup is exactly the same as Confinement Soup (page 92), but it is not reduced. It is served clear, garnished with tiny meatballs (following) and the small rivels on page 56. Individual servings should contain 3 or 4 meatballs and dumplings each and a sprinkling of parsley. To add a bit more color, dice 1 or 2 small carrots and 2 celery stalks and cook in the clear soup when reheating. (Do not serve the vegetables that cooked in the basic soup.)

Danish Meatballs
·········◆·········

¼ pound lean chuck beef and ¼ pound lean veal, very finely
  ground together 3 times
2 teaspoons grated onion
3 to 4 tablespoons flour
1 extra-large egg, lightly beaten
Generous pinch of salt and black pepper

·················

Combine all ingredients lightly but thoroughly with a fork, starting with 3 tablespoons of flour and adding more only if needed to make a mixture that is sticky but workable. Chill for 30 minutes.

Using 2 teaspoons dipped in hot water or the wet palms of your hands, shape mixture into tiny balls about ½ inch in diameter. Drop into rapidly boiling salted water, reduce to a low simmer, cover loosely, and cook for about 7 minutes or until meatballs are puffy and float to the surface. Remove with a slotted spoon, drain, and keep warm until serving. Reheat in the soup.

·················

YIELD: 26 TO 30 MEATBALLS;
ENOUGH FOR ABOUT 6 SERVINGS OF SOUP

NORWAY
◆◆◆

CHICKEN SOUP WITH APPLES AND VEGETABLES
Hünsekjüttsuppe
········◆········

O ne might conjecture that this soup reflects the kinship of the Norsemen with Normandy, for chicken soup with apples and leeks is favored in both regions.

....

1 quart Basic Chicken Soup (page 28)
3 tablespoons unsalted butter
1 leek, white portion only, cleaned and thinly sliced
1 small carrot, peeled and finely diced
A 2-inch piece of parsnip, peeled and finely diced
3 tablespoons flour
2 medium Granny Smith or other tart apples,
    peeled, quartered, and cut into ¹/₂-inch vertical slices
1¹/₂ cups diced cooked chicken breast
Salt and white pepper, to taste

....

Heat broth to a simmer. Melt butter in a saucepan and slowly sauté leek, carrot, and parsnip for about 7 minutes or until they begin to soften but do not take on color. Stir in flour and cook for 5 minutes, stirring until well blended. Turn into hot soup, stirring vigorously. Simmer gently for about 10 minutes or until soup is smooth and slightly thick.

Add apple slices and chicken, and simmer about 10 minutes or until apples and vegetables are tender but slightly firm. Adjust seasonings.

....

YIELD: 4 TO 6 SERVINGS

SWEDEN
◆◆◆

CHRISTER'S CHICKEN AND SAVOY CABBAGE SOUP
Hönssoppa med Savoykål
·········◆·········

C hrister Larsson, the talented Swedish chef who holds forth at his handsome restaurant Christer's, in New York City, generously developed this soup for me, based on vegetables and the airy dill favored in his native land. Browning the chicken and vegetables and the long, slow simmering give this golden-brown soup a lusty richness. It is most elegantly garnished with chicken dumplings, but for plainer tastes—or cooks pressed for time—poached breast meat can be substituted.

···················

FOR THE SOUP
Two 3¹/₂- to 4-pound chickens, preferably young fowl
1 large carrot, scraped
1 large leek, white portion only, well washed
2 celery stalks
1 medium onion
2 bay leaves
1 teaspoon black peppercorns
12 allspice berries
4 garlic cloves
1 fresh thyme sprig, or ¹/₂ teaspoon dried leaf thyme
4 quarts water, or more as needed
1¹/₂ pounds savoy cabbage
4 tablespoons (¹/₂ stick) butter or mild-flavored vegetable oil
4 medium boiling potatoes, peeled and cubed (optional)
Swedish Dilled Chicken Dumplings (page 97)

FOR THE GARNISH
Minced fresh dill

···················

Preheat the oven to 375° F.
Remove breast meat from both chickens, discarding the skin.

Reserve breast meat for dumplings. Cut remaining chicken with skin and bones into convenient large sections. Arrange in a baking pan. Cut carrot, leek, celery, and onion into large chunks and arrange around chicken. Roast for about 30 minutes or until all are light golden brown. Turn several times so chicken pieces brown all over and vegetables are moistened with chicken drippings.

Place browned chicken and vegetables in a close-fitting 7-quart soup pot. Skim fat off roasting pan juices, then add clear juices to pot. Add a little water to the roasting pan and scrape in coagulated juices and add to soup pot.

Add bay leaves, peppercorns, allspice berries (do not substitute ground allspice), garlic, thyme, and water. Bring to a boil, reduce to a simmer, and skim off all foam. Partly cover pot and simmer soup, very slowly, for $3\frac{1}{2}$ to 4 hours or until chicken is thoroughly off bones. Replenish water as it evaporates to keep at 4-quart level. Stir intermittently.

Remove and discard all solids and spices. Thoroughly skim all fat from soup.

Cut cabbages into quarters, wash well, and cut out heavy white cores. Shred finely as for coleslaw. Heat butter or oil in a 12- to 14-inch heavy-bottomed skillet and stir in cabbage. Sauté slowly, stirring frequently, for about 10 minutes or until cabbage is golden brown but not black. Add cabbage to soup along with potatoes, if you are using them, and simmer, partly covered, for 20 to 30 minutes.

Drop dumplings carefully into simmering soup and cook for 5 to 6 minutes or until they float to the surface.

Adjust seasonings with salt and pepper and serve in wide, heated soup plates. Garnish each portion with a sprinkling of fresh dill and 2 dumplings (for a first course) or about 5 for a main course.

This soup tastes best when prepared 24 hours in advance. Store with dumplings, covered, in the refrigerator. Skim fat off again before reheating.

....

YIELD: ABOUT 12 FIRST-COURSE PORTIONS; 8 MAIN-COURSE PORTIONS

NOTE: If you prefer not to prepare the dumplings, poach whole reserved chicken breasts in the soup for the last 30 minutes of cooking, before the cabbage is added. Reserve in a warm place. After cabbage is cooked, dice or shred chicken and reheat in soup.

Swedish Dilled Chicken Dumplings

·········◆·········

1 small red onion, finely diced
2 tablespoons (¹/₄ stick) unsalted butter, or 1 slice finely chopped
*   lean bacon*
Reserved chicken breast meat (from soup)
2 chicken livers
1 tablespoon salt
¹/₂ teaspoon ground allspice
Generous pinch of grated nutmeg
1 teaspoon ground black pepper
1 medium potato, peeled and boiled
1 egg
¹/₂ cup milk
2 to 4 tablespoons flour, as needed
1 cup minced fresh dill

···················

Begin to prepare dumplings about 1 hour before they are to be cooked. Sauté the onion in butter or, for more flavor, with chopped bacon that has been slightly melted, until onion is soft but not brown, about 7 minutes. Reserve.

Cut chicken meat and livers into chunks, removing sinews and connective tissue, and place in a food processor. Add salt, spices, potato and egg and process for 3 to 4 minutes or until ground but still a bit coarse. Alternatively, process in milk and flour until mixture is the consistency of thick oatmeal. Mixture should be sticky and fall from a spoon in clumps. Stir in sautéed onion and ¹/₂ cup dill. (If you do not have a processor, use a meat grinder with the finest blade and put the chicken, liver, and potatoes through alternately, mixing spices and egg in by hand, then adding flour and milk and other ingredients as described.)

The dumpling mixture can be cooked at once or held for 30 minutes in the refrigerator, which makes it a little easier to handle.

Shape dumplings either with 2 oval soup or dessert spoons dipped in hot water or with slightly wet hands. Ideally they should be in large ovals, each formed from one rounded spoonful of the mixture, or in balls about 1¹/₂ inches in diameter. Dumplings are ready to be dropped into soup.

Dumplings can be prepared 1 or 2 hours before serving, leaving dumplings in soup and keeping pot uncovered. Reheat thoroughly before proceeding.

···················

YIELD: 28 TO 32 LARGE DUMPLINGS

BELGIUM
◆◆◆

CHICKEN WATERZOI
Waterzoi à la Gantoise
········· ◆ ·········

S ometimes prepared with fish and eel, around Ghent this leek-scented soup is made with chicken. The name derives from the Flemish dialect in which *water* means just that, and *zooi*, or *ziedem*, means simmered. But simmered water hardly begins to describe the richness of this main-course soup.

·················

FOR THE SOUP
One 5-pound fowl or equivalent in broilers, quartered, with all
    giblets except liver
3 quarts water, or as needed
6 tablespoons (³/₄ stick) unsalted butter
2 large onions, coarsely chopped
3 medium leeks, white portions only, chopped
1 large or 2 small parsley roots, scraped and diced; or 1 small
    parsnip; or 1 large carrot, chopped
3 celery stalks, chopped
1 large bay leaf
¹/₂ teaspoon ground thyme, or 3 fresh sprigs
1 cup dry white wine
3 or 4 parsley sprigs
8 to 10 white peppercorns
1 teaspoon salt, or to taste
4 egg yolks
1 cup heavy cream
2 to 3 tablespoons lemon juice
Ground white pepper, to taste

FOR THE OPTIONAL GARNISH
1 or 2 boiled, peeled
    small potatoes per serving
Chopped fresh parsley

·················

Place chicken and giblets in a 7- or 8-quart soup pot and add water to cover. Bring to a boil, cover partly, and simmer for 30 minutes, skimming off foam as it rises to the surface.

Heat butter in a saucepan and sauté chopped vegetables for 7 or 8 minutes or until they soften and begin to turn golden. Stir into soup with all melted butter. Add bay leaf, thyme, wine, parsley, peppercorns, and salt. Continue simmering, partly covered, until chicken is completely tender and begins to fall from the bone, about 2 hours.

Remove chicken and trim off all bones and skin. Cut the chicken meat from thighs and breasts into long strips and reserve. Save drumsticks and wings for snacks.

Strain soup into a clean 5-quart soup pot and discard all vegetables and giblets. Let cool, undisturbed, for 20 to 30 minutes, then skim off as much fat as possible. You should have 9 to 10 cups of soup. If there is more, boil rapidly, uncovered, until it is reduced.

The soup can be prepared up to this point and stored, covered, in the refrigerator for 1 day.

Using a fork, beat egg yolks and cream in a 1-quart bowl. Slowly spoon in 2 cups of the hot soup, beating constantly with a wire whisk or fork. Then pour egg mixture in a slow stream into barely simmering soup, beating constantly. Add reserved chicken and heat thoroughly but do not let soup boil. Season with lemon juice, additional salt, and ground white pepper.

Serve soup with strips of chicken in heated wide bowls and, if you like, 1 or 2 small boiled potatoes in each portion. Sprinkle with chopped parsley.

YIELD: 4 TO 6 MAIN-COURSE SERVINGS

VARIATION

A leaner Chicken Waterzoi is prepared without the egg yolk and cream thickening. Season the finished and skimmed broth with lemon juice and sprinkle ¼ cup fresh bread crumbs on each portion, then top with parsley.

FRANCE

◆◆◆

GARNISHED CONSOMMÉ
Consommé Garní

.... ◆ ....

From an esthetic standpoint, chicken consommé is held in high esteem, and some 40 variations are listed in *Larousse Gastronomique.* (There are many more consommés, but others are based on meat, game, or fish.) The range is from the elaborate *consommé à l'ambassadrice,* which is decked out with truffled chicken quenelles and tiny profiteroles filled with foie gras and chervil, to the simple *consommé aux pàte d'italie* (garnished with one of the Italian pasta specialties on page 132, cooked right in the broth), the Consommé à la Semoule (page 113), and *consommé à la parisienne,* for which finely diced carrots, the white portion of leek, turnips, and onion are lightly braised in butter until they wilt but take on no color before being added to the broth with diced or sliced Royal Custard (see page 36). If those same vegetables are browned in the butter, then simmered in the soup, the result is the lustier *consommé brunoise* and the additional garnish may be the same custard, or a fine pasta, or 1 poached egg per portion, or rice or barley cooked in the broth. For either of the latter consommés, you will need 1 cup finely diced vegetables in equal proportions and 2 tablespoons unsalted butter in which to sauté them, for 6 cups of simmering consommé.

Consommé should be reduced (see page 22) and strained, but I do not think it needs to be clarified for the above preparations. If, however, you want it to be very clear, follow the instructions on page 23.

WHIPPED EGG AND CHICKEN BROTH
Sabayon de Poulet

.... ◆ ....

As luxurious as this and the recipe for Baked Chicken Custard (page 101) may seem to us, both were recommended for invalids in *The Epicurean,* written by Charles Ranhofer, the famed chef at Delmonico's in New York City during its turn-of-the-century heyday.

My personal favorite is Consommé Pritanier, a springtime refresher garnished with tiny, new, green spring vegetables—diced new white onions, green peas, just the tips of the smallest asparagus, ½-inch slices of green beans, and finely diced baby carrot—are simmered until almost tender in lightly salted water, and then finished in the hot soup and seasoned with chervil. One mixed cupful of vegetables will do for 6 cups of consommé.

Although he recommends it for invalids, he also includes the dishes on several formal banquet menus.

Although not sweet or a dessert, this soup is prepared in the manner of Italian *zabaglione* or German *Weinschaum*. It is a frothy and fragrant restorative, best sipped from a cup, and makes an exquisite forerunner to a main course of simple grilled fish, meat with a green vegetable, or a seafood salad. It is also a stylish first course for brunch if no aperitif or any egg dishes are to be served.

....

4 egg yolks
1 1/2 cups degreased Basic Chicken Soup (page 28), prepared with
    optional leeks, thyme, and bay leaf, at room temperature
Salt and white pepper, to taste
1 tablespoon dry sherry or Madeira, or to taste

....

Beat egg yolks in a bowl and slowly whisk in chicken soup. Place in the top of a double boiler and set over very hot, but not boiling, water that does not touch the bottom of the upper pan. Cook over simmering water, beating constantly and briskly with a wire whisk for about 5 minutes, being careful that water does not get so hot that eggs curdle. The mixture should be pale and frothy and thick enough to coat the back of a wooden spoon. Remove from the heat and whisk in salt, pepper, and sherry. Serve immediately in heated cups.

....

YIELD: 3 TEACUPS
OR 6 DEMITASSE–CUP SERVINGS

BAKED CHICKEN CUSTARD
Crème Bain-Marie de Volaille

.... ◆ ....

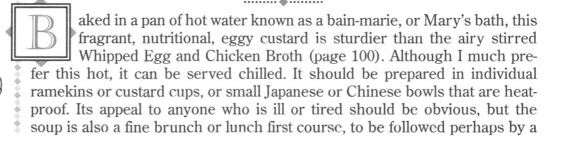

Baked in a pan of hot water known as a bain-marie, or Mary's bath, this fragrant, nutritional, eggy custard is sturdier than the airy stirred Whipped Egg and Chicken Broth (page 100). Although I much prefer this hot, it can be served chilled. It should be prepared in individual ramekins or custard cups, or small Japanese or Chinese bowls that are heatproof. Its appeal to anyone who is ill or tired should be obvious, but the soup is also a fine brunch or lunch first course, to be followed perhaps by a main-course salad or delicate sandwiches and a green salad, but no other egg dishes.

....

6 egg yolks
2 cups warm, degreased Basic Chicken Soup (page 28), prepared
    with optional leeks, thyme, bay leaf, and cloves
Salt and white pepper, to taste

....

Heat the oven to 325° F.

Set 6 ramekins or custard cups in a shallow baking pan large enough to hold them without having them touch. Boil water in a kettle.

Lightly beat egg yolks, then beat in warm (but not hot) chicken broth. Pour through a sieve, taste a bit on your finger, and adjust seasonings. This is very good when slightly peppery.

Fill the ramekins or cups to within $1/4$ inch of rim. Slide out the shelf in the lower third of the oven and set pan with custard cups on rack. Pour in rapidly boiling water to come halfway up sides of ramekins or cups, then slide shelf into oven very carefully so custard does not overflow.

Bake for 35 to 45 minutes or until custard is firm. Do not increase heat, or custard may disintegrate; custard in a shallow ramekin will set faster than that in a deep custard cup. A thin crust that may crackle will form on top.

Remove cups from water, dry ramekins, set on small plates, and serve immediately with teaspoons or demitasse spoons. Or to chill, let cool thoroughly at room temperature, then top each ramekin with plastic wrap and place in refrigerator for 5 hours or overnight.

....

YIELD: 6 SERVINGS

CHICKEN BOURRIDE
Bourride de Poulet

.........◆.........

L ike bouillabaisse, this creamy, richly garlicked main-course soup of Provence is usually prepared with fish, but lends itself readily to chicken. With the garlic mayonnaise, aïoli, it is also related to a Grand Aïoli, a meal of soup followed by a huge platter of assorted fish or a whole poached chicken surrounded by vegetables for an elegant boiled-in-one-pot dinner.

....

France has the most intriguing and diverse repertory of chicken soups in Europe, although one hears little about its curative or comforting powers today. In times past, chicken soups in many elegant forms were recommended as restoratives, most especially with the addition of eggs, cream, or pounded chicken meat.

FOR THE SOUP

One 3¹/₂- to 4-pound chicken, cut into 8 pieces
¹/₃ cup olive oil
2 celery stalks, thinly sliced
2 or 3 fennel stalks, cut into ¹/₄-inch strips (about ²/₃ cup)
1 large carrot, cut into ¹/₄-inch-thick rounds
1 large leek, white portion only, thinly sliced
2 garlic cloves
Salt and freshly ground black pepper, to taste
1 cup dry white wine, heated
3 cups degreased Basic Chicken Soup (page 28) or Improved
    Canned Chicken Broth (page 30), heated
1 fresh thyme sprig, or ¹/₂ teaspoon dried leaf thyme
1 small bay leaf
2 or 3 fennel sprigs, or ¹/₂ teaspoon crushed fennel seeds
1 hot red chili pepper, seeded; or
    ¹/₂ teaspoon dried red pepper flakes
5 or 6 saffron threads, crushed
Aïoli Sauce (recipe follows)
8 to 10 small toasted French bread slices

FOR THE OPTIONAL GARNISHES
¹/₄ pound vermicelli
1 or 2 boiled small new potatoes per serving
1 small head green cabbage, cut into wedges and cooked
3 small zucchini, cut into 1¹/₂-inch round slices and cooked
Minced fresh parsley

Let chicken come to room temperature. Heat oil in a 5-quart nonreactive casserole, preferably of enameled cast-iron. When oil is hot, add celery, fennel, carrot, leek, and garlic and sauté slowly, stirring frequently, for about 10 to 15 minutes or until vegetables soften but do not brown. Cover for 2 or 3 minutes so vegetables steam in their juices.

Add chicken, sprinkle with salt and pepper, and stir through the vegetables. Pour in wine and let boil for 2 or 3 minutes, then add soup along with herbs and spices. Simmer gently but steadily, partly covered, for about 1 hour or until chicken is completely tender. Stir during cooking to prevent scorching and add more stock if necessary, although it should not be. Remove chicken when tender and discard bay leaf, thyme, and fennel.

The soup can be prepared up to this point and stored, covered, in the refrigerator, overnight. Aïoli Sauce can be prepared just before serving, or a few hours in advance if it is refrigerated.

Before serving, remove skin from chicken and skim fat from soup. Chicken can be served on or off the bone, as you like. Return trimmed chicken to the soup to heat thoroughly.

Cook vermicelli for garnish in lightly salted boiling water until tender, and do the same with any other vegetables you want to serve with the chicken.

Just before serving, remove soup from heat and beat in ⅓ cup Aïoli Sauce. Reheat but do not boil. Serve soup with vermicelli in heated cream soup or similar small bowls and pass toasted bread.

Arrange chicken on a platter or on individual plates with potatoes, cabbage, and zucchini. Spoon some of the soup with the vegetables that cooked in it over all as a sauce. Sprinkle with parsley and serve with additional Aïoli Sauce on the side.

....

YIELD: 4 TO 6 SERVINGS OF SOUP PLUS MAIN COURSE

VARIATION

For a less formal presentation, the soup can be served as a one-dish meal in a wide bowl with boned and skinned pieces of chicken, potato, and vegetables. In that case, eliminate the vermicelli and, if you like, substitute rice for potatoes. Sprinkle with parsley and pass toast and Aïoli Sauce on the side.

Aïoli Sauce
.... ◆ ....

 his is essentially an egg yolk and olive oil mayonnaise strongly flavored with crushed garlic. It is best prepared in a bowl with a wire whisk, or with a mortarF and pestle, but it can be done in a blender.

....

5 garlic cloves
Pinch of coarse salt
4 egg yolks, at room temperature
About 1½ to 2 cups mild-flavored olive oil, at room temperature
2 to 3 slices firm white bread without crusts, soaked in ½ cup cold
*   water (optional)*
½ teaspoon salt, or to taste
Pinch of freshly ground white pepper
2 to 3 tablespoons fresh lemon juice, to taste

....

Cut garlic cloves in half vertically and remove any green inner core to avoid an overly sharp flavor. The garlic can be crushed to a fine paste with coarse salt using a mortar and pestle, or it can be put through a garlic press and then mashed with the salt. Blend in the egg yolks, using the pestle or a wire whisk. (If you use a blender, puree the garlic with salt and yolks.)

Gradually trickle in the olive oil, beating constantly with a whisk or with the blender on slow speed. Watch carefully after you have added 1½ cups of oil to be sure yolks can absorb more without oil separating. If the mixture curdles, beat in 1 tablespoon boiling water and blend or beat slowly until it is smooth.

The soaked bread can be beaten in at this point to add body and mellow flavor. Squeeze all the water from bread; you should have about 3 table-spoonfuls of soaked bread. Beat it in to mixture. If you prefer an intense, oily sauce, do not add bread. Season with salt, pepper, and lemon juice.

This sauce may be served immediately or stored in the refrigerator for 2 or 3 hours. It should be served at room temperature.

YIELD: ABOUT 2 CUPS

VARIATION

Aïoli Made with Cooked Egg Yolks

Because of salmonella problems, some cooks worry about the raw eggs in aïoli. Hard-cooked egg yolks can be pureed with olive oil, but I find that a greasy, unharmonious alternative, especially when stirred into the soup. It is better and easier to prepare the aïoli from a decent store-bought true mayonnaise that has been cooked; my choice is Hellmann's or Best Foods. The results are acceptable if slightly less elegant and distinctive. Do not add bread to this mixture, as it will become too sticky.

5 garlic cloves
Pinch of coarse salt
1 cup prepared mayonnaise, at room temperature
1 cup mild-flavored olive oil, at room temperature
¼ teaspoon salt, or to taste
Pinch of ground white pepper, or to taste
2 to 3 tablespoons fresh lemon juice, to taste

Cut garlic cloves in half vertically and remove the green inner core to avoid an overly sharp flavor. Crush with salt using a mortar and pestle, or press through a garlic press, then crush in a bowl with the coarse salt. Beat in mayonnaise.

Slowly trickle in olive oil, beating constantly and briskly with a wire whisk. Add salt, pepper, and lemon juice.

....

YIELD: 2 TO 4 MAIN-COURSE SERVINGS

CHICKEN BOUILLABAISSE
Bouillabaisse de Poulet

········◆········

M eaning "boiled from below"—*buoilli à baisse*—this method of rapid boiling to create a slightly reduced, intense broth lends itself to chicken as well as to the fish and seafood used in the Marseilles classic. That was an invention of "nouvelle cuisine" chefs who first switched chicken for fish in bouillabaisse, just as they substituted fish for meats in the Alsatian sauerkraut dish, *choucroute garni*—innovations intended to free the formalized French language of cuisine and allow for new concepts. Cooking the chicken without its skin assures a lean broth, in keeping with the character of the original. It can be prepared with fresh tomatoes, but unless they are at peak season, canned offer more flavor. Because chicken is less fragile than fish, this can be prepared hours or even a day ahead of serving, but will then have to be carefully degreased while cold. The broth is served as a first course and the chicken with vegetables as a main course. Both are garnished with *rouille*, the fiery pink cousin to aïoli.

....

FOR THE SOUP
One 3¹/₂- to 4-pound chicken, cut into 8 pieces
¹/₄ cup mild-flavored olive oil
1 medium onion, coarsely chopped
4 garlic cloves, chopped
1 large leek, white portion only, coarsely chopped
5 or 6 small canned Italian-style plum tomatoes (a 14¹/₂-ounce can),
*   coarsely chopped, with their liquid*
2 or 3 feathery sprigs of fresh fennel, or ¹/₂ teaspoon dried fennel
*   seeds, crushed*
5 or 6 saffron threads, or ¹/₈ teaspoon ground saffron
1 small bay leaf

*A 2-inch strip of orange peel (dried on the rack of a 450° F. oven
    for about 7 minutes, or until edges curl and are slightly brown)
Pinch of cayenne pepper, to taste (optional)
Salt and pepper
3 to 4 cups Basic Chicken Soup (page 28), as needed
10 or 12 slices of French bread, toasted
Rouille (recipe follows)*

*FOR THE OPTIONAL GARNISH
Minced fresh parsley
2 peeled and boiled small potatoes, or ⅓ to ½ cup cooked rice for
    each portion*

....

Pull off all skin from chicken pieces, without cutting into the meat. Trim off all visible bits of yellow fat. Set chicken aside at room temperature.

Heat oil in a 4- to 5-quart casserole, preferably of enameled cast-iron and oval in shape. When oil is warm, add onion, garlic, and leek, and sauté slowly but steadily, stirring often, for about 5 minutes. Cover and simmer over low heat for another 5 minutes or until vegetables begin to soften but are only faintly golden. Stir in tomatoes and their juices, and add fennel, saffron, bay leaf, orange peel, and cayenne pepper. Simmer, uncovered, for 7 or 8 minutes.

Add chicken pieces with a little salt and pepper and turn through the vegetable mixture. Pour in just enough soup to come to the level of the chicken. Partly cover pot and boil vigorously for about 30 minutes, adding broth if needed and stirring to be sure nothing scorches. Chicken should be tender by that time. If not, simmer longer unless you are preparing this in advance and will be reheating it. Discard fennel, bay leaf, and orange peel.

The soup can be prepared ahead up to this point, but if so, chicken should be only barely tender as it will cook during the reheating. If this is to be served within 4 hours of cooking time and the kitchen is cool, keep bouillabaisse at room temperature, loosely covered. Otherwise, cool, cover, and store in the refrigerator for up to 2 days. When stored, this soup will become greasier than when freshly cooked, because of added fat seeping out of the chicken. If bouillabaisse is served immediately after being cooked, fat need not be skimmed from surface as it gives the dish character.

Just before serving, uncover and bring to a rapid boil, and boil for about 5 minutes. Serve soup separately as a first course with toasted bread slices topped with Rouille. Then serve chicken on a plate with the cooked vegetables as a sauce along with more Rouille, and, if you like, with boiled potatoes or rice.

....

YIELD: 2 TO 4 MAIN-COURSE SERVINGS

Rouille

.... ◆ ....

Follow exactly the recipe for Aïoli Sauce or variation (pages 104, 105) but beat in ¼ teaspoon cayenne pepper and 6 to 8 crumbled saffron threads that have been soaked in a few drops of lemon juice or olive oil. Eliminate saffron if you dislike it. As an alternative to cayenne pepper, you can use ½ teaspoon dried red pepper flakes crushed with the garlic and salt. Just before serving, stir 3 tablespoons of the bouillabaisse broth into the Rouille.

....

YIELD: 2 CUPS

CREAM OF CHICKEN SOUP FEDORA
Créme de Volaille Fédora

.... ◆ ....

According to the charming directory and history of soups, *Dictionnaire des Potages*, by Michel Caron and Ned Rival, published in 1964, this elegant soup was created by Adolphe Dugléré, chef at the famed Café Anglais in Paris. First served in 1882, it honored the hit play *Fédora*, starring Sarah Bernhardt and Vincent Sardou. Like all dishes by this chef, it includes tomatoes that lend a pretty blush to the broth. I prefer using tomato puree, not tomato paste or whole tomatoes, and I like the bite of cayenne pepper, although it is not traditional.

....

FOR THE SOUP
One 4- to 4½-pound chicken, quartered, with all giblets except liver
1 veal knuckle bone
8 to 10 cups water, as needed
2 medium carrots, quartered
2 small white turnips, quartered
1 large leek, white and green portions
2 celery stalks with leaves
1 medium onion, studded with 5 or 6 whole cloves
Salt
8 to 10 black peppercorns
½ cup cooked white rice
3 tablespoons water
¼ cup milk

4 tablespoons canned crushed tomatoes or puree (not paste)
Pinch of cayenne pepper, to taste (optional)
2 egg yolks
¹/₂ cup crème fraîche or heavy cream
¹/₄ pound vermicelli, broken into thirds

FOR THE OPTIONAL GARNISH
Minced fresh parsley or basil
Dash of hot paprika
Diced peeled fresh tomato

....

Place chicken, giblets, and veal bone in a 5-quart soup pot and add 8 cups water, which should be enough to cover. Add more if needed, but if you have to exceed 10 cups, the pot is too wide and you will not have a strong broth. Bring to a boil, reduce to a simmer, and skim foam as it rises to the surface.

When foam subsides, add vegetables, a pinch of salt, and peppercorns. Simmer gently but steadily, partly covered, for about 1¹/₂ hours.

Remove all vegetables, the giblets, and the chicken breasts from the soup. Leave veal bone, thighs, and drumsticks in the soup. Remove skin and bones from chicken breasts and return bones to the soup. Simmer soup, partly covered, for another 30 minutes. Meanwhile, cut chicken into julienne strips or, better yet, pull them into shreds and keep warm.

Place rice in a small, heavy saucepan with the water and milk and simmer slowly, partly covered, until rice has absorbed the liquid. When soup has cooked with bones, strain it into a clean, 3-quart pot and discard chicken and bones. Skim or blot fat off soup. Stir tomato puree into soup and add rice. Simmer gently, partly covered, for about 15 minutes or until rice swells and gives the soup a creamy look. Adjust seasonings, adding cayenne to taste.

Beat egg yolks into cream and set aside.

Cook broken vermicelli in rapidly boiling salted water until tender, about 5 minutes. Drain quickly and rinse under cold running water so strands will not stick. Set aside in warm place.

Slowly ladle a little of the simmering soup into the egg yolk mixture, beating constantly. When you have beaten in about 2 cups of soup, pour egg yolk mixture back into remaining soup set over very low heat. Beat constantly as you pour. Heat soup until slightly thickened but do not boil or it will curdle. Adjust seasonings.

Place equal amounts of chicken and vermicelli in each bowl, ladle in soup with rice and serve. Garnish to taste.

....

YIELD: 6 TO 8 SERVINGS

HENRI'S CHICKEN-IN-THE-POT
Poule-au-Pot, Henri IV

········◆·········

C hicken and vegetables served in the soup they were cooked in is virtually a worldwide favorite, as you can see throughout this book. The French version dates back to the seventeenth century, when it was dubbed "Portugal Broth for the Queen" and included various meats. It is often identified as the favorite of France's King Henry IV. Traditionally, the chicken is poached whole with a mildly flavored meat stuffing that can be eliminated. However, because the quality of the chicken meat is important, it is best to truss the bird before cooking. If you intend to use stuffing, be sure to buy a chicken that has not been so carelessly butchered that it lacks enough skin to close across the cavity; it should also have the crop skin intact at the neck.

···················

FOR THE STUFFING
1¹/₂ cups fresh white bread crumbs
¹/₂ to ²/₃ cup milk
3 chicken livers, trimmed and chopped
¹/₄ pound lean ground pork
¹/₄ pound lean mild-flavored French- or Italian-style pork sausage
*   meat, or ¹/₄ pound ground cooked ham or prosciutto*
Pinch of nutmeg, preferably freshly grated
1 egg
¹/₂ teaspoon salt, or to taste
Black pepper, preferably freshly ground
2 tablespoons finely minced fresh parsley

FOR THE SOUP
1 young fowl (pullet) or roasting chicken, 4¹/₂ to 5 pounds, plus all
*   giblets except liver*
1 small veal knuckle bone (optional)
5 to 6 cups Basic Chicken Soup (page 28)
5 to 6 cups water
4 medium carrots, cut up
1 medium onion, studded with 5 or 6 whole cloves
4 medium white turnips, quartered
3 leeks, white and green portions

4 celery stalks with leaves
1 small bay leaf
4 or 5 parsley sprigs
8 to 10 black peppercorns
2 fresh thyme sprigs or ¹/₂ teaspoon dried leaf thyme
1 small head green cabbage (about 1¹/₂ pounds), cut into
    8 wedges, half-cooked in lightly salted water (optional)

FOR THE OPTIONAL GARNISH
Coarse salt
Minced fresh parsley
8 to 10 slices toasted French bread, or ¹/₃ pound cooked vermicelli

....

Soak bread crumbs in milk for about 10 minutes, or until mushy and most of the milk is absorbed. Squeeze out excess milk and discard. Pull bread apart with your hands to avoid clumps. Using 1 or 2 forks, mix bread with livers, pork, and sausage meat or ham until well blended. Add nutmeg, egg, salt, and a few grindings or a generous pinch of black pepper and the parsley. Mix well. Do not taste this mixture for seasoning as it contains raw pork. To test for seasoning, make a tiny ball about ³/₄ inch in diameter and cook, covered, in lightly salted, simmering water or soup for about 7 minutes or until thoroughly cooked. Taste and add more salt, pepper, or nutmeg to the uncooked stuffing mixture as needed.

Stuff the cavity of the chicken loosely and sew the opening closed with needle and thread. Even though you do not stuff the crop, draw the skin across the back of the bird to close the opening, fastening it by sewing or by inserting 2 short skewers through skin and backbone. Whether stuffed or not, the chicken should be trussed.

Place chicken in a close-fitting 6- to 7-quart soup pot along with giblets and the bone if you use it, and add soup and water to cover. Bring to a boil, reduce to a simmer, and skim foam as it rises to the surface. When foam subsides, add 2 carrots, onion, 2 turnips, 2 leeks, 2 celery stalks with leaves, the bay leaf, parsley, peppercorns, and thyme. (The remaining vegetables will be cut differently and cooked in the soup just before serving.)

Simmer gently but steadily, partly covered, for about 1¹/₂ hours if you use the broiler, or 2¹/₂ to 3 hours if you use the fowl. Do not worry if a few bits of uncooked stuffing float out into the soup at the beginning of cooking. Add a little more water during cooking if chicken is not at least seven eighths covered. Turn chicken carefully once or twice during cooking, using the trussing cord to turn and being sure not to poke a whole through the chicken skin.

When drumsticks can be moved freely in their joints, chicken is done. Do not allow it to overcook until it is falling apart. Carefully remove chicken and reserve in a warm place. Discard bones, giblets, and all vegetables or herbs. Skim or blot fat from soup and strain into a cleaned pot. Degrease again if necessary.

The soup can be prepared to this stage about 30 minutes before serving as long as chicken is covered, on a platter, and kept in a warm place. Otherwise it will be hard to reheat stuffing without overcooking chicken.

Prepare remaining vegetables. Carrots can be cut into chunky slices of about 1 ½ inches each or coarsely diced. Cut each turnip into 6 or 8 wedges. Cut celery into 1-inch pieces. Leeks should be whole, although the green portion should be split so sand can be washed out. Return chicken to strained soup with fresh vegetables, and parboiled cabbage, if you use it, and simmer 15 to 20 minutes or until vegetables are tender. Adjust seasonings.

Just before serving, remove chicken from soup and remove all trussing cord. Carve off hind quarters as for a turkey and, using poultry shears, cut through backbone of chicken. Hold apart and remove stuffing, which should look much like a meat loaf. Serve quarters or slices of chicken with slices or chunks of stuffing.

Chicken, stuffing, vegetables, and soup with vermicelli can be served together as a one-course meal in wide, deep soup bowls. Knives and forks will be needed, as well as soup spoons. Or serve soup as a first course with vermicelli or toast slices on the side. Then serve chicken, sliced stuffing and vegetables with a little extra broth spooned over them, and on flat plates. Add a sprinkling of parsley and pass coarse salt at the table.

....

YIELD: 4 MAIN-COURSE SERVINGS

VARIATIONS

Alsatian Chicken Soup
Bouillon de Poule, Alsacienne

.... ◆ ....

Prepare the soup using the Basic Chicken Soup (page 28) made with 10 to 12 cups of water and a 4¹/₂- to 5-pound fowl or broiler and optional veal knuckle bone, leeks, turnip, parsnip, celery root, parsley root, thyme, bay leaf, and cloves in the amounts indicated, plus 1 whole peeled garlic clove. Prepare the soup exactly as in the master recipe, trimming chicken of bones and skin, and discarding vegetables and skimming fat from soup's surface. Garnish with semolina or marrow dumplings (see pages 113-114).

....

YIELD: 6 TO 8 SERVINGS

Alsatian Chicken Soup with Semolina
Consommé à la Semoule

.... ◆ ....

8 cups hot degreased Basic Chicken Soup (page 28)
1 tablespoon mild salad oil
²/₃ cup semolina (farina or Cream of Wheat)
Chopped fresh parsley

....

The soup should be gently simmering, covered. Heat oil in an 8-inch skillet and stir in semolina. Stir over low heat for about 5 minutes or until semolina begins to take on a faint golden color. Turn into soup and simmer, partly covered, for 15 minutes. Serve in cups or bowls, sprinkling each portion with parsley.

....

YIELD: 6 TO 8 SERVINGS

Alsatian Marrow Dumplings
Quenelles à la Moelle
·········◆·········

Uncooked marrow from four or five 2-inch pieces of beef marrow
    bone
Unsalted butter, softened, as needed
2 cups fresh white bread crumbs
1/3 cup semolina (farina or Cream of Wheat)
2 eggs, lightly beaten
1/2 teaspoon grated nutmeg
Salt and pepper, to taste
2 tablespoons minced fresh parsley and/or chervil

Five or 6 hours before you start this recipe, scoop the marrow out of the bones. Place in a small, heavy-bottomed saucepan and melt slowly. This will take about 7 or 8 minutes. Strain through a sieve lined with a double thickness of dampened cheesecloth. Chill for 3 to 5 hours or until set. You should have about 1/2 cup marrow. If not, add a little softened unsalted butter to make up the difference. Mash with fork until creamy.

Stir in bread crumbs, semolina, eggs, nutmeg, salt, pepper, and herbs until well mixed. Chill in refrigerator for 30 minutes to 1 hour.

Using wet hands or 2 teaspoons, shape mixture into rounds or ovals a little less than 1 inch in diameter. Form all before you begin cooking. Drop carefully into steadily but gently simmering soup and cook, half-covered, for about 10 minutes or until dumplings float to the surface and a test dumpling proves to be cooked through.

These are best eaten immediately, but if necessary they can be removed from the broth with a slotted spoon and kept in a warm spot for about 30 minutes before being served in the hot soup.

·········

YIELD: ABOUT 36 DUMPLINGS;
FOR 6 TO 12 SERVINGS OF SOUP

GERMANY, AUSTRIA, AND SWITZERLAND

◆◆◆

GERMAN-STYLE CHICKEN BROTH OR SOUP

Hühnerkraftbrühe or Hühnersuppe

·········◆·········

This is Basic Chicken Soup (page 28), prepared with the veal knuckle bone and all optional root vegetables, in amounts indicated. Root vegetables define the flavor of this soup, and herbs such as thyme and bay leaf are rarely added in traditional German versions, but 4 or 5 cloves studded into the onion may be added along with a pinch of powdered mace, and salt and pepper.

Serve with either of the following garnish choices: 1 or 2 raw egg yolks placed in each bowl before hot soup is poured in; or the Egg Noodles, Pinched Noodles, Soup Nuts, Royal Custard, Egg Flakes, or Slivered Crepes that appear on pages 33 through 39. Marrow Dumplings (page 114) and semolina as prepared for Alsatian Chicken Soup with Semolina (page 113) are also much loved in Germany, Austria, and the German parts of Switzerland, as are Liver Dumplings (page 120). Cooked thin asparagus tips, the tiniest green peas, and/or tiny cooked flowerets of cauliflower are also favored, especially in spring, as are minced parsley and chervil.

A COLD AND RAINY NIGHT IN HAMBURG

· · · · · · · · · · · · · · · · · · · ◆◆◆ · · · · · · · · · · · · · · · · · · ·

Among my most memorable encounters with chicken soup, few are more cherished than one of a cold and rainy November night in Hamburg in 1953. After driving across the Lüneberger moors all day and getting to my hotel close to midnight, I was chilled and starved, and I knew room service had ended hours before. Explaining my plight to the chambermaid, I was offered Hühnerkraftbrühe, or chicken broth. Disheartened but resigned, I accepted and was rewarded with a deep, thick white porcelain bowl full of steaming, golden broth. As I dipped into it, I found a bonus—two egg yolks had been placed raw in the bowl, and as I cut into them, they poached gently into fine ribbons. Rarely have I slept more soundly or more sweetly.

CREAM OF CHICKEN SOUP WITH CARAWAY
Hühnercremesuppe mit Kümmel

········◆········

The caraway seeds add exotic undertones to this gentle soup. It is very much like one my grandmother used to serve for winter breakfasts. Hers did not include wine, but it was garnished with tiny squares of toast.

....

8 cups German-Style Chicken Soup (page 115)
4 tablespoons (¹/₂ stick) unsalted butter
5 tablespoons all-purpose flour
Salt and white pepper, to taste
2 teaspoons caraway seeds
2 egg yolks, lightly beaten (optional, see Note)
1 cup heavy cream
¹/₂ cup dry white wine, heated

....

Let soup come to a slow simmer. Prepare a roux by melting butter in a 1-quart saucepan. When butter is hot, stir in flour. Sauté, stirring, for about 5 minutes or until flour is golden but not brown. Pour in 2 cups hot soup and stir until smooth. Turn this into remaining soup and simmer for 10 minutes, seasoning with salt and pepper and caraway seeds that have been crushed in a mortar and pestle. If you do not have a mortar and pestle or a spice mill, wrap the seeds in cheesecloth to make a tight little ball and tap it against a cutting board using a mallet or meat tenderizer, or even a light hammer.

The soup can be prepared to this point 1 hour before serving and held at room temperature.

Heat soup slightly just before serving. Beat egg yolks with cream in a bowl. Slowly ladle in hot soup, beating constantly, until you have added 2 cups. Pour that mixture into hot soup away from the heat, beating constantly. Add warm wine and heat but do not boil. Serve in heated cups or cream soup bowls.

....

YIELD: 6 TO 8 SERVINGS

NOTE: Egg yolks can be eliminated, in which case use 5 tablespoons butter and 6 tablespoons flour for the roux and proceed with the rest of the recipe.

GIBLET RAGOUT SOUP
Hühnerragoutsuppe

rugality can have savory results much appreciated throughout central Europe.

FOR THE SOUP
1 pound chicken gizzards and hearts
1 pound combined chicken wings, necks, and backs
8 to 9 cups water, as needed
1 teaspoon salt
6 to 8 black peppercorns
1 medium onion, studded with 4 white cloves
3 tablespoons unsalted butter
2 medium carrots, diced
1 small parsley root or ½ parsnip, diced
¼ small celery root (celeriac), diced
2 celery stalks, diced
2 tablespoons flour
Pinch of sugar, if needed

FOR THE OPTIONAL GARNISH
⅔ cup sour cream
6 chicken livers
Cooked flowerets of 1 small cauliflower
¼ pound mushrooms, sautéed

Clean all giblets and trimmings. Place in a 3-quart, close-fitting soup pot and add water, which should cover giblets. If not, add a little more, not to exceed 9 cups. Add salt, peppercorns, and clove-studded onion. Bring to a boil, reduce to a simmer, and skim off foam as it rises to the surface. Keep soup simmering gently for 30 minutes after foam subsides.

Heat butter in a 10-inch skillet and gently sauté vegetables, stirring frequently, for 3 or 4 minutes or until they brighten and just begin to soften. Sprinkle with flour and stir over low heat until flour is absorbed and begins to turn yellow, about 2 minutes. Turn this mixture into the simmering soup, beating to blend. Ladle a little of the hot soup into the skillet and scrape up all coagulated flour and return it to soup pot.

Simmer gently but steadily, partly covered, for 30 minutes more or until all giblets and trimmings are very tender. Remove all meats and onion.

Discard onion and cloves. Trim and coarsely chop the tender meat of gizzards and hearts, discarding chewy tissue. Pick meat from neck, backs, and wings. Chop and return to the soup. Simmer for 10 minutes and adjust seasonings, adding a tiny pinch of sugar if soup seems acidic.

Serve in small soup bowls. To garnish, top each portion with a tablespoonful of sour cream that has warmed to room temperature. Or trim, chop, and sauté the chicken livers in 3 tablespoons butter and divide among portions of soup. Or do the same with cauliflower flowerets or mushrooms.

YIELD: 6 TO 8 SERVINGS

VARIATIONS

Creamed Giblet Soup

An elegant alternative. Cook giblets and trimmings with onion as described above, add raw vegetables after 30 minutes, and continue cooking for another 30 minutes. Prepare a sauce by heating 4 tablespoons unsalted butter and stirring 4 tablespoons flour. Sauté, stirring, for about 4 minutes or until flour is golden but not brown. Pour in about 2 cups of soup stock and beat until smoothly blended, then turn that mixture into soup, beating constantly. Simmer for 10 minutes, then stir in $^1/_2$ cup heavy cream or beaten sour cream.

Giblet, Mushroom, and Barley Soup

This has a deep golden richness. It is prepared exactly like the master recipe but with the following additions. Soak 3 or 4 dried black mushrooms (Polish or Russian, if possible, but porcini will do) in a cup of hot water for 30 minutes, then drain and chop coarsely. Add to soup with vegetables and $^1/_4$ cup rinsed pearl barley. Let all simmer together for 30 minutes. Garnish with minced fresh dill or parsley (or both) and, if you like, 2 teaspoons of sour cream atop each portion.

CURRIED CREAM OF CHICKEN SOUP
Hühnersuppe mit Curry

·········◆·········

urry, with warmly exotic overtones that contrast to gloomy weather, is a popular seasoning throughout Germany, Austria, Switzerland, and Scandinavia.

···················

FOR THE SOUP
One 3¹/₂- to 4-pound chicken
¹/₃ cup unsalted butter
2 medium onions, chopped
1 medium celery root (celeriac), diced
2 tablespoons good curry powder
1 teaspoon salt
White pepper, to taste
Pinch of cayenne pepper (optional)
Pinch of turmeric (optional)
8 cups water, as needed
2 tablespoons rice flour or potato starch
3 tablespoons cold water
1 cup heavy cream
Cayenne pepper, to taste
2 cups cooked white rice

FOR THE OPTIONAL GARNISH
Chopped pistachios or toasted coconut flakes

···················

Cut chicken into 8 pieces. Keep at room temperature for 30 minutes before beginning to cook and pat very dry.

Heat butter in a 5-quart soup pot and when hot, brown chicken pieces a few at a time, reserving those that are browned. It should take about 7 minutes per batch. Turn to brown all sides. When all chicken is brown and removed, add onions and celery root to remaining butter in pot and sauté slowly for 6 or 7 minutes, until they begin to soften and turn yellow. Return chicken pieces to pot and stir in curry powder, cayenne, and turmeric; sauté slowly with vegetables, stirring, for 7 or 8 minutes.

Add water to cover and season with salt and freshly ground pepper. Simmer gently but steadily for about 1 hour or until chicken is tender. Remove chicken pieces. Reserve dark meat for other uses. Trim off all skin, bones, and cartilage from white meat and cut or shred into spoonable pieces.

Skim fat from soup, then strain, and return to rinsed pot. Dilute rice flour or potato starch in cold water and stir into soup, simmering gently until it thickens. Stir in cream. Heat but do not boil. Adjust seasonings, and add cayenne. Place some chicken and cooked rice in heated individual bowls and ladle in hot soup, garnishing as you like.

....

YIELD: 8 SMALL SERVINGS

Liver Dumplings
Leberknödel

.... ◆ ....

This is a very popular soup garnish in Germany, Austria, and throughout Eastern Europe. Pork liver is the favorite, but beef or calves' liver will do. This recipe has been adapted from one that appears in my book *The German Cookbook*.

....

³/₄ pound pork, beef, or calves' liver
5 slices white bread with crusts, or the equivalent in crusty
    Italian white bread or rolls
1 cup warm chicken broth or milk
2 ounces kidney fat, or 2 tablespoons (¹/₄ stick) butter or bacon fat
1 small onion, chopped
2 eggs
1 teaspoon salt
¹/₂ teaspoon grated nutmeg
¹/₂ teaspoon dried thyme (optional)
Grated rind of 1 lemon
¹/₂ cup minced fresh parsley (optional)
Dried homemade white bread crumbs, as needed
10 cups water or clear homemade or canned chicken broth

....

Trim all tubes and membranes from liver. This must be done thoroughly or the grinding will be difficult. Soak crumpled bread in chicken broth or milk until liquid is cool and absorbed. Using the fine blade of a meat grinder, grind liver, bread, fat or butter, and onion. This grinding can be done in a food processor, but you must be quick and careful, using the pulse frequently, or the liver will liquefy.

Beat in eggs, salt, nutmeg, thyme, lemon rind, and parsley. Add bread crumbs a tablespoon at a time until mixture can be handled but is still fairly moist. With wet hands, shape into round dumplings about 1¹/₂ inches in diameter.

Drop a test dumpling into gently boiling, lightly salted water or broth that you will not be serving. Cover and simmer steadily for about 18 to 20 minutes. Dumpling should float and be cooked through. Cook remaining dumplings, 6 or 8 at a time. Drain and keep warm until serving in chicken broth.

Dumplings will keep for 2 or 3 hours before becoming soggy. Reheat for a few minutes in soup.

....

YIELD: 10 TO 12 DUMPLINGS; FOR 5 TO 6 SERVINGS OF SOUP

ITALY

◆◆◆

ITALIAN-STYLE CHICKEN SOUP
Brodo di Pollo

.........◆.........

G iven the myriad forms of Italian pasta, it should be no surprise that chicken soup seems to be just one more vehicle for it, in varying widths, as the tiny squares called *quadrettini*, or stuffed, as tortellini or cappelletti. Also popular are dried shapes such as pastina, the rice-shaped orzo, the seedlike semini, the short tubular ditalini, and even larger shapes such as Apuglia's "little ears," *orecchiette*.

....

FOR THE SOUP
Ingredients for Basic Chicken Soup (page 28), without parsley
4 to 6 whole cloves
2 canned Italian plum tomatoes (about ¹/₃ of a 14¹/₂-ounce can)
2 small or 1 large bay leaf
2 garlic cloves (optional)
2 small leeks, white and green portions (optional)
1 medium boiling potato, peeled (optional)
4 or 5 large sage leaves, or 1 sage sprig (optional)

Lidia Bastianich, who oversees the cooking of dishes from her native Istrea and Friuli in her fine New York restaurant Felidia, recalls in her charming autobiographical cookbook La Cucina di Lidia, *"When someone was ill or recovering from childbirth, the aroma of chicken soup filled the house, in keeping with accepted folk wisdom."*

FOR THE GARNISH
Pastas as described on page 121
Chopped fresh parsley
Grated Parmesan cheese

....

Insert cloves into the onion called for in the basic recipe. Add with tomatoes and bay leaves, along with vegetables and sage, and proceed with basic recipe. Serve with any of the suggested garnishes, or use as called for in the following recipes.

....

YIELD: 6 TO 8 SERVINGS

CAPON BROTH
Ristretto di Cappone
.... ◆ ....

The recipe for this bracing, richly aromatic broth comes from the brilliant Italian chef Theo Schoenegger, who at this writing holds forth at the exceptional San Domenico restaurant in New York. He is a native of the mountainous Tyrolean province of Alto Adige, close to the Austrian border, and serves this soup with his region's tortellini.

....

FOR THE SOUP
One 6- to 7-pound capon, well cleaned
3 to 3$^1/_2$ quarts water, as needed
2 celery stalks with leaves
2 medium carrots
2 canned Italian plum tomatoes (about $^1/_3$ of a 14$^1/_2$-ounce can)
2 medium leeks, white and green portions
1 fresh sage sprig (5 or 6 large leaves), or 3 or 4 leaves dried sage
2 bay leaves
4 or 5 whole cloves
2 teaspoons salt, to taste

FOR THE OPTIONAL GARNISH
Chopped fresh parsley
Grated Parmesan cheese
Tortellini (page 132), vermicelli, or small pasta
Italian Chicken Meatballs (page 134)

....

If the sensibilities of their guests are not offended, good Montovani, a few minutes before going to the table, dissolve a proper quantity of grated Parmesan in a cup of hot chicken broth, then pour in a half-glass of sparkling white wine such as Lambrusco. With its brimming white foam, this is a match for the best aperitivo.

—FROM *CUCINA MONTOVANA, DI PRINCIPE E DI POPOLI* (MANTUA'S KITCHEN, OF PRINCES AND OF THE POPULACE)

Place whole capon in a close-fitting 7- to 9-quart soup pot of enameled cast-iron or stainless steel. Add water to cover, not to exceed 3 ½ quarts. Bring to a boil, reduce to a simmer, and skim off foam as it rises to the surface. When foam has subsided, add all vegetables, cloves and herbs, and salt. Partly cover pot and simmer soup very gently for 4 hours or until capon meat begins to fall off the bone. Skim fat from surface intermittently during cooking.

Remove chicken, herbs, and vegetables from soup. Reserve chicken, to be served in soup or kept for other purposes. Discard vegetables.

Let soup cool for several hours, then skim off as much fat as possible. Bring to a boil, reduce to a steady simmer, and cook, uncovered, for 1 to 2 hours or until soup is reduced by half. Add salt to taste. Cool uncovered at room temperature, then cover and store in refrigerator overnight. Remove all solidified fat and proceed as directed in various recipes.

This soup can be reheated and served plain or sprinkled with parsley. Or serve with any of the pasta garnishes.

....

YIELD: 6 TO 8 SERVINGS

WINE SOUP
Zuppa di Vino, or Ginestrata

.........◆.........

Chicken broths laced with wine have been popular as delicacies, restoratives, and appetite whetters in Italy since the Renaissance. Often bound with egg yolks, the soup takes on a pale yellow hue. As explained by the scholarly Giuliano Bugialli in his great classic, *The Fine Art of Italian Cooking*, that color accounts for its antique name, *ginestrata*, after the broom flowers, ginestre.

This fine recipe is another prize from Theo Schoenegger.

....

FOR THE SOUP
2 cups Capon Broth reduced by one-half (page 122),
2 cups dry white wine
6 egg yolks
1 cup heavy cream
½ teaspoon salt, or to taste
⅛ teaspoon freshly ground black pepper, or to taste
Pinch of ground cinnamon, or to taste
Pinch of freshly grated nutmeg, or to taste

FOR THE GARNISH
1 tablespoon finely minced fresh chives
¹/₂ cup small cubed croutons

....

Heat reduced capon broth. Place wine in a 1-quart saucepan and boil rapidly, uncovered, until reduced by one half to 1 cup. Combine with reduced broth and let cool for about 15 minutes.

In a bowl, beat egg yolks lightly, then beat in cream and all seasonings except chives. Bring capon and wine broth to a boil and slowly add it to the egg yolk mixture, beating constantly. When half of the broth has been added, pour the egg yolk mixture into the remaining hot broth away from the heat, beating constantly.

Heat the mixture thoroughly but do not boil. Serve in heated cups or small bowls, sprinkling each portion with chives and croutons.

....

Yield: 2 to 4 servings

VARIATIONS

1. Marsala can be substituted for the white wine and a pinch of sugar added at the end to give this a sweet flavor that is especially soothing to convalescents.

2. For a more golden color and exotic flavor, crush 3 or 4 threads of saffron and simmer in the broth for 7 or 8 minutes before adding wine. This was a typical addition to Renaissance *ginestrata*.

BROTH
WITH CHICKEN LIVERS, PEAS, AND
RICE OR PASTA
Pasta in Brodo con Fegatini e Piselli

........◆........

his is a specialty of Italy's Veneto region and is popular from Verona to Venice. For best results, prepare it just before serving as it can become cloudy and bitter if livers soak.

....

Cheese is added to most Italian chicken soups, and here, as throughout Europe, eggs are relied on for texture, color, and nutrients. All of which suggests that the cholesterol cops who extol the Mediterranean diet for its low-fat content tend to acknowledge only the evidence that supports their view and ignore anything that might refute it. However, if you must cut fats from your diet, egg and cheese can be eliminated from many of the soups that follow, although the results will be thinner and less satisfying.

FOR THE SOUP
6 cups Italian-Style Chicken Soup (page 121)
1 cup cooked rice or small pasta such as risone or orzo
1 1/2 cups fresh peas, or one 10-ounce package unthawed frozen
  tiny green peas
6 chicken livers, trimmed and cut into 1/2-inch pieces
3 or 4 fresh sage leaves, or 2 or 3 dried leaves
  (do not use ground sage)
2 tablespoons (1/4 stick) unsalted butter
Salt and pepper, to taste

FOR THE GARNISH
Minced fresh parsley
Grated Parmesan cheese

Heat broth and add cooked rice or pasta and peas. Simmer until peas are tender but firm, about 5 minutes. Meanwhile, sauté liver pieces in butter until they lose all traces of redness and are thoroughly cooked. Do not brown them or they will become hard. Remove liver from pan with a slotted spoon and add to soup along with sage, discarding pan juices. Simmer for about 8 minutes and adjust seasonings. Spoon into heated soup bowls and sprinkle with parsley. Pass cheese at the table.

YIELD: 4 TO 6 SERVINGS

ESCAROLE IN CHICKEN SOUP
Scarola in Brodo

This healthful, verdant soup is a traditional first course. If garnished with chicken and rice or pasta, it is a fine light lunch main course, followed by a fruit or lemon tart.

FOR THE SOUP
8 cups Italian-Style Chicken Soup (page 121)
1 very fresh head of escarole, about 1 to 1 1/4 pounds
Salt, to taste
2 tablespoons (1/4 stick) unsalted butter
Freshly ground black pepper, to taste

FOR THE OPTIONAL GARNISH
1 cup cooked rice or cooked small pasta such as orzo or the small
*   bow-ties called tripolini*
1 cup diced cooked chicken breast meat
*   or Chicken Meatballs (page 134)*
Grated Parmesan cheese

. . . .

Chicken soup should be clear, strained, and well skimmed of fat. If cold, bring to a very low simmer while you prepare escarole.

Trim off any tough or bruised outer leaves of the escarole. Cut off brown stem bottom and separate leaves. Wash well until free of sand. Place escarole in a large saucepan, preferably of enameled cast-iron or stainless steel, and add just enough cold water to come up to the level of the escarole. Add a pinch of salt and bring to a boil, partly covered. Simmer steadily for 5 to 7 minutes or until leaves just begin to wilt. Drain and cool a little, until you can squeeze out as much liquid as possible. You can do this by pressing escarole against the sides of a colander with a wooden spoon or by squeezing bunches in your hands. Cut leaves into large crosswise strips.

Melt butter in the well-dried pot in which escarole cooked or in a smaller saucepan. Stir in escarole, coating it with butter and add a little salt and pepper. Cover and allow to sweat over very low heat for 4 or 5 minutes, stirring once or twice.

Bring soup to a moderate simmer and add escarole with any pan juices, of which there should be very little. Simmer, partly covered, for about 10 minutes or until escarole is tender but not mushy.

If you are using cooked rice or pasta, add it to the soup for the last 5 minutes of cooking. If you are using diced chicken, keep it close to the stove so it will not be too cold, but do not reheat in the soup. Divide chicken among portions and spoon soup, escarole, and rice or pasta over it.

If you use none of the garnishes, serve soup with escarole only. In any case, pass grated cheese at the table.

. . . .

YIELD: 6 TO 8 FIRST-COURSE SERVINGS

ITALIAN EGG DROP SOUP
Stracciatelle

T his soup is especially favored in Rome. Semolina adds fluffiness and spinach, though not traditional, lends a verdant freshness. Flour is sometimes used instead of semolina for a silkier result, as described for Egg Flakes (page 37). I prefer the body and texture that semolina imparts.

6 cups hot Italian-Style Chicken Soup (page 121)
2 eggs
2 tablespoons grated Parmesan cheese
2 tablespoons semolina (farina or Cream of Wheat) (optional)
5 ounces (half a 10-ounce package) frozen chopped spinach,
*   thawed and well drained (optional)*

Have soup simmering gently. Beat eggs lightly in a bowl with grated cheese and semolina, if you use it. Slowly stir in 1 cup of the hot broth and mix until blended.

If you are using spinach, add it to the simmering soup and cook for 2 minutes. Bring soup to a gentle boil and beat in egg mixture with a fork so it breaks into clumps. Let cook gently for another 2 or 3 minutes and serve immediately.

YIELD: 4 TO 6 SERVINGS

THE HONEST VOLUPTUARY

P ublished in Venice in 1475, De Honesta Voluptate *(The Honest Voluptuary) is the work of Bartolomeo de Sacchi di Piadena, better known as Platina. It includes many recipes for soups, most especially capon broth. Typical of the aromatic dishes popular in his time, it simmers for seven hours with bacon, pepper, cinnamon, cloves, sage, and bay leaves. Platina suggests that it can be served to the ailing and the hearty alike, but warns, "Beware of adding salt, for that can be the cause of ailments. Nothing is wrong with a few spices, but use even less when this is served to an ailing person."*

His frugal recipe for potage from capon skin calls for cutting into small pieces the skin of a boiled capon that then simmers in the previously made capon broth for half an hour, with a few strands of saffron for a golden glow. "Put it into dishes and sprinkle with spices and grated cheese. Our Archigallus used to enjoy this when circumstances permitted." The circumstances being, I suppose, that the skin of a cooked capon was available.

CHICKEN SOUP WITH POACHED EGG
Zuppa alla Pavese

········◆········

Although this can be prepared with an egg that has been fully poached in water or extra broth before being added to the soup, it is far more delicate and in character to let the hot soup cook the egg right in the bowl. If possible, use a deep round bowl rather than one that is wide and shallow, so that the egg will set quickly. This is traditionally a first course or a snack for anyone feeling under the weather. With the addition of a small green salad or some fresh fruit, it makes a satisfying light lunch or meal.

··················

FOR EACH SERVING
1 1/2 to 2 cups hot Italian-Style Chicken Soup (page 121)
1 slice good white bread, without crust
1 tablespoon butter
1 egg

FOR THE GARNISH
Minced fresh parsley
Grated Parmesan cheese

··················

Have very hot soup ready in a saucepan. Bread may be left in a square or, for a refined look, trim it to a circle that fits the bottom of your bowl. Heat butter in a small skillet and brown the bread slice, turning once so both sides toast. It should take 2 or 3 minutes for each side.

Place toasted bread in bowl and bring soup to a rapid boil. Break egg on top of toast and pour in boiling soup. Top with parsley, if you like, and sprinkle on grated cheese at the table.

In a few seconds, the white of the egg will be cooked. Break the yolk with a spoon as you eat, so it runs out and sets in ribbons.

NOTE: To prepare several portions of this soup, fry all toast slices first, then add to bowls. Top each with an egg, then quickly pour boiling soup over all.

GREEN MINESTRONE WITH CHICKEN AND PESTO
Minestrone Verde al Pesto
........◆........

Pesto sauce, with its fragrant trinity of garlic, basil, and Parmesan, gives this soup of green and white vegetables distinct Ligurian overtones. Untraditional though it may be, chicken proved to be an enhancement, lending a mellowness to the broth. Served without chicken meat in it, the soup is a satisfying first course. With chicken meat, it is a sturdy main course. No other vegetables would be needed in such a meal, nor would any cheese. An appetizer of cold seafood or a country pâté and a simple nut torte or crunchy cookies for dessert should round things out nicely. Split peas lend a velvety flavor background for the other vegetables, but they can be omitted to have a lighter soup, perhaps better suited to summer. Unlike the classic pesto sauce, this one contains no pignoli nuts, as I dislike their flavor and grittiness in the soup. It is also possible to eliminate cheese from the pesto and pass some separately at the table.

....

FOR THE SOUP
One 3¹/₂- to 4-pound chicken, quartered, with
    neck and all giblets except liver
10 cups water, or as needed
1 celery stalk whole with leaves and 2 celery stalks, diced
1 small carrot
1 small onion, whole, and 1 medium, chopped
3 parsley sprigs
8 to 10 black peppercorns
²/₃ cup green split peas (optional)
2 tablespoons (¹/₄ stick) butter and 2 tablespoons mild olive oil,
    or 4 tablespoons olive oil
2 large leeks, white portions only, thinly sliced
¹/₂ pound string beans, trimmed and cut into ¹/₂-inch lengths
1 pound small zucchini
1 small (about 1¹/₂ pounds) green cabbage, preferably savoy
Leaves of 1 large bunch young and tender Swiss chard,
    well washed and coarsely chopped (optional)
¹/₂ cup rice or 4 medium boiling potatoes, peeled
    and cubed
Salt and pepper, to taste

FOR THE OPTIONAL GARNISH
Pesto Sauce (page 131)
Grated Parmesan cheese

. . . .

Place chicken and giblets in a close-fitting 5-quart soup pot, preferably of enameled cast-iron, and add up to 10 cups of water, which should cover the chicken. Bring to a boil, partly covered, then reduce to a simmer and skim foam as it rises to the surface. When foam subsides, add the whole celery stalk, carrot, whole onion, parsley, and peppercorns. Keep at a low simmer for about 3 hours, stirring every 30 minutes, until chicken begins to fall from bones. Replenish water if chicken is not covered during the first 2 hours of cooking.

While chicken is cooking, prepare split peas. Wash them in 2 changes of cold water and pick over to remove stones or discolored peas. Place in saucepan with about 3 to 4 cups of water and boil for 2 or 3 minutes. Drain off water and rinse peas. Add about 3 to 4 cups fresh water and bring to a boil and cover; let stand for about 30 minutes.

Remove chicken from soup and discard giblets, vegetables, and peppercorns. If you plan to serve chicken meat in soup, remove skin, bones, and cartilage and break breast and thigh meat into spoonable pieces. Strain soup through a sieve and skim off fat. Return to rinsed soup pot and add soaked, drained split peas. Simmer gently, partly covered, for about 20 minutes while preparing the other vegetables.

Heat butter and oil in a 10-inch skillet. Add chopped onion, leeks, and diced celery and sauté gently, stirring frequently, for 8 to 10 minutes or until vegetables soften but are not brown. Add to soup with string beans and simmer gently, partly covered, for about 10 minutes.

Wash zucchini well, trim off ends, and cut into vertical quarters. Using a small paring knife or a spoon, scoop out inner pulp with seeds. Slice remaining zucchini shell into ³/₄-inch pieces.

Cut cabbage into quarters, wash under running cold water, and trim out white core. Shred cabbage as for coleslaw, eliminating tough white ribs. Add zucchini and cabbage to soup and simmer gently for another 20 minutes.

If you use Swiss chard, trim off all white stems and veins. Stems can be cooked as a separate vegetable another day. Wash leaves well and chop or slice coarsely. You should have 3 to 4 cups. Place in saucepan with enough water to cover and parboil for about 3 minutes or until leaves begin to wilt. Drain well and add leaves to soup, discarding their cooking water.

The soup can be prepared up to this point and stored, covered, in the refrigerator for up to 24 hours. Bring to room temperature before reheating.

About 20 minutes before serving, add rice or potatoes to soup and cook until tender. Season with salt and pepper, but do not oversalt as pesto will be added.

Serve in heated bowls, with or without chicken. Pass Pesto Sauce at the table. I prefer this without extra cheese sprinkled on top, but it can be passed at the table.

Leftover minestrone can also be stored, covered, in the refrigerator for up to 24 hours or frozen for 6 weeks, but rice will expand considerably so soup will need thinning with water or broth in the reheating. Potatoes may disintegrate a bit, but that can be pleasantly soothing.

....

YIELD: ABOUT 8 FIRST-COURSE SERVINGS WITHOUT CHICKEN;
6 MAIN-COURSE SERVINGS WITH CHICKEN

Pesto Sauce
········◆········

4 garlic cloves
1 teaspoon coarse salt
2 cups loosely packed whole fresh basil leaves, well washed
1/2 cup olive oil
4 tablespoons grated Parmesan (optional)
Salt, to taste

....

Cut garlic cloves in half vertically and remove and discard inner green-tipped sprout. Cut garlic into small pieces and, using a blender or mortar and pestle, crush to a paste with coarse salt. You can also crush garlic through a press and then mix with salt. Slice basil leaves and add to garlic. If using a mortar and pestle, trickle oil in slowly, working it in as for mayonnaise. If you are using a blender, add 1/3 cup oil and blend at moderate speed until you have a smooth emulsion, adding the rest gradually.

If you add cheese, stir it in by hand. Add salt as needed.

Extra pesto can be spooned into a narrow, small bowl or jar and topped with 1/2-inch layer of olive oil. Cover and store in refrigerator for up to 1 week or in freezer for up to 1 month.

....

YIELD: ABOUT 1 CUP;
ENOUGH FOR 6 TO 8 SERVINGS OF SOUP

VARIATION

Cheeseless pesto can be made simply by blending the garlic and basil as above, using only ⅓ cup olive oil, or as much as the green mixture will absorb without "leaking," or separating.

Chicken dumplings will be juicier if you use some dark meat.

Meat-Filled Pasta Dumplings
Tortellini and Cappelletti

·········◆·········

Some say tortellini should be cut from squares and be pointed while cappelletti should be round; some say just the opposite. I think you should choose for yourself since neither shape alters the way the final result tastes or is prepared. Squares are easier to cut and fold, if that helps you decide.

The tortellini filling is adapted from the savory originals prepared by Theo Schoenegger at the San Domenico restaurant in New York.

····················

FOR THE FILLING
2 tablespoons beef marrow, from 3 or 4 thin slices of
    marrow bone (optional)
2 to 3 tablespoons (¼ stick) unsalted butter
½ skinless and boneless chicken breast (1½ to 2 ounces), prefer
    ably in 1 piece
1½ to 2 ounces boneless pork loin or the heart of a small pork loin
    chop, preferably in 1 piece
1 or 2 thin slices (1 ounce) Italian mortadella sausage
½ cup grated Parmesan cheese
1 egg
Pinch of grated nutmeg, or to taste
Salt, to taste
Pinch of ground black pepper, to taste

FOR THE PASTA WRAPPING
Egg Noodle dough (page 33) made with 1½ cups flour, 1 whole
    egg plus 1 yolk, ½ teaspoon salt, and 1 tablespoon water

····················

Prepare filling 3 to 5 hours before making pasta. Marrow bones should be cold but thawed if they were frozen. Using a sharp-pointed knife, dig marrow out of bones. You should have about 2 tablespoons of crumbled pieces.

Heat 2 tablespoons butter in an 8- or 9-inch skillet or, if not using marrow, use 3 tablespoons. Gently sauté marrow, chicken breast, and pork, turning meat several times so it cooks through but remains moist. This should take about 8 to 10 minutes.

Place cooked meats, pan drippings, and mortadella in a grinder or in a food processor bowl. Grind through the finest blade, or process using pulsing on and off for about 4 minutes, or until meats are blended and finely ground, but not pulverized. Scrape down sides of bowl once or twice during grinding.

In a bowl, combine ground meats with cheese, egg, and seasonings. You may taste this for seasoning as meat is cooked. Adjust as needed. Place in refrigerator, loosely covered, for 3 to 5 hours.

Prepare dough according to instructions. Roll dough out to about ⅛ inch thickness and roughly into a 12-inch square, keeping unrolled dough wrapped in plastic so it will stay moist. Fill and form tortellini as soon as each sheet is rolled. Cut dough into 2-inch squares or circles, using a cookie cutter for the latter.

Place about ¾ teaspoonful of filling on one side of each square or circle. If you make squares, fold into triangle. Fold circles in half, pinching edges closed as you do so. Carefully turn outer points of triangles or half-circles together, forming a ring. If you have cut circles, fold top edge down. If you cut squares, leave point standing.

Roll remaining dough and fill each batch. When all are formed, spread on a clean towel and let dry at room temperature for 2 hours before cooking. Turn several times so all sides dry. Or cover with another towel and chill for 5 or 6 hours or overnight before cooking. You can also freeze them, but in that case, dry for 2 hours before storing in plastic freezer bags or containers. Do not thaw before cooking.

To cook, bring about 4 quarts of water to a boil in a deep saucepan and add 2 tablespoons of salt. Drop tortellini in gently, rolling them off the towel if possible so you do not handle each and spoil its shape. Boil gently, partly covered, for 7 to 12 minutes. The fresher the pasta, the less cooking time needed. Taste to be sure all pinched corners are thoroughly cooked, but do not let pasta get too soft.

Remove from water with a slotted spoon and divide among soup bowls. Pour in hot broth and serve.

....

YIELD: ABOUT 80 TORTELLINI OR 125 CAPPELLETTI; FOR 8 TO 12 SOUP SERVINGS

VARIATION

Cappelletti, or little hats, are small tortellini, easy to pick up by spoonfuls in soup. Cut dough into 1½-inch squares and use about ½ teaspoonful of filling for each.

Italian Chicken Meatballs
Polpettini di Pollo

These are similar to the meatballs mentioned as the garnish for Passover chicken soup made by Tuscan Jews (page 45). Jews who observe kosher laws would eliminate the cheese.

½ pound skinless and boneless chicken meat,
    preferably white and dark meat combined
1 egg, lightly beaten
3 to 5 tablespoons dried bread crumbs, as needed
3 tablespoons grated Parmesan cheese
1 tablespoon finely minced Italian flat-leaf parsley leaves
½ teaspoon salt, or to taste
⅛ teaspoon freshly ground black pepper, or to taste
Grated rind of ½ lemon

Grind white and dark chicken meat together using the finest blade of a meat grinder, or in a food processor using the pulse and flicking it on and off for 3 or 4 minutes until meat is smooth but still has some texture.

Mix in egg and 3 tablespoons bread crumbs, the cheese, and remaining ingredients. Add more bread crumbs gradually until mixture is the consistency of thick cooked oatmeal. If you want to check seasonings, make 1 small ball, about ½ inch in diameter, with the wet palms of your hands and simmer in broth or salted water for 7 or 8 minutes or until done. Taste and add salt or pepper as needed. Do not taste this mixture raw.

Shape balls about 1 inch in diameter, using 2 teaspoons or the wet palms of your hands. Cook, partly covered, in gently simmering soup for about 10 minutes or until dumplings float and one tests done.

YIELD: ABOUT 12 CHICKEN DUMPLINGS; FOR ABOUT 6 SERVINGS OF SOUP

Bread and Cheese Noodle-Dumplings
Passatelli or Passetini

········◆········

Passatelli look like scraggly, brownish noodles, but are really dumplings. They are formed of bread crumbs, eggs, and cheese mixed to a thick mass, then forced through a food mill or potato ricer into simmering broth. They derive their name from being passed—*passato*—through the mill.

Some cooks use a greater proportion of cheese to bread crumbs, winding up with the same combined amount as called for below. In *Mangiari Di Romagna*, an old cookbook of that region, it is explained that in poorer families, a greater proportion of bread crumbs was used, while those who could afford to, used more cheese, thereby creating a class system for passatelli.

Giancarlo Quadalti was the skillful chef at the New York restaurant Amarcord, now, alas, closed. After trying his light but pungent passatelli, I asked for the recipe and he obliged. Parsley is not traditional in passatelli, but it is Giancarlo's special touch. In the classic cookbook, *La Scienza in Cucina e L'Arte Di Mangiar Bene* (Science in the Kitchen and the Art of Eating Well), Pellegrino Artusi, the Escoffier of Italian cuisine, suggests substituting 1 teaspoon of very finely grated lemon rind for the nutmeg, a touch that results in a more typical Italian flavor.

These are quick and easy to prepare once you get the hang of it, but it's a good idea to rehearse before serving them to guests.

··················

2 eggs
²/₃ to ³/₄ cup toasted fresh unseasoned bread crumbs, as needed
²/₃ to ³/₄ cup freshly grated Parmesan cheese, as needed
1 tablespoon very finely minced Italian flat-leaf parsley
¹/₈ teaspoon ground white pepper, or to taste
¹/₄ teaspoon grated nutmeg, or 1 teaspoon finely grated lemon rind
8 to 10 cups Italian-Style Chicken Soup (page 121)
Grated Parmesan cheese

··················

The best utensil for forming passatelli is a food mill fitted with the disk that has the largest holes. Alternatives are a potato ricer or a colander, with holes that are between ¹/₄ and ³/₈ inch. If you use a colander, you will need a wooden spoon, spatula, or flat mallet to rub the dough through the holes. If

"Go to Cesarina," Federico Fellini advised me when I interviewed him years ago for a story in Vanity Fair. *"They specialize in the food of my home region, Emilia-Romagna, like* passatelli in brodo *exactly as my mother did." Naturally, I followed his suggestion and was beguiled by this unusual and delicious soup garnish at the restaurant favored by denizens of Rome's* Cinecittá.

holes are smaller than 1/4 inch, the passatelli will be too thin.

Break eggs into a bowl, beat lightly, and stir in 2/3 cup each of bread crumbs and cheese, along with the parsley, white pepper, and nutmeg. Mix, then knead with your hands, pressing between palms and gradually adding equal amounts of bread crumbs and cheese until you have a damp, firm mass that is very slightly crumbly when broken, much like stiffly cooked polenta but softer than pie dough.

This dough can be prepared up to 30 minutes in advance of cooking and stored, covered, in the refrigerator. It should stand 10 minutes at room temperature before being cooked.

Heat soup to boiling point in a 3-quart saucepan, then reduce to a low simmer. Place dough in the mill or other device and, holding it over the soup pot, press or rub through the mill or ricer, letting the long broken squiggles drop directly into the soup. Simmer for about 1 minute, then turn off heat and allow to stand 2 or 3 minutes before serving. If soup boils, passatelli will disintegrate, so keep heat low.

If you have trouble working the dough through the holes, stop after 1 minute and remove cooked passatelli with a sieve or slotted spoon and set aside so they do not overcook while you press the rest of the dough into the soup. Return all to soup when finished, and let stand without cooking for 2 or 3 minutes.

Although passatelli are at their best and lightest when served as soon as they are cooked, it is possible to cook them up to 30 minutes ahead. To do that, remove from the broth after 2 minutes of cooking, using a sieve or a slotted spoon. Keep them in a warm spot and reheat in very hot (but not cooking) soup for 2 or 3 minutes before serving.

Ladle soup and passatelli into heated bowls and pass extra grated Parmesan at the table.

....

YIELD: 6 TO 8 SERVINGS

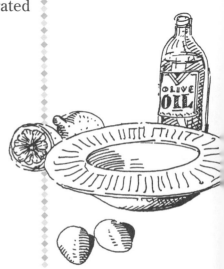

PORTUGAL
◆ ◆◆

MINTED CHICKEN-RICE SOUP WITH EGG AND LEMON
Canja

········◆········

In her cookbook *A Taste of Portugal*, Shirley Sarvis writes that *canja* is a term for all chicken soups in that country, but there is quite a different explanation of the term for the completely different Brazilian Canja (page 73). The egg-lemon version is, however, one of Portugal's national dishes, an apparent holdover from the Moors or, perhaps, adopted during Portuguese explorations of Arab lands. It is prepared exactly like Basic Egg-Lemon Chicken Soup (page 164) and is garnished with paper-thin lemon slices and fresh mint leaves. As you can see, the Alentejana region of Portugal has a lustier version, minus egg and lemon.

ALENTEJANA CHICKEN, SAUSAGE, AND RICE SOUP
Canja de Galinha à Alentejana

········◆········

This is a thick, meaty main-course soup, and with its bacon and pork sausage, is typical of the Alentejana region of Portugal. It is much like a liquid jambalaya and is best preceded by a green salad or cold vegetables such as artichokes, mushrooms, or asparagus with a vinaigrette dressing, and followed by sherbet or fresh fruit. A light, bland white bread with a good crust, most typically Cuban or Sicilian, goes well with this. German *speck* adds a sophisticated ripeness and is much leaner than most bacon in our markets.

··················

FOR THE SOUP
One 3½- to 4-pound whole chicken
8 to 10 cups water, as needed
2 medium onions, cut in half
2 fresh thyme sprigs, or 1 teaspoon dried leaf thyme
2 or 3 fresh cilantro (coriander) sprigs, or 2 or 3 parsley sprigs
1 bay leaf
1 teaspoon salt
8 to 10 black peppercorns
¼ pound Portuguese linguiça sausage or Spanish chorizo
¼ pound very lean smoked bacon, German speck, or
    dry Italian prosciutto, in 1 piece
2 garlic cloves
1 teaspoon coarse salt
1 tablespoon paprika, sweet or hot or in combination
3 tablespoons tomato puree, or 1½ tablespoons tomato paste
1 cup dry red wine, or to taste
1½ cups white rice, preferably short-grained

FOR THE GARNISH
Chopped fresh parsley or cilantro (coriander)
Cuban or Sicilian-style bread

....

Place chicken in close-fitting 5-quart soup pot and add 8 cups water, using more only if needed to cover chicken, but not exceeding 10 cups. Bring to a boil, reduce to a simmer, and skim off foam as it rises to the surface. When foam subsides, add onions, thyme, parsley or cilantro, bay leaf, salt, and peppercorns. Simmer, partly covered, for 1 hour.

Parboil sausage in 1 quart water for about 15 minutes. Add bacon and continue parboiling for 5 minutes. Add to soup, discarding water. Continue simmering soup gently, partly covered, for 1 to 1½ hours or until chicken begins to fall from the bone. Using a slotted spoon, remove chicken, sausage and bacon, onion, herbs, and peppercorns.

Cut garlic into small pieces. Using a mortar and pestle, crush garlic to a fine paste with coarse salt, or crush garlic through a press and mash with salt. Mix into a paste with the paprika, using sweet if you like mild flavor, hot if you like it fiery, or a combination. Taste the soup to decide how much spiciness is needed. Stir into soup along with the tomato puree or the thicker tomato paste. Add wine and simmer for 10 minutes or until flavors are blended; adjust to taste. Let cool for 30 minutes, then skim off fat.

Add rice to soup and simmer steadily, partly covered, for about 30 minutes or until rice is very soft and soup has taken on a creamy opaqueness.

Meanwhile, take chicken meat off bones, discard skin, and trim off all gristle and cartilage. Cut or tear chicken meat into spoonable pieces. Peel and cut sausage into ¹/₂-inch-thick slices and dice bacon or ham. Return meats to soup and adjust seasoning, adding salt, pepper, or wine as needed. Simmer 10 to 15 minutes and serve, dividing chicken, meats, and rice among portions. Garnish with parsley or cilantro and pass bread at the table.

This soup has a richer flavor if made a day ahead and stored, covered, in the refrigerator. If you plan to do that, do not add rice or it will expand too much and make the soup overly thick. Rather, simmer rice in soup during the reheating for about 20 minutes. Remove all fat before it melts, then let soup come to room temperature before starting to reheat. Simmer gently, partly covered, setting pot over an asbestos mat or metal insulator. Stir, adjust seasonings, and add a little wine, stock, or water if soup becomes too thick.

YIELD: 6 MAIN-COURSE SERVINGS

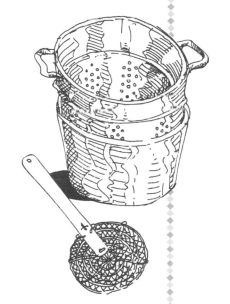

SPAIN

MADRID CHICKEN, SAUSAGE, AND VEGETABLE HOTPOT
Cocido Madrileño

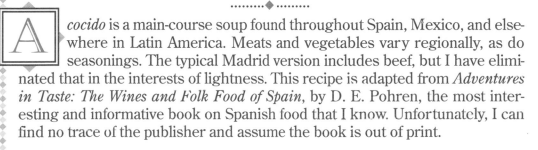

A *cocido* is a main-course soup found throughout Spain, Mexico, and elsewhere in Latin America. Meats and vegetables vary regionally, as do seasonings. The typical Madrid version includes beef, but I have eliminated that in the interests of lightness. This recipe is adapted from *Adventures in Taste: The Wines and Folk Food of Spain*, by D. E. Pohren, the most interesting and informative book on Spanish food that I know. Unfortunately, I can find no trace of the publisher and assume the book is out of print.

FOR THE SOUP
1 cup (¹/₂ pound) dried chickpeas (garbanzos)
One 5-pound fowl or roasting chicken, quartered, with
    all trimmings and giblets except liver
2 pieces beef or veal marrow bones (optional)
10 cups water, as needed
¹/₄ pound lean bacon or salt pork, in 1 piece and without rind
¹/₂ pound boneless serrano ham, prosciutto, or German
    speck in 1 piece
2 medium leeks, white and green portions
3 medium carrots, scraped
1 large onion
2 small white turnips, scraped
1 large garlic clove
1 small bay leaf
3 or 4 parsley sprigs
2 fresh thyme or mint sprigs, or to taste
6 to 8 peppercorns
6 chorizo sausages (about 1 pound)
1 small head green cabbage (about 1¹/₂ pounds), cored and
    shredded as for coleslaw
6 small new potatoes, peeled
Cayenne pepper or dried red pepper flakes, to taste (optional)

FOR THE OPTIONAL GARNISH
¹/₂ pound cooked vermicelli for broth
2 cups hot broth simmered with 3 tablespoons canned tomato puree
    (not paste) as sauce for main course

Wash and pick over chickpeas, eliminating stones, if any, and shriveled peas. Place in bowl with about 4 cups cold water and soak 5 or 6 hours or overnight.

Drain off any remaining water, and place peas in a close-fitting 7-quart soup pot along with chicken and parts. Add water as needed to cover chicken. Bring to a boil, reduce to a simmer, and skim off foam as it rises to the surface. When foam subsides, partly cover pot and let soup simmer gently for 1¹/₂ hours, adding water if needed to keep chicken covered.

Meanwhile, blanch bacon or salt pork in boiling water to cover for 5 minutes, then drain. Add to chicken with ham, leeks, carrots, onion, turnips, garlic, bay leaf, parsley, thyme or mint, and peppercorns. Simmer, partly covered, for about 40 minutes or until chicken and peas are tender.

While soup is cooking, prick sausages with a fork or skewer and brown for about 5 minutes in a 10- to 12-inch skillet. Add shredded cabbage and 1 cup of water or enough to cover bottom of the pan with a thin film. Toss cabbage to coat with sausage drippings. Simmer partly covered for about 10 minutes, stirring once or twice, until cabbage begins to soften.

Add to soup along with potatoes. Simmer, partly covered, for about 25 minutes, until cabbage and potatoes are tender. Remove chicken, meats, bones, and herbs, discarding the bones and herbs. Trim skin and bones from chicken. If you want to serve chicken in soup, dice or shred it into spoonable pieces; otherwise leave it in large sections. Dice or slice bacon and ham and keep warm.

Skim all grease from soup. Adjust seasonings, adding salt to taste, and depending on the strength of the sausages, cayenne pepper or pepper flakes.

Broth can be served as a first course with a little cooked vermicelli in each portion. Chicken and meats, with chickpeas, cabbage, sliced carrots, and whole potatoes can be a second course. Pass a bowl or gravy boat of the hot broth blended with the tomato puree as a sauce to be spooned over individual portions.

Or all meats and vegetables can be cut up and served together in the soup as a one-dish meal, in which case, slice sausages, removing the casings.

This soup tastes best if made 24 hours before it is to be served. Store covered in the refrigerator, but do not add cooked vermicelli. Prepare that when you have skimmed and reheated the soup.

....

YIELD: 4 TO 6 MAIN-COURSE SERVINGS

Chapter 8

EASTERN EUROPE AND RUSSIA

*Czech Republic, Georgia, Hungary,
Moldavia, Poland, Romania,
Russia, Ukraine, Yugoslavia*

EASTERN EUROPEAN CHICKEN SOUP
........◆........

T he recipe for Basic Chicken Soup (page 28) made with the pot vegetables applies here. Bones may or may not be used.

Traditional garnishes are the various Egg Noodle variations (pages 33–36), Soup Nuts or Puffs (page 38), and Slivered Crepes (page 39); liver dumplings, especially popular in the Czech Republic (see pages 146 and 152); and the Meat and Pastry Turnovers, Piroshki, or Pierogi, in Poland, Russia and Ukraine (page 158).

UJHÁZY CHICKEN AND VEGETABLE SOUP
Ujházyleves
........◆........

I n the early 1900s, the Hungarian actor Ede Ujházy was a loyal patron of the historic and still exquisite Gundel restaurant in Budapest. His favorite dish was said to be chicken soup, and he gradually created this complex triumph that bears his name. Beef bones and tomatoes are sometimes called for, but I prefer the soup without them. Semolina dumplings are added along with liver dumplings, but that is pretty heavy going. I prefer vermicelli and/or the liver dumplings.

....

FOR THE SOUP
One 4- to 5-pound stewing or soup chicken, or equivalent,
*   quartered, with neck and all giblets except liver*
One 3- to 4-inch beef bone (optional)
10 to 12 cups water, as needed
2 medium carrots, peeled
½ small celery root (celeriac), or 2 celery stalks with leaves
1 small parsnip or ½ parsnip and 1 small white turnip, peeled
1 medium onion
4 parsley sprigs
1 large garlic clove, unpeeled
10 black peppercorns
Salt, to taste
2 small kohlrabi, peeled and cut into matchstick strips; or

½ cauliflower, cut into flowerets; or ½ small head savoy cabbage, slivered
1 small green bell pepper, seeded and sliced
2 tablespoons tomato puree (not paste); or 2 peeled fresh or canned tomatoes, cut into chunks (optional)
2 tablespoons (¼ stick) unsalted butter
¼ pound fresh mushrooms, thinly sliced
1 cup shelled green peas, fresh or frozen

FOR THE OPTIONAL GARNISH
Minced fresh parsley or chives
1 poached egg for each portion
¼ pound cooked vermicelli and/or Hungarian Liver Dumplings (page 146)

Place chicken, giblets, and bone in a 6- to 7-quart enameled or stainless-steel soup pot. Add about 10 cups of cold water, just enough to cover the chicken. Bring to a boil, reduce to a simmer, and cook, partly covered, skimming foam as it rises to the surface. When foam subsides, add the carrots, celery root, parsnip, onion, parsley, garlic, peppercorns, and salt, using only about 2 teaspoons salt.

Simmer steadily but gently, partly covered, for about 2 hours or until chicken is completely tender. This will take about 30 to 45 minutes less time with broilers than with a fowl. Add water to maintain original level. Remove chicken, giblets, and bones. Discard bones along with chicken skin. Cut or shred chicken meat into spoon-size pieces, trimming off all veins, sinews, and cartilage. Set aside with diced meaty portions of giblets.

Strain soup into a large bowl, pressing all liquid from vegetables. Discard peppercorns, parsley, onion, and garlic. Other vegetables may be diced and put back into soup; use only those that are not too greasy and devoid of flavor. Skim soup and return to rinsed pot. Add chicken and the kohlrabi, cauliflower or cabbage, green pepper, and puree or tomatoes if you use them. Simmer, partly covered, for 15 to 20 minutes or until vegetables are tender.

While vegetables simmer, melt butter in a small skillet and when hot, add mushrooms and sauté, stirring, over moderate heat until they are faintly golden brown. Do not let the butter brown. Add mushrooms with pan juices to soup.

The soup can be prepared to this point up to 1 hour before serving. Keep partly covered at room temperature.

Ten to 15 minutes before serving, reheat soup to a simmer and add peas. Simmer fresh peas for about 8 minutes; thawed frozen peas will be done in 1 to 2 minutes; frozen peas require about 4 minutes. Adjust seasonings.

Serve with any or all garnishes. If you wish to garnish soup with eggs, poach in soup for 4 minutes while peas are cooking. Allow 1 egg for each portion.

....

YIELD: 6 TO 8 FIRST-COURSE SERVINGS; 4 TO 6 MAIN-COURSE SERVINGS
NUMBER OF SERVINGS WILL VARY WITH GARNISHES USED

Hungarian Liver Dumplings
Majas Gomboc
.... ◆ ....

Follow the recipe for Liver Dumplings on page 120, using chicken or calves' liver. Eliminate the nutmeg and substitute dried marjoram for the thyme, all in the amounts called for. Shape into 1-inch balls and cook as directed. Serve about 3 dumplings in a first-course soup, 5 in a main-course portion.

....

YIELD: ABOUT 18 TO 20 DUMPLINGS

GOULASH SOUP
Gulyasleves
.... ◆ ....

Goulash soup is traditionally made of beef, but I found that dark chicken meat produces a leaner, savory result. White meat is too dry and bland to stand up to the other strong flavors. Do not add salt until the soup has finished cooking, owing to the amount in the broth.

This is a main-course soup, and served with rye bread or pumpernickel, is often the entire meal. A green salad would be the most appropriate first course if you want one, and a sherbet or fresh fruit would make the best dessert, if needed.

....

FOR THE SOUP
3¹⁄₂ to 4 pounds chicken thighs and drumsticks
6 to 8 cups Basic Chicken Soup (page 28) or clear canned chicken
*   broth, as needed*
2 tablespoons (¹⁄₄ stick) butter or light vegetable oil

2 medium onions, coarsely chopped
1 large green bell pepper, seeded and diced
¹/₂ teaspoon ground black pepper
1¹/₂ tablespoons sweet Hungarian paprika
¹/₄ to ¹/₂ teaspoon hot Hungarian paprika, or to taste (optional)
1 tablespoon caraway seeds, lightly crushed
2 large garlic cloves
1 teaspoon dried marjoram or leaf thyme
2 small canned tomatoes, chopped; or 4 tablespoons light tomato
*   puree (not paste)*
3 medium boiling potatoes, peeled and diced
Salt, to taste

FOR THE OPTIONAL GARNISH
¹/₄ pound cooked Pinched Noodles (page 35), Egg Noodles
*   (page 33), or egg barley (see page 41), and sour cream*

....

Disjoint the chicken and remove skin. Cut as much meat as possible from bones, discarding fat and sinew. Trim 2 tablespoons raw fat from chicken and set aside. Cut meat into ¹/₂-inch cubes. You should have 2¹/₂ to 3 cups of chicken. Set aside at room temperature. Simmer skin and bones in homemade or canned broth for 30 minutes. (Do not add salt.) Skim foam as it rises to the surface. Remove skin and bones and strain broth. Let cool a bit, then skim off fat and reserve broth. Trim solid bits of cooked meat from bones and reserve. Discard bones and skin.

Place raw chicken fat in a 3¹/₂- to 4-quart saucepan, preferably of enameled cast-iron or heavy-bottomed stainless steel. When fat is melted, add butter or oil. When hot, add onions and sauté gently, stirring often for about 7 minutes or until onions soften but do not take on color. Add green pepper and sauté for 3 or 4 minutes, stirring frequently.

Stir in pepper, both paprikas, crushed caraway seeds, garlic, and marjoram or thyme. Sauté gently for 2 or 3 minutes, then stir in chicken until pieces are well coated with spices. Cover loosely and braise over very low heat for about 10 minutes, stirring to prevent scorching, until chicken loses raw look.

Add 6 cups hot chicken broth, the bits of chicken meat trimmed from cooked bones, and the tomatoes or puree. Reserve remaining broth. Simmer soup gently, partly covered, for about 25 to 30 minutes or until chicken is almost tender.

Cool, uncovered, for about 1 hour, then skim off fat. Bring to a simmer, add potatoes, and cook, partly covered, for 15 to 20 minutes or until chicken and potatoes are tender. Add reserved chicken broth if soup thickens as potatoes cook.

Skim fat from surface. Adjust seasonings and serve with any or none of the optional garnishes. If you serve sour cream, let it come to room temperature and pass it at the table.

This soup can be stored, covered, in the refrigerator, for 3 days and also freezes well. For best results, potatoes should be cooked just before serving.

YIELD: 6 TO 8 FIRST-COURSE SERVINGS; 3 TO 4 MAIN-COURSE SERVINGS

CHICKEN AND SAUERKRAUT SOUP

Versions of this silky, piquant white soup are especially popular in Poland, the Czech Republic, and Hungary. The first version is basically Hungarian, with Polish and Czech variations following. In his enticing and most unusual cookbook, *Transylvanian Cuisine*, Paul Kovi, a native of that Hungarian region and a partner in New York's Four Seasons restaurant, describes a Saxon sauerkraut and chicken pot soup somewhat like the one below. It is known as *szász káposztaleves tyúkússal* or as *kriläwend*. By the latter name, Kovi writes, "it is a delicacy of Transylvanian-Saxon ecclesiastical cuisine, prepared in late winter for festive occasions."

FOR THE SOUP
One 6-pound fowl or stewing chicken, or two 3-pound chickens,
*   with neck and all giblets except liver*
10 to 12 cups water, as needed
2 large carrots, scraped
$1/2$ medium celery root (celeriac), peeled
2 celery stalks with leaves
2 leeks, white and green portions, split vertically
1 small parsnip or 2 parsley roots, scraped
1 bay leaf
3 or 4 pieces dried cracked ginger, or $1/2$ teaspoon ground ginger
8 to 10 black peppercorns

2 pounds sauerkraut, preferably fresh from a barrel or in plastic
packages, but not canned, with juice
4 tablespoons (¹/₂ stick) unsalted butter
2 medium onions, coarsely chopped
3 tablespoons flour
3 small carrots, diced (optional)
2 large celery stalks, diced (optional)
1 medium onion, coarsely chopped; or white portions of 2 small
leeks, thinly sliced (optional)
4 egg yolks, or 4 tablespoons flour
1 cup sour cream
1 tablespoon freshly grated horseradish
Salt, to taste
Freshly ground black pepper, to taste

FOR THE OPTIONAL GARNISH
Hot peeled boiled potatoes, cut into cubes or whole if small
Pierogi (page 158)

....

If using fowl, disjoint into 8 pieces. Trim 2 tablespoons raw fat from the chicken and set aside. Then chop each breast and thigh in half through the bones. Rinse and place in a 7-quart enameled or stainless-steel soup pot. Add giblets and 10 cups of water, as needed to cover chicken. Partly cover and bring to a boil. Reduce to a simmer and skim foam as it rises to the surface. When foam subsides, add carrots, celery root, celery, leeks, parsnip, bay leaf, ginger, and peppercorns. Simmer gently, partly covered, for 1¹/₂ to 2 hours or until chicken is tender and loosening from bones. Add water during cooking to maintain original level.

Remove chicken from soup and separate meat from skin and bones. Cut or shred meat into spoon-size pieces. Strain soup, discarding vegetables and seasonings, and when cool, skim off fat. Return chicken to soup.

While soup cooks, drain sauerkraut through a strainer set over a bowl, reserving juice. If sauerkraut is very sour, rinse under cold running water for a few seconds, then squeeze out water. Melt raw chicken fat slowly in a 2¹/₂-quart enameled or stainless-steel pot that has a heavy bottom. Add butter and when it has melted, sauté onions until faintly golden brown, about 8 minutes. Add sauerkraut and stir through onions, using a fork to pull sauerkraut apart. Cover and braise over very low heat, without adding liquid, for about 10 minutes, stirring once or twice to prevent scorching. Sprinkle in flour and turn through the sauerkaut until absorbed. Add sauerkraut juice and simmer gently but steadily, partly covered, for 20 to 30 minutes or until sauerkraut loses

I've loved chicken soup since childhood, but regrettably, what my mother did with the chicken is no longer done, so now chicken soup, while still special, is not what it was. My mother always bought a chicken with unborn eggs in it and lots of fat. The fat would be rendered and the unborn eggs would be fried in it with onions. That was a pre-appetizer, along with the fat cracklings called gribbenes. Let me tell you, gribbenes and unborn eggs were better than Godiva chocolates.

—EDWARD I. KOCH,
MAYOR EMERITUS OF
NEW YORK CITY

its crunch. The fresher the sauerkraut, the longer that will take.

Reheat degreased chicken soup and, when simmering, add sauerkraut mixture with all of its liquid.

The soup can be prepared ahead up to this point. Store, covered, in the refrigerator for 1 day.

About 20 minutes before serving, reheat soup to a simmer. To serve it with vegetables, simmer the diced carrots, celery, and onion or leeks in the soup for 10 minutes or until tender. Thicken with either egg yolks or flour. Eggs produce a lusher result, but flour is leaner. Beat whichever you are using into the sour cream in a mixing bowl. When well blended, trickle in some hot soup, beating constantly with a whisk. When 2 cups of soup have been added, slowly pour thickening mixture back into soup, off the heat, beating constantly with a whisk. Add horseradish, salt, and pepper to taste.

Reheat but do not boil soup if you used eggs. If you used flour, let simmer for 8 to 10 minutes. Serve immediately if made with eggs. If made with flour, soup can be held for 2 hours, partly covered, at room temperature and reheated before serving. Serve with or without potatoes that have been cooked in lightly salted water.

....

YIELD: 8 TO 10 FIRST-COURSE SERVINGS;
4 TO 6 MAIN-COURSE SERVINGS

POLISH OR CZECH CHICKEN AND SAUERKRAUT SOUP

..........◆..........

Follow the previous recipe, but substitute 8 allspice berries, lightly crushed, for the ginger and add 1 tablespoon dried marjoram. Add 3 large dried Eastern European or Italian mushrooms (porcini) that have been soaked for 20 minutes in hot water. Cook with the chicken and pot vegetables. Omit the horseradish. Garnish with boiled potatoes and 1-inch-thick slices of kielbasa. If you like, heat 1½ pounds of Polish kielbasa sausage in the soup just before it is thickened, then remove and keep warm.

VOJVODINA CHICKEN VEGETABLE SOUP WITH HORSERADISH

········◆········

A n autonomous province in the Pannonian plain, north of the Danube and Sava rivers, Vojvodina was annexed by Serbia in 1990. Formerly it was considered Yugoslavia's bread basket. Influences of both Slavic and Hungarian settlers are obvious in this lusty soup that includes horseradish among its root vegetables. This recipe derives from one in the little *Yugoslav Cookbook* and another in *The Balkan Cookbook*.

····················

FOR THE SOUP
One 4- to 5-pound soup or stewing hen, or equivalent in broiler
*   chickens, jointed in 8 pieces, with neck and all giblets except liver*
8 to 10 black peppercorns
10 cups water, or as needed
1 medium onion, unpeeled
3 medium carrots, scraped
2 celery stalks with leaves
1 parsley root, scraped, if available
¹/₂ large parsnip, scraped, or 1 whole parsnip if parsley root is
*   unavailable*
1 small celery root (celeriac), peeled and cut in half; or 3 celery
*   stalks with leaves*
2 garlic cloves, unpeeled
1 medium kohlrabi bulb, peeled; or 1 white turnip, peeled, and 3 or
*   4 green cabbage leaves*
A 3-inch piece fresh horseradish, scraped and split in half; or
*   1 tablespoon prepared horseradish, drained*
1 medium leek, white portion only, split and washed
3 or 4 parsley sprigs
3 medium boiling potatoes, peeled and cubed
Salt, to taste
Ground black pepper, to taste

FOR THE GARNISH
Cooked egg noddles
Slavic Liver Dumplings (page 152)

····················

Place chicken pieces, giblets, and peppercorns in a 5- to 6-quart enameled cast-iron or stainless-steel soup pot and add 10 cups of water, to cover chicken. Bring to a boil, partly cover, and reduce to a simmer, continuing for about 25 minutes. You may skim foam off if you like, but that is not traditional, as the added flavor and "meat value," or albumen, is much valued.

Meanwhile, roast the onion in its skin to impart a rich flavor and color. Place on a small baking pan in the upper third of a 450° F. oven for about 10 minutes or until skin is a deep golden brown; watch carefully so it does not blacken. Add to soup, along with all other ingredients except potatoes. Simmer gently, partly covered, for 1 hour or until chicken is falling from bone and vegetables are tender.

Remove chicken and vegetables. Discard peppercorns, onion remains, garlic, parsley sprigs, and remnants of stalk celery and cabbage leaves if you used them, and horseradish.

Dice and reserve remaining root vegetables. Remove chicken meat from skin and bones, and dice. Pick edible meat from giblets. Strain soup and degrease. Return soup to rinsed pot, adding vegetables and meat. Add potatoes and simmer gently, partly covered, for about 20 minutes or until potatoes are tender. Adjust seasonings.

The soup can be prepared ahead and stored, covered, in the refrigerator for 2 days. Potatoes may be cooked with this, or added in the reheating for a thinner, less starchy soup.

Serve boiling hot, adding noodles and/or liver dumplings to each portion.

....

YIELD: 4 TO 6 MAIN-COURSE SERVINGS

Slavic Liver Dumplings
.........◆.........

Follow recipe for Liver Dumplings on page 120, using chicken livers. Season only with salt, pepper, and minced parsley. Shape into 1-inch balls and simmer, partly covered, for 7 or 8 minutes directly in the finished soup. Allow 3 to 4 dumplings for each portion of soup, with 1/2 cup cooked noodles.

....

YIELD: 18 TO 20 DUMPLINGS

No part of the world has taken chicken soup more seriously than this one. It is often reserved for special occasions such as weddings when a pinch of saffron may be added to intensify its golden color.

GEORGIAN OR ARMENIAN LEMON CHICKEN SOUP
Chikhirtma

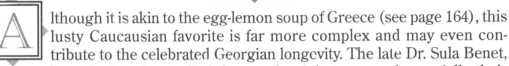

A lthough it is akin to the egg-lemon soup of Greece (see page 164), this lusty Caucausian favorite is far more complex and may even contribute to the celebrated Georgian longevity. The late Dr. Sula Benet, the anthropologist who studied the people of that area and especially their food, included three recipes for this soup in her book, *How to Live to Be 100*. In her carefully detailed cookbook, *The Food and Cooking of Russia*, Lesley Chamberlain writes that this soup is also claimed by Armenians, who garnish it with a little cooked rice, barley, or vermicelli.

In *The Georgian Feast*, Darra Goldstein suggests basil as an alternative garnish. I especially love its clean and minty accent, and find it a good choice for those who detest fresh cilantro (coriander).

FOR THE SOUP
One 3¹/₂- to 4-pound chicken, quartered, with neck and all giblets
    except liver
8 cups water, or as needed
Salt, to taste
8 to 10 black peppercorns
2 tablespoons (¹/₄ stick) unsalted butter or reserved chicken fat
1 large onion, chopped
2 tablespoons flour
¹/₂ teaspoon ground cardamom, or seeds of 8 cardamom pods,
    crushed
¹/₂ teaspoon ground cinnamon
¹/₄ teaspoon ground saffron
1¹/₂ tablespoons red wine vinegar, or to taste
3 fresh cilantro sprigs (optional)
3 egg yolks
¹/₃ to ¹/₂ cup strained lemon juice, to taste

FOR THE GARNISH
Chopped fresh parsley, basil, cilantro, dill
Cooked rice, barley, or vermicelli

Place chicken in 5-quart enameled or stainless-steel soup pot and add just enough water to cover. Add 1 teaspoon salt and the peppercorns. Bring to a boil, reduce to a simmer, and skim off foam as it rises to the surface. Simmer gently, partly covered, for about 2 hours or until chicken is tender and falling from the bone.

Remove chicken and trim meat from skin and bones. Cut or shred meat into spoon-size pieces and reserve. Remove peppercorns from soup and skim fat from surface, reserving 3 tablespoons of it if used instead of butter. Return soup to rinsed pot with chicken pieces.

Heat chicken fat or butter in a skillet and slowly sauté onion, stirring, until light golden brown but not black. Blend in flour and sauté, stirring, for 3 or 4 minutes until it turns a pale cocoa color. Stir in spices and sauté over very low heat for about 1 minute. Turn flour mixture into gently simmering soup, beating with a whisk so that flour dissolves in the liquid.

Add vinegar a ¹⁄₂ tablespoon at a time, to taste. Tolerances for it vary, and remember that much of the flavor will dissipate when the soup is reheated. Add cilantro sprigs if you use them. Simmer, partly covered, for 15 minutes.

The soup can be made ahead up to this point and kept, partly covered, at room temperature for 1 hour or in the refrigerator for 1 day.

Just before serving, bring soup to a gentle simmer. Beat egg yolks and lemon juice together in a small bowl and slowly trickle in 2 cups hot soup, beating constantly with a whisk. Slowly pour egg mixture into soup away from direct heat, beating constantly. Adjust seasonings with salt, pepper, and lemon juice. Reheat but do not boil. Sprinkle each serving with any combination of herbs, and for the Armenian version, add a tablespoonful of cooked rice, barley, or ¹⁄₂ cup cooked vermicelli.

YIELD: 4 TO 6 SERVINGS

GEORGIAN WALNUT SOUP
Kharcho

........◆........

Walnuts add a crunchy texture and fresh-air flavor that comes as a pleasant surprise. This soup, with its aromatic overtones of wine vinegar, cinnamon, scallions, and cilantro, clears clogged nasal passages in an instant and is a bracing uplifter.

FOR THE SOUP
6 cups Basic Chicken Soup (page 28) or Improved Canned
    Chicken Broth (page 30)
2 skinless and boneless chicken breasts, at room temperature
3 to 4 tablespoons (¹/₂ stick) unsalted butter, as needed
1 small onion, chopped
1 garlic clove, minced (optional)
²/₃ cup finely chopped (not ground) walnuts
3 tablespoons red wine vinegar, or to taste
¹/₄ teaspoon ground cinnamon, or to taste
Salt, to taste
8 to 10 scallions, white and green portions, coarsely chopped
6 parsley sprigs
4 fresh cilantro (coriander) sprigs (optional)

FOR THE GARNISH
Chopped fresh parsley and/or cilantro

....

Degrease the soup thoroughly and simmer in a 2¹/₂- to 3-quart enameled or stainless steel saucepan. Dice the chicken meat.

Heat 3 tablespoons butter in a small skillet and add chicken pieces. Sauté over moderate heat for about 5 or 6 minutes or until chicken begins to brown. Add onion, garlic, walnuts, and additional butter if needed. Sauté gently, stirring, until onion and nuts are light golden brown. Add vinegar and let boil for a second or two.

Stir the chicken mixture into the simmering soup, adding cinnamon and salt, and a little more vinegar if you want a sharper edge. Simmer for 10

CHORBA

Chorba, *basically of Turkish origin, appears as the word for "soup" throughout the Balkans, the Middle East, and North Africa, albeit in a variety of spellings such as* tschorba, shorba, *or* corbe. *As is so neatly explained in* The Balkan Cookbook *by Vladimir Mirodan, in Romania and surroundings,* chorbe *(in contrast to* zup*) designates soups that are "soured" with lemon juice, vinegar, the fermented cider that is* kvas*, pomegranate juice, or sour cherries, mirabelle plums, or gooseberries.*

A pinch of sour salt (citric acid) is sometimes added for an enticingly piquant accent. Although considered unhealthful in large doses, sour salt is used in tiny amounts, and it would be hard to reach a dangerous level. It comes in crystal form and can be purchased in the spice sections of many supermarkets (especially in Jewish and Eastern European neighborhoods) or at pharmacies.

minutes. Add scallions, parsley, and cilantro and simmer for 10 minutes, then remove parsley and cilantro and adjust seasonings.

This soup can be made in advance up to this point and stored, covered, in the refrigerator for 1 day.

Reheat soup to boiling point and serve sprinkled with parsley or cilantro.

....

YIELD: 4 TO 6 SERVINGS

POLTAVA BORSCHT

.... ◆ ....

I n the true borscht belt that is Ukraine, each town and region seems to have a special variation of that thick and sustaining soup. In Poltava, chicken substitutes for beef, adding a golden shimmer to the beet red soup.

....

FOR THE SOUP
10 cups Basic Chicken Soup (page 28), prepared with a 3¹/₂-
*   to 4-pound chicken*
5 tablespoons rendered chicken fat (see page 50) or bacon; or
*   6 tablespoons fat skimmed from soup; or 5 tablespoons unsalted*
*   butter; or a 5-tablespoon combination of fats*
2 medium carrots, scraped and grated into long strips
1 small parsley root or ¹/₂ small parsnip, scraped and grated into
*   long strips*
1 medium onion, chopped
5 tablespoons flour
5 medium beets, peeled and grated into long strips
1 tablespoon sugar
1 teaspoon salt, or to taste
3 tablespoons red wine vinegar
2 tablespoons tomato paste
3 medium potatoes, peeled and cubed
A 1¹/₂-pound head green cabbage, cored and cut into slivers
8 black peppercorns
1 bay leaf
2 or 3 crystals sour salt (citric acid; optional)

2 or 3 large garlic cloves, minced
Salt, to taste
Ground black pepper, to taste
Fresh lemon juice, to taste
Sugar, to taste

FOR THE GARNISH
Sour cream
Minced fresh parsley and dill
Piroshki (page 158)

....

The soup should be strained, skimmed, and returned to a rinsed 5-quart enameled or stainless-steel soup pot. Add cooked, boned, skinned, and cut-up chicken meat to soup.

Heat 3 tablespoons of whichever fat (or combination of fats) you use in a 10-inch heavy-bottomed skillet. When hot, stir in carrot, parsley root or parsnip, and onion and sauté over moderate heat, stirring, until vegetables are golden brown, 8 to 10 minutes. Add flour and continue to stir and sauté until it too becomes a pale cocoa brown. Stir in beets, sugar, salt, vinegar, and tomato paste, blending well. Add 2 or 3 tablespoons chicken soup if mixture is very dry. Cover loosely and braise over very low heat, stirring frequently, for 8 to 10 minutes, adding a little more soup as needed to prevent scorching.

Bring soup to a simmer and stir in beet mixture to blend ingredients. Add potatoes, cabbage, peppercorns, bay leaf, and sour salt. Simmer gently, partly covered, for about 25 minutes or until all vegetables are very tender.

This soup tastes best if prepared to this point and held for 24 hours, covered, in the refrigerator. Reheat before serving.

Just before serving, heat remaining fat and lightly brown minced garlic. Add to hot soup and simmer for 15 minutes before serving, adjusting seasonings with salt, pepper and, if needed for the right sweet-sour balance, lemon juice and sugar.

Garnish each portion with a dollop of sour cream and sprinklings of dill and parsley. Eliminate bay leaf and peppercorns as you serve.

....

YIELD: 6 TO 8 FIRST-COURSE SERVINGS;
4 MAIN-COURSE SERVINGS

Meat and Pastry Turnovers
Piroshki (Russian) or Pierogi (Polish)

●●●●●●●●◆●●●●●●●●

ften made with yeast dough or puff pastry, these plump meat-filled favorites are more easily and quickly accomplished with sour cream pastry that is rich and flaky. These are equally good with soup or as hot appetizers passed with drinks.

....

FOR THE FILLING
3 to 4 tablespoons (¹/₂ stick) unsalted butter, as needed
1 large onion, finely chopped
1 pound lean ground beef, at room temperature
3 tablespoons flour
¹/₄ cup minced fresh dill
2 tablespoons minced fresh parsley
2 hard-cooked eggs, chopped
Salt, to taste
Ground black pepper, to taste

FOR THE PASTRY
2 eggs
1 cup sour cream
3¹/₂ to 4 cups all-purpose flour, as needed
1 teaspoon salt
1 teaspoon baking powder
¹/₂ cup (1 stick) unsalted butter
1 egg yolk beaten with 3 tablespoons water

....

Prepare filling before making pastry, so it can cool. However, do not prepare meat filling more than 1 hour before filling pastry and baking, as it will become too wet.

Heat 3 tablespoons butter in a 10- to 12-inch skillet and sauté onion very slowly until it begins to soften, about 8 minutes. If should not take on color. Add beef and, with a fork, break clumps apart. Stir and sauté over moderately high heat so that liquid evaporates and meat browns slightly. If pan seems dry, add 1 more tablespoon butter. Reduce heat and sprinkle in flour, stirring to distribute through meat.

Turn meat into a bowl and add dill, parsley, chopped egg, and salt and freshly ground black pepper to taste. Mix well and let cool at room temperature or in the refrigerator while you prepare the pastry.

For pastry, preheat the oven to 400°F. Beat eggs into sour cream and set aside. Sift flour with salt and baking powder into a wide mixing bowl or into the bowl of a food processor. Cut butter into small pieces and work into flour by processing for 3 or 4 seconds, flicking the pulse several times, or with your fingertips or a pastry blender, until you have a coarse meal.

Gradually stir in egg yolk and sour cream mixture until you have a soft dough that is not too sticky to be handled. Turn out onto a floured pastry board and, with the heel of your hand, knead 2 or 3 times until smooth. Divide dough into 2 flat rounds. Wrap each in waxed paper or plastic wrap and chill for 30 minutes.

Remove one ball of dough at a time from refrigerator. Roll each on a lightly floured board with a floured rolling pin to a little less than ¼-inch thickness. If dough is sticky, sprinkle both sides with a little more flour.

Cut into circles with a 3-inch cookie cutter or into 3-inch squares with a knife. Set aside and roll out remaining ball of dough.

Place 1 tablespoonful of meat filling on 1 half of each circle or square. Fold over into triangles or half-circles and pinch edges firmly closed. Brush tops with egg yolk and water mixture. Bake on lightly buttered cookie sheet for about 20 minutes or until golden brown. Let cool for 7 or 8 minutes before serving.

The baked turnovers can be frozen for up to 3 weeks. Do not freeze them unbaked. Wrap in freezer paper, or first in plastic wrap and then in aluminum foil. To reheat, unwrap and let stand at room temperature for about 20 minutes. Arrange on ungreased cookie sheet and bake in a 350°F. oven for about 20 minutes, or until crisp outside and hot inside.

....

YIELD: ABOUT 40 TURNOVERS;
FOR 10 TO 20 SERVINGS OF SOUP

Siberian Pelmeni

.... ◆ ....

Traditionally served in either clear lamb or chicken broth, these are made exactly like Kreplach (page 51). Follow that recipe for the dough and filling, using cooked or raw beef or lamb as the meat with 3 tablespoons finely minced fresh dill. Roll, cut, fill, shape, and cook as described. Serve in clear chicken soup into which you stir sour cream and a generous amount of minced dill. Allow 2 teaspoons room-temperature sour cream and 1 teaspoon minced dill for each cup of soup.

MOLDAVIAN SOUR SOUP
Chorbe Moldoveniaske
········ ◆ ········

A province of Romania, Moldavia puts zing in its chicken-based soup with a lacing of vinegar and some hot and sweet paprika.

···················

FOR THE SOUP
8 cups Basic Chicken Soup (page 28) or Improved Canned
    Chicken Broth (page 30)
2 chicken breasts (if using canned broth)
3 tablespoons rendered chicken fat (see page 50), or 4 tablespoons
    fat skimmed from soup, or 3 tablespoons unsalted butter
2 medium carrots, scraped and cut into matchstick strips
1 medium onion, chopped
1 small parsley root or 1/2 parsnip, scraped and cut into match
    sticks
4 tablespoons flour
1 teaspoon sweet paprika
1/4 to 1/2 teaspoon hot paprika, to taste
2 tablespoons red wine vinegar
2 small crystals sour salt (citric acid; optional)
3 medium boiling potatoes, peeled
Salt, to taste
Ground black pepper, to taste

FOR THE GARNISH
Sour cream
Chopped fresh dill and/or parsley
Piroshki (page 158)

···················

Degrease chicken soup and bring to a simmer. If chicken breasts have been cooked with the soup, trim off skin and bones, cut or shred into spoon-size pieces, and reserve. If raw, cook them without skin and bones in canned broth for about 25 minutes or until tender; cut as suggested and reserve.

Heat chicken fat or butter in an 8- to 10-inch heavy-bottomed skillet and sauté carrots, onion, and parsley root or parsnip, stirring frequently until vegetables are light golden brown. Sprinkle with flour and stir in, sautéing over low heat until flour is light golden brown, about 6 or 7 minutes. Stir in both paprikas and sauté for a minute or two, until paprika no longer smells raw. Remove from heat and stir in vinegar.

When I was at the Yale School of Drama, I got very bad tonsillitis. Although my parents then lived in Manhattan, they still went back to our old neighborhood in Brooklyn for chicken soup made by L & E Caterers. They drove the soup to me in New Haven, taking it across state lines. I think that was probably soupnapping.

—WENDY WASSERSTEIN, PLAYWRIGHT, *THE SISTERS ROSENSWEIG*

Turn sautéed mixture into simmering soup, adding sour salt, if you use it, and potatoes. Simmer, partly covered, for 20 minutes or until potatoes are tender. Adjust seasonings. Serve with a dollop of sour cream in each portion and sprinklings of parsley and/or dill, with Piroshki on the side.

....

YIELD: 6 TO 8 FIRST-COURSE SERVINGS;
3 TO 4 MAIN-COURSE SERVINGS

Chapter 9

MIDDLE EAST, NORTH AFRICA,
and Culinary Cousins

◆◆

◆

Albania, Armenia, Bulgaria, Egypt, Greece,
Gulf States, Iran, Iraq, Jordan, Kuwait, Lebanon, Libya,
Morocco, Saudi Arabia, Syria, Tunisia, Turkey, Yemen

◆

BASIC EGG-LEMON CHICKEN SOUP
Kotosoupa Avgolemono

.........◆.........

This is the most typical, nearly ubiquitous soup of the countries in this chapter, from Greece, Albania and Bulgaria through Armenia to Egypt and beyond. With its thickening of egg yolks and accents of fresh lemon juice, it appears with minor variations throughout that sprawling region. It must be served as soon as it is made, because it cannot be reheated once the egg yolks are beaten in. Cloves are sometimes added in Greece, a bay leaf in Albania and Turkey, cinnamon in Lebanon and Tunisia, and cumin or cardamom in Egypt. Even when diced chicken is added, this is a first-course soup.

....

FOR THE SOUP
8 cups Basic Chicken Soup (page 28), or Improved Canned
    Chicken Broth (page 30)
¹/₂ cup white rice
5 or 6 whole cloves, or 1 bay leaf, or a 2-inch stick of cinnamon, or
    ¹/₄ teaspoon powdered cumin or crushed seeds of 2 cardamom
    pods, or ¹/₄ teaspoon ground cardamom (optional)
3 egg yolks
3 to 4 tablespoons fresh lemon juice
Salt, to taste
White pepper, to taste

FOR THE OPTIONAL GARNISH
3 cups finely diced cooked chicken breast (see Note)
1 tablespoon chopped fresh parsley

....

Heat degreased chicken soup to a slow boil in a 2¹/₂- to 3-quart enameled or stainless-steel saucepan with rice and whichever spice you use, if any. Partly cover and cook gently but steadily for about 35 minutes or until rice is very tender but intact. Remove soup from heat and pick out whole spices.

In a small bowl, lightly beat egg yolks and 3 tablespoons of lemon juice with a fork until thin. With a ladle, slowly trickle in hot but not simmering soup, beating constantly with a whisk. When you have added 2 cups of soup, slowly pour egg mixture back into hot soup, beating constantly with a whisk. Adjust seasonings with salt, pepper, and additional lemon juice.

Add chicken, if using, and heat but do not boil for about 5 minutes, then serve immediately. Garnish each portion with parsley.

....

YIELD: 4 TO 8 FIRST-COURSE PORTIONS

NOTE: Adding chicken breast meat is simple if you are cooking the soup from scratch, as you will have it on hand. When starting with homemade or canned broth, add 2 skinless chicken breasts (about 1 to 1½ pounds) to the soup along with the rice. Both should be done at the same time. Remove chicken, pick meat off the bones and dice or shred.

VARIATIONS

Tunisian Chicken, Rice, and Parsley Soup
Chorba Jaj

Follow recipe for Egg-Lemon Soup, using cinnamon and bay leaf but not cumin or cardamom. Add a pinch of cayenne pepper, to taste, with other seasonings. Garnish each portion with a generous sprinkling of chopped fresh parsley leaves and chopped fresh mint leaves.

Turkish Wedding Soup
Sehriye Corbasi

Follow recipe for Egg-Lemon Soup, adding the bay leaf but eliminating the rice. Simmer for 10 minutes and then add ¾ cup of 1½- to 2-inch lengths of vermicelli and chicken, if you are using it. Cook for 10 minutes, then add egg yolks and lemon, as above. For the garnish, melt 3 tablespoons unsalted butter and stir in 2 teaspoons sweet paprika until well blended. Drizzle a swirl of this bright topping on each portion.

Armenian Royal Soup
Arkayagan Abour

Prepare Bulgur Meatballs (page 174) without mint. Cook as described and keep warm. Follow recipe for Egg-Lemon Soup, but eliminate rice. Finish with egg yolks and lemon as described and ladle over meatballs divided among individual soup bowls.

"The finest and most respected recipe to come out of the Caucasus" is how royal soup was described in the cookbook Dinner at Omar Khayyam's, *by George Mardikian, the proprietor of that excellent but long-gone San Francisco restaurant known for its Armenian food despite its Persian name. He noted that it was served only on very special occasions, such as the birth of a boy or the return of the oldest son from a twenty-year pilgrimage. (Girl babies and prodigals apparently rated no special soup.) Mardikian claimed that the recipe is 1,500 years old and at its most traditional is garnished with venison meatballs.*

TURKISH CHICKEN YOGURT SOUP WITH RICE OR BARLEY
Tavuk Corbasi Yogurtlu

········ ◆ ········

P iquant chicken and yogurt soup is second only to egg-lemon soup in its widespread popularity throughout this region. It may be served with or without bits of chicken and is a first-course soup. Flour is optional, but provides a fluffy texture. Hot pepper and/or sweet paprika gives this added bite and color, but both are optional and not typical outside of Turkey.

8 cups Basic Chicken Soup (page 28) or Improved Canned
    Chicken Broth (page 30)
1 bay leaf
$^1/_8$ teaspoon harissa (Moroccan chili paste), or $^1/_4$ teaspoon dried
    red pepper flakes (optional)
$^1/_2$ cup white rice or $^1/_4$ cup washed pearl barley
4 tablespoons flour (optional)
1 teaspoon sweet paprika
1 cup plain yogurt
3 egg yolks
3 tablespoons cold water
Salt, to taste
White pepper, to taste
2 cups diced cooked white meat of chicken (optional)
4 tablespoons ($^1/_2$ stick) butter
1 tablespoon dried mint, or 2 tablespoons minced fresh mint leaves

········ ◆ ········

Simmer degreased chicken soup in a $2^1/_2$- to 3-quart enameled or stainless-steel saucepan with bay leaf, harissa or pepper flakes, and rice or barley. Cook, partly covered, for 25 minutes for rice or 40 minutes for barley. Blend flour, paprika, and yogurt and beat into soup. Simmer for about 15 minutes or until rice or barley is very tender. Remove from heat and discard bay leaf.

With a fork, lightly beat egg yolks and water in a bowl until thin. Using a ladle, slowly trickle some hot soup into egg yolks, beating constantly with a whisk. When you have added 2 cups of soup, slowly pour egg yolk mixture into hot but not simmering soup, beating constantly. Adjust seasonings and add chicken if you are using it. Heat for about 5 minutes, but do not boil. Ladle soup into individual bowls.

Melt the butter and warm mint together for a minute or two, then trickle onto each portion of soup. Serve immediately.

....

YIELD: 4 TO 8 SERVINGS

VARIATION

Armenian Yogurt and Meatball Soup
Madzounov Kufta Abour

........◆........

Follow above recipe but eliminate hot pepper and paprika. Garnish with Bulgur Meatballs (page 174).

EGYPTIAN CHICKEN BROTH WITH LEMON AND GARLIC
Khoulaset feraakh bel lamoon wal tom

........◆........

This lemony, garlic-scented broth should work wonders for colds and frazzled nerves. It must be served scalding hot as soon as it is prepared. The recipe below is my version of one in the fascinating and comprehensive cookbook *Egyptian Cuisine*, by Nagwa E. Khalil.

....

FOR THE SOUP
One 3 1/2- to 4-pound chicken, cut up, with all giblets except liver
8 cups water, or as needed
Crushed seeds of 1 cardamom pod, or pinch of ground cardamom
A 3-inch-wide strip of lemon peel
4 celery stalks with leaves, cut up
3 or 4 parsley sprigs
2 or 3 sprigs fresh cilantro (coriander) (optional)
6 large garlic cloves, chopped
Salt and pepper, to taste
3 to 4 tablespoons lemon juice, to taste

FOR THE GARNISH
Cooked rice
Diced chicken breast meat
Chopped parsley and/or fresh mint or cilantro

....

Place chicken and giblets in a 4- to 5-quart enameled or stainless-steel soup pot with just enough water to cover. It should not take more than 9 cups. Bring to a boil, reduce to a simmer, and skim foam as it rises to the surface.

Dry lemon peel on a piece of foil in a 400°F. oven for about 10 minutes, or until edges begin to curl and turn light golden brown. Add to soup and simmer, partly covered, along with celery, parsley, cilantro, and garlic. Simmer gently but steadily, partly covered, for about 1 hour or until chicken is falling from bones. Strain soup, reserving chicken but discarding other solids.

Return soup to rinsed pot and simmer briskly, uncovered, for about 30 minutes or until soup is reduced by one half. Adjust seasonings with salt and pepper and lemon juice only after soup is reduced.

This is best appreciated when served clear and hot, with or without added herbs. For more substance, serve with 1 or 2 tablespoons cooked rice or diced white chicken meat.

....

YIELD: ABOUT 4 CUPS; 2 TO 4 SERVINGS

MOROCCAN
SPICY CHICKEN NOODLE SOUP
WITH LENTILS OR CHICKPEAS

.... ◆ ....

For this recipe I combined elements of two Moroccan soups— *Harira*, usually prepared with both lamb and chicken, and *Shorabit Djaj Sharia*, finished with lemon juice and sometimes egg yolks. *Harira* is traditionally served at the end of each day's fast during the month of Ramadan.

....

FOR THE SOUP
One 3¹/₂- to 4-pound chicken, quartered, with all giblets except liver
2 teaspoons salt, or to taste

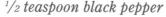

¹/₂ teaspoon black pepper
8 to 10 cups water, as needed
1 large onion, chopped
3 tablespoons olive oil or unsalted butter
2 celery stalks with leaves
5 or 6 parsley sprigs
3 cilantro (coriander) sprigs
2-inch cinnamon stick, or 1 teaspoon ground cinnamon
1 teaspoon turmeric
¹/₈ teaspoon harissa (Moroccan chili paste), or ¹/₄ teaspoon dried
    red pepper flakes, or to taste
1 cup crushed canned tomatoes
²/₃ cup lentils or chickpeas, washed and soaked; or 2 cups cooked,
    canned lentils or chickpeas, rinsed and drained
1 cup broken-up vermicelli, in 1- to 1¹/₂-inch lengths
3 egg yolks, or 3 tablespoons flour
3 tablespoons lemon juice, or to taste

FOR THE GARNISH
Chopped parsley and/or fresh cilantro (coriander)
Harissa

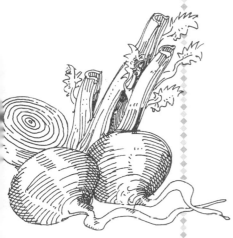

Combine chicken and giblets, salt, and pepper in a 4- to 5-quart enameled or stainless-steel soup pot with water to cover. Bring to a boil, reduce to a simmer, and skim off foam as it rises to the surface.

Sauté onion in hot olive oil or butter in a small skillet, and when lightly browned, add to soup along with celery, parsley, cilantro, all spices, and tomatoes. If you are using dried, soaked lentils or chickpeas, add them now.

Simmer soup gently but steadily, partly covered, for about 1 hour or until chicken is falling from the bones and dried beans are tender. Add more water as needed to maintain original level.

Remove and reserve chicken and trim meat, discarding bones and skin. Remove and discard wilted celery, parsley, and cilantro from soup along with cinnamon stick. Cut or shred chicken into spoonable pieces and return to soup.

The soup can be prepared up to this point and stored, covered, in the refrigerator for 1 day.

About 20 minutes before serving, simmer vermicelli in soup and, if you use them, the canned chickpeas or lentils rinsed in cold water. Simmer 10 minutes or until beans are hot and vermicelli are soft.

To thicken, blend flour into ¹/₃ cup of soup, making a thin paste. Pour that back into soup, beat with a whisk and simmer 10 minutes. Flavor with lemon juice and adjust other seasonings. Or thicken by beating egg yolks with lemon juice in a small bowl. Using a ladle, slowly trickle in hot but not simmering soup, beating constantly with a whisk. When 2 cups of soup have been added, slowly pour egg yolk mixture into hot soup, beating constantly with a whisk.

Adjust seasoning and heat soup for 5 minutes but do not boil. Sprinkle each portion with parsley and/or cilantro and pass extra harissa for those who want a more fiery accent.

....

YIELD: ABOUT 8 FIRST-COURSE SERVINGS; 4 TO 5 MAIN-COURSE SERVINGS

RED LENTIL SOUP
WITH CHICKEN
Shorabit Addas

.........◆.........

In her well-detailed cookbook *The Arabian Delights*, Anne Marie Weiss-Armushu writes that the delicate, tea-rose-colored red lentil soup prepared with lamb is a standard for breaking the daily fast during the month of Ramadan in Syria, Lebanon, and Saudi Arabia. She also lists variations in seasonings and accent ingredients for this same soup in Turkey, Kuwait, Gulf States, Iraq, Egypt, Libya, Armenia and Yemen, and notes that a proverb in Fez warns that this soup must be "as smooth as silk." Its creaminess results from the slow cooking of the tiny, bright coral lentils. I have adapted it to chicken with savory results and added Moroccan touches of ginger, chili pepper, and saffron. For a milder, more innocent flavor, eliminate those spices.

....

FOR THE SOUP
One 3¹/₂- to 4-pound chicken, quartered, with all giblets except
    liver
10 cups water, or as needed
2 tablespoons olive oil or unsalted butter
1 medium carrot, diced
2 celery stalks, diced
1 medium onion, chopped

1 garlic clove
1¹/₂ cups red lentils, rinsed in 2 changes of cold water
¹/₂ cup canned crushed tomatoes
Pinch of ground ginger, or to taste (optional)
Pinch of ground saffron (optional)
*¹/₈ teaspoon harissa (Moroccan chili paste), or ¹/₄ teaspoon dried
    red pepper flakes (optional)*
Salt, to taste
Black pepper, to taste
1 cup broken-up vermicelli, in 1- to 1¹/₂-inch lengths (optional)

FOR THE GARNISH
Chopped fresh parsley and/or cilantro (coriander)
Lemon wedges
Cooked rice

....

Place chicken and giblets in a 4- or 5-quart enameled or stainless-steel soup pot and add water to cover. Bring to a boil, reduce to a simmer, and skim all foam as it rises to the surface. When foam subsides, simmer soup, partly covered, as you prepare vegetables.

Heat olive oil or butter in a small skillet and sauté carrot, celery, and onion until they soften and begin to turn light golden brown, about 7 minutes.

Add to simmering soup along with garlic, lentils, tomatoes, and all spices. Simmer gently but steadily, partly covered, for 1 to 1¹/₂ hours or until chicken is falling from bone and lentils are disintegrating. To prevent scorching, stir frequently and add water as soup thickens. Remove chicken and reserve dark meat for another use. Trim breast meat from skin and bones, dice or shred, and return to the soup. Adjust seasonings.

The soup can be prepared ahead up to this point and stored, covered, in the refrigerator for 1 day. Add water during reheating to prevent scorching.

If adding vermicelli, do so 15 minutes before serving and simmer in soup. Garnish each portion with parsley and/or cilantro and pass lemon wedges at the table. Rice should be served on the side, in a small dish, to be eaten along with the soup. Do not serve rice if soup contains vermicelli.

....

YIELD: ABOUT 8 TO 10 FIRST-COURSE SERVINGS;
4 TO 5 MAIN-COURSE SERVINGS

VARIATION

Chicken Soup with Lentils and Swiss Chard
Shorbet Addss bel Salq

·········◆·········

This soup's name changes a bit from one country to the next throughout the region. It is also a favorite in Lebanon, Syria, and Tunisia. Spinach is often used instead of Swiss chard, but I find it less subtle. Follow the master recipe, substituting brown lentils for the red and using 1 extra onion and 2 extra garlic cloves. Eliminate all spices except salt and pepper, and substitute 1 teaspoon crushed caraway seeds or $1/2$ teaspoon ground cumin. Add well-washed leaves of 1 bunch of Swiss chard for the last 20 minutes of cooking time, or a 10-ounce package of unthawed frozen Swiss chard for the last 10 minutes of cooking time. Garnish with parsley and fresh cilantro, and add a sour note with lemon juice or a winy drizzle of pomegranate syrup.

MIDDLE EASTERN CHICKEN AND VEGETABLE SOUP

·········◆·········

E specially popular in Egypt and Iran, this soup with its varying vegetables and garnishes is a standby throughout the area. Use a mix of seasonal vegetables as available, but for the authentic look, try for a color scheme of green, orange, yellow, and white. Avoid the strong-flavored or runny vegetables such as broccoli, kale, eggplant, beets, and spinach. Cardamom adds an especially Egyptian accent, while cumin is preferred in Iran and other countries. I am partial to the astringently scented cardamom.

This is basically a main-course soup, but a cupful can be served as a first course.

·················

FOR THE SOUP
One 3¹/₂- to 4-pound chicken, quartered, with all giblets except liver
10 cups water, or as needed
Crushed seeds of 2 cardamom pods, or ¹/₄ teaspoon ground
   cardamom, or ¹/₂ teaspoon ground cumin
2 teaspoons salt, or to taste
¹/₂ teaspoon black pepper, or to taste
1 cup soaked dried chickpeas, or 2 cups canned chickpeas
3 fresh tomatoes, peeled and seeded; or 5 canned, peeled plum
   tomatoes with 1 cup of their juice
1 medium onion, coarsely chopped; or 2 small leeks, white and
   green portions, sliced
2 small white turnips, peeled and diced; or a ¹/₂-pound piece of
   rutabaga (yellow turnip), peeled and cubed
2 medium carrots, sliced
2 medium zucchini, seeded and cubed
2 small yellow summer squash, seeded and cubed
2 celery stalks, diced
2 medium boiling potatoes, peeled and cubed; or 1 large white
   potato and 1 large sweet potato, peeled and cubed
¹/₄ pound string beans, cut into 1-inch lengths
3 tablespoons lemon juice
3 egg yolks (optional)

FOR THE GARNISH
Lemon wedges
Chopped parsley and/or fresh cilantro (coriander), mint, or dill
Middle Eastern Chicken Meatballs (page 174) or Bulgur Meatballs
   (page 174)
Cooked rice

....

Place chicken and giblets in a 5-quart enameled cast-iron or stainless-steel soup pot and add water to cover pieces. Bring to a boil, reduce to a simmer, and skim off foam as it rises to the surface. When foam subsides, add seasonings, spices, and uncooked chickpeas. (Do not add canned chickpeas at this point.)

Simmer gently but steadily, partly covered, for about 1 hour or until chickpeas and chicken are almost completely tender. Add water during cooking to maintain original level. Add all remaining vegetables and cook for about 30 minutes more or until all ingredients are very soft. Remove chicken and trim off bones and skin. Dice or shred meat and return to soup, adding canned chickpeas, if using.

The soup is best freshly made, but it can be prepared ahead up to this point and stored, covered, in the refrigerator for 1 day.

Heat soup and adjust seasonings. To finish, simply add the lemon juice, but for added richness, thicken lemon juice with egg yolks. Beat them in a small bowl with lemon juice and, with a ladle, slowly trickle in hot but not simmering soup, beating constantly with a whisk. When 2 cups of soup have been added, slowly pour back into remaining soup, beating constantly. Heat for 5 minutes but do not boil.

Garnish each portion with lemon wedges and parsley and/or cilantro or dill, and 3 or 4 meatballs. Rice should be served separately on a small side dish, but if you like, just add some to each portion of soup and stir in.

YIELD: 8 TO 10 FIRST-COURSE SERVINGS;
4 TO 6 MAIN-COURSE SERVINGS

Middle Eastern Chicken Meatballs

Follow recipe for chicken meatballs on page 134, but omit cheese. Add $\frac{1}{2}$ teaspoon dried mint leaves, 1 teaspoon finely grated lemon rind, and a pinch of turmeric, cumin, or cinnamon.

YIELD: ABOUT 12 MEATBALLS; 4 TO 6 SERVINGS

Bulgur Meatballs
Kibbeh

Although popular throughout the Middle East, *kibbeh* is especially associated with Lebanon, Jordan, and Syria. Bulgur can be found in health food stores and in many supermarkets packaged as cracked wheat pilaff or wheat salad (tabbouleh). Just discard the envelopes of seasonings (or save them for other dishes) and use the grain as described below.

1 cup cracked wheat (bulgur)
2 cups warm water
1 medium onion, grated
1 pound ground lean lamb or beef
1 teaspoon salt, or to taste
½ teaspoon black pepper, or to taste
Pinch each of ground cinnamon and cloves
1 teaspoon grated lemon rind (optional)
1 teaspoon chopped fresh mint leaves, or ½ teaspoon
*   dried mint (optional)*
2 quarts homemade or canned clear chicken soup

Wash bulgur in 2 changes of cold water and drain. Cover with the warm water and soak for 30 minutes. Drain and squeeze out as much water as possible. Combine with all other ingredients in a mixing bowl. With wet hands, knead mixture until very smooth and thoroughly blended.

This can be prepared up to this point and stored, loosely covered, in the refrigerator for several hours.

Bring soup to a steady simmer in a 2½- to 3-quart saucepan. With hands or 2 teaspoons wet with cold water, shape meatballs about ½ to ¾ inch in diameter and simmer steadily in soup, partly covered. Cook in 2 batches so pan is not overcrowded. Cook for about 8 minutes or until meatballs float to surface and one tests done. Remove with a slotted spoon, drain, and keep warm.

These can be made up to 1 hour before they are served and reheated in the soup if necessary.

YIELD: ABOUT 50 MEATBALLS; FOR 10 TO 15 SERVINGS OF SOUP

Chapter 10

SUB-SAHARAN AFRICA

Ethiopia, Ghana, Ivory Coast,
Nigeria, Senegal,
Sierra Leone

ETHIOPIA
◆◼◆

SPICY CHICKEN SOUP
Yedoro Shorba
·········◆·········

Here again *shorba* means soup, as in the Middle East, North Africa, and some Balkan countries (see page 155). *Yedoro Shorba* varies from the mildly aromatic restorative at The Blue Nile to this bracingly pungent version.

Butter adds richer overtones, but the soup is also traditionally made with a vegetable oil such as sunflower or corn. For flavor, a mix of white and dark meat chicken is best. For leanness, use only breast meat.

···················

2 skinless chicken breasts and 1 chicken thigh, or
    3 skinless chicken breasts on the bone
Cold water to cover, about 3 cups
1 lemon
5 cups water
2 tablespoons unsalted butter, or sunflower, corn, or safflower oil
1 medium red onion, chopped
4 whole garlic cloves, crushed in a mortar or through a press
1¼-inch-thick slice fresh ginger, peeled and crushed with a knife
    blade or in a mortar
Pinch of ground cumin, to taste
Crushed seeds from cardamom pods, or ¼ teaspoon ground
    cardamom, or to taste
1 small fresh hot red chili pepper, or ¼ teaspoon dried red pepper
    flakes (optional)
Salt, to taste
Black pepper, to taste
1 small fresh rosemary sprig, or ½ teaspoon dried rosemary leaves

···················

Trim all visible fat from chicken. Cover chicken with cold water. Cut lemon into quarters and squeeze juice of 1 quarter into soaking water, adding squeezed rind as well. Let soak for 10 minutes. Discard water.

Chop chicken into chunks roughly 1½ inches square. Meat can remain on the bones or be trimmed off, and the bones cooked in the soup and discarded before serving. Sprinkle chicken and bones with juice of remaining lemon quarters and marinate for 15 minutes.

Combine drained chicken and bones in a 2½-quart enameled or stainless-steel saucepan, adding 2 cups of water. Heat butter or oil in a small skillet and cook onion gently until soft but not yet taking on color. Add to chicken along with garlic, ginger, cumin, cardamom, chili pepper, ½ teaspoon salt, and a pinch of freshly ground black pepper. Simmer gently, partly covered, for about 15 minutes.

Pour in 3 cups of water and continue simmering for 10 minutes or until chicken is completely tender. Add rosemary in the last 2 or 3 minutes. Adjust seasonings and simmer for a minute or two. Remove rosemary and bones if separated from chicken. Serve at once, dividing chicken among portions.

This soup tastes best when freshly made, but it can be covered and stored in the refrigerator for up to 2 days.

Serve soup very hot, in cups or small bowls for a first course, or in larger bowls as a light one-course pick-up.

....

YIELD: 2 TO 4 SERVINGS

VARIATION

The Blue Nile's Spicy Chicken Soup contains no cumin, cardamom, chili pepper, or rosemary. Two chopped, canned medium tomatoes and 1 cup of their juice are added with the first 2 cups of water. The chicken is chopped into

PILLOW TALK

*A*fter tasting the gentle ginger- and onion-scented chicken soup prepared for me at The Blue Nile, the colorful little New York restaurant where savory Ethiopian fare is served at basket tables, I asked the proprietor, Arraya Selassie, why it was never on the menu. "Because we eat it only when we are sick," he said,

agreeing with Daniel J. Mesfin, who writes in Exotic Ethiopian Cooking, "This is not an everyday soup, but one prepared for children and convalescents."

How chicken soup came to be considered a cure in Ethiopia is anybody's guess. I fantasize that it was pillow talk between Solomon and the

Queen of Sheba. "And now I tell you of a soup like the best wine, that goeth down sweetly, causing the lips of those that are asleep to speak," the wise king of Israel might have whispered, borrowing from his famous Song. Quite possibly he added, "Of course, Sheba, you'll need a kosher butcher."

chunks and served on the bone. The hot red chili paste, *berberé*—much like Moroccan harissa or Szechuan chili paste—can be added at the table to suit the fortitude of individual palates.

GHANA

◆◆◆

CHICKEN AND EGGPLANT SOUP
Nkakra
········◆········

The Ghanaian name literally translates to "plain soup," but that hardly seems to do this lush soup justice. Recipes generally call for "garden eggs," referring to a variety of eggplant that is small and ivory colored. This soup may be mild or spicy.

························

FOR THE SOUP
2 medium eggplants or 6 small Italian or Asian purple or white
*   eggplants, peeled and diced*
1 pound skinless and boneless chicken, preferably mixed breast and
*   thigh meat, cut into spoonable pieces*
2 green bell peppers, seeded and finely chopped
1 hot red chili pepper, seeded and finely chopped; or ¹/₂ teaspoon
*   dried hot chili pepper (optional)*
8 cups water, or as needed
6 medium yellow onions, finely chopped
4 canned tomatoes, seeded and finely chopped
1 teaspoon salt, or to taste
¹/₂ teaspoon ground black pepper, or to taste

FOR THE GARNISH
Steamed rice
Yam or Cassava Fufu (pages 187, 189)

····················

Although Ghanaian recipes do not call for peeling the eggplants or salting them to extract bitter juices, I prefer doing both, especially if eggplants are the usual large purple variety. Placed peeled, diced eggplant in a colander, tossing in 1 tablespoon salt. Cover with a plate and weight down. Let stand for about 30 minutes, or until dark juices run out. Rinse lightly and pat dry.

In an enameled or stainless-steel 3-quart saucepan or soup pot, combine eggplant with chicken pieces and peppers. Add 6 cups of water. Simmer gently, partly covered, skimming foam from surface. Cook until vegetables are tender, about 20 minutes. Add onions, tomatoes, salt, and pepper and 2 cups water so that chicken and vegetables are covered. Simmer gently, partly covered, for another 15 or 20 minutes, or until chicken is tender and vegetables are almost disintegrated. Adjust seasonings. Serve with a side dish of steamed rice or *fufu*.

This soup can be prepared an hour or so before serving and held at room temperature until reheating.

....

YIELD: 4 SERVINGS

VARIATION

Ghanaian Okra Soup
Nkruma-nkwan

..........◆..........

Prepare exactly as for master recipe, but while eggplant and peppers cook with chicken, boil 1/2 pound washed whole okra in salted water to cover for about 5 minutes. Drain, split, remove seeds, and chop. Add to simmering soup along with onions and tomatoes. (If you can get only frozen okra, thaw, seed, and chop, then add to soup with onions and tomatoes.) This soup will be pleasantly thick. Serve as above, with *fufu*.

IVORY COAST

◆◆◆

IVORY COAST PEPPER SOUP
Pepe-Soupe

········◆········

For the descriptions of these outstanding dishes, I am indebted to Sekou Diabate, a native of the Ivory Coast who guides the impeccable seafood department at the gourmet grocery store Agata & Valentina, in New York City. Adapted from his descriptions, this recipe and the ones that follow are among the most savory in this book. "We make our chicken soups very spicy when we are sick," says Mr. Diabate, "because we often have fevers from colds and sometimes malaria, and it is considered good to sweat."

With its ground peanut paste and chopped peanuts, this is a first cousin to the groundnut soup-stews favored throughout West African countries, such as Ghana, Nigeria, Sierra Leone, and Senegal. Supermarket peanut butter, smooth or chunky, can be used, but the unsweetened type, available at health food stores, is preferable. So is homemade peanut butter, easily made by grinding shelled, husked, and roasted unsalted peanuts to a fine paste in a food processor. Allow 1 pound shelled peanuts to make 1 cup peanut butter and, flipping the pulse every 2 or 3 seconds, and scraping down sides of the bowl with a rubber spatula intermittently, process to a fine paste and until oil begins to separate, in 5 to 7 minutes. Store in a tightly covered jar in a cool place until ready to use.

·················

FOR THE SOUP
1/2 chicken, about 2 pounds
6 cups water, or as needed
1 cup tomato juice, or 1/2 cup seasoned canned tomato sauce
2 thin slices peeled fresh ginger (optional)
1 garlic clove, chopped (optional)
1 to 2 teaspoons salt, to taste
1/2 teaspoon ground black pepper, or to taste
1 large onion, chopped

1 fresh hot red chili pepper, seeded and chopped; or
   ¹/₂ teaspoon dried red pepper flakes
³/₄ cup chunky peanut butter, preferably unsweetened;
   or 1 cup finely ground fresh, unsalted, roasted peanuts
1 teaspoon crushed dried leaf thyme

FOR THE OPTIONAL GARNISH
Chopped roasted peanuts and fufu (see pages 187-189)

Chop chicken into small pieces, cutting through skin and bones. Place in a 2½-quart enameled or stainless-steel saucepan or soup pot, and add 2 cups of the water. Partly cover and boil gently for 5 minutes.

Add tomato juice or sauce, 2 more cups of water, ginger, garlic, salt, pepper, chopped onion, and chili pepper. Simmer gently, partly covered, for 20 minutes. Remove chicken pieces and discard skin and bones. Cut meat into slivers and return to soup, beating in peanut butter or ground peanuts; add thyme.

Simmer gently for another 10 to 15 minutes or until chicken is completely tender. Add 1 or 2 cups water if soup is greatly reduced and cook 10 minutes more. Stir frequently and add water if mixture is too thick. It should be the consistency of a light cream soup. Adjust seasonings.

Serve in cups as a first course or in bowls as a main course. If you like, sprinkle each portion with chopped peanuts and serve with *fufu*. Best when fresh, this soup can be covered and stored in the refrigerator for 1 day.

YIELD: 2 TO 4 SERVINGS

VARIATIONS

Ghanaian Groundnut Stew
Hkatenkwan

This is prepared almost exactly like Ghanaian Okra Soup (page 181) and can be made with or without eggplant. The main difference is the addition of ³/₄ to 1 cup smooth or chunky peanut butter. Stir peanut butter into the soup along with the tomatoes, salt, and pepper and cook as indicated. A little more hot chili flavor is preferred with this version.

Optional garnishes are chopped roasted peanuts sprinkled on each portion and yam or cassava. For really elaborate presentations, side dishes such as chopped hard-cooked eggs, fried plantain slices, and diced tomatoes seasoned with lemon juice and chili pepper can be passed at the table, as garnishes are for gazpacho.

....

YIELD: 2 TO 4 SERVINGS

Sierra Leone and Nigerian Groundnut Chicken Soup-Stew

.........◆.........

Follow recipe for the Ivory Coast Pepper Soup, but begin by browning the chicken pieces in 3 tablespoons peanut oil along with 2 chopped garlic cloves and the onion, ginger, and chili pepper, as called for. Simmer the browned mixture with tomato juice or sauce and 5 cups of water for about 25 minutes or until chicken is almost tender. Stir in peanut butter and simmer 15 minutes longer. Salt to taste. Optional garnishes are chopped roasted peanuts sprinkled on each portion and cassava.

This version has a richer if heavier flavor.

....

YIELD: 2 TO 4 SERVINGS

IVORY COAST GUMBO SOUP
Soupe Gumbo

.........◆.........

Fresh okra is far preferable to frozen in this Ivory Coast recipe. I find canned okra completely unsatisfactory. Chicken bouillon cubes add authentic flavor, but I can live without them. If you use them, add salt at end of cooking and with caution. As you might guess from the word *gumbo*, this is a forerunner of the Louisiana specialty (see page 59). *Gumbo* is the West African Bantu word for okra, brought to this country by slaves who cooked the soup in the masters' kitchen and, along the way, added lustier seasonings and the now-classic browned flour roux.

....

FOR THE SOUP
¹/₂ chicken or breasts and thighs, about 2 pounds
¹/₂ pound whole fresh okra, or a 10-ounce package frozen whole okra
6 to 8 cups water, as needed
1 medium onion, sliced into thin rings
²/₃ cup seasoned canned tomato sauce
1 fresh hot red chili pepper, or ¹/₂ teaspoon cayenne pepper
2 small or 1 large chicken bouillon cube (optional)
Salt, to taste
Ground black pepper, to taste

FOR THE GARNISH
1 cup cooked white rice

Trim chicken meat from bones and skin, discarding the latter. Chop or dice chicken meat and set aside with bones.

Cook whole fresh okra in 4 cups water for 8 to 10 minutes, or until they begin to soften. Cook frozen okra for only 4 or 5 minutes. Remove okra with a slotted spoon and reserve half of the cooking water in the pot. Split okra; remove and discard seeds. Working in a wooden bowl or on a cutting board, mash okra to a pulp using your fist or a wooden spatula or mallet. Do not puree in a blender, food processor, or through a sieve, as results will be too fine.

Stir mashed okra into cooking water, adding 4 cups more water along with the chicken bones, onion, tomato sauce, chili pepper, and boullion cube. Simmer gently, partly covered, for about 20 minutes or until bones are cooked and no longer have any traces of red. Add more water if needed to have 4 cups.

Remove bones and add reserved, raw chicken meat. Simmer, partly covered, for about 20 minutes or until chicken is tender, and season to taste with salt, pepper, and cayenne. Serve in small bowls as a first course. A small mound of rice can be set in the gumbo or, as is more customary, on a small side dish to be eaten between spoonfuls of soup.

This soup tastes best when fresh, but it can be stored, covered, in the refrigerator for 1 day.

YIELD: 4 TO 6 SERVINGS

VARIATION
Senegalese Mafé

Follow master recipe, but add 3 additional cups of water, 2 cups finely slivered green cabbage, 2 peeled and cubed sweet potatoes, 3 sliced carrots, 2 sliced celery stalks, and 3 peeled and diced white turnips. Cook with raw chicken and ⅔ cup peanut butter for the last 20 minutes. Add more water if needed and adjust seasonings.

....

YIELD: 6 TO 8 FIRST-COURSE SERVINGS;
3 TO 4 MAIN-COURSE SERVINGS

IVORY COAST POTATO SOUP
Soupe à la Patat

.........◆.........

This soup gains intensity from steaming the chicken skin with seasonings in very little water, as a first step. Potatoes add a comforting touch.

....

1 small chicken, about 3 pounds
1 garlic clove, minced
1 teaspoon crushed dried leaf thyme
¼ to ½ teaspoon dried red pepper flakes
6 small boiling potatoes (about 1½ pounds), peeled
8 cups water, or as needed
1 to 2 teaspoons salt, to taste
¼ to ½ teaspoon ground black pepper, to taste

....

Remove all skin from chicken. Chop chicken with bones into 2-inch chunks. Place chicken skin in a 3-quart enameled or stainless-steel saucepan or soup pot. Add garlic, thyme, red pepper flakes, 2 potatoes thinly sliced, and 3 cups of water. Partly cover and simmer very gently for 10 to 15 minutes or until potatoes are tender. Remove potatoes, mash, and return to pot.

Add remaining 4 whole potatoes, chicken pieces on bones, and 5 cups of water, or just enough to cover chicken and potatoes. Add 1 teaspoon salt and ¼ teaspoon pepper. Partly cover and simmer for about 25 minutes or until chicken and potatoes are done. Adjust seasonings. Discard skin. Serve chicken in the soup, on the bone. Allow 1 potato per portion as a first course, 2 for a main course.

This soup is best served within 30 minutes of preparation. If necessary, reheat gently so potatoes do not disintegrate. However, leftovers can be stored, covered, in the refrigerator for 1 day, but expect the potatoes to fall apart in a comfortably homey way.

YIELD: 2 TO 4 SERVINGS

FUFU

Substantial starchy accompaniments to soups are as popular in West Africa as bread, potatoes, pastas, and rice are in Europe and Asia, and for the same reasons: they add nutrients and bulk. Aesthetically, they serve to renew the palate between spoonfuls so the flavor of the soup does not pall. *Fufu* is a dense, sticky, near-porridge much like stiff cornmeal, but it becomes lighter when eaten with soup. It is made of the flour or meal of potato, rice, corn, cassava, plantains, or yams. It is generally pressed into lemon-size balls or large, cake-size rounds, and is served in the soup or on the side.

Any of the following can be served with the West African soups.

Yam Fufu

This is my favorite form of *fufu*, for both flavor and color.

2 medium yams or sweet potatoes, about 1 1/2 pounds
3 cups water, or to cover
2 teaspoons salt, or to taste

Peel yams and cut into slices between 1/4 and 1/2 inch thick. Immediately drop slices into a 2- to 2 1/2-quart pot of salted water so potato does not discolor.

Partly cover, bring to a boil, then simmer steadily but gently for about 35 minutes or until potatoes are tender but not falling apart.

Drain thoroughly and return to pot. Set over low heat and shake pot back and forth for 4 or 5 seconds until potatoes dry. Turn off heat but leave pot on the burner. Using a potato masher, mash potatoes as finely as possible. If you do not have a potato masher, turn potatoes onto a board or platter and mash with a fork or puree through a food mill. Do not use any sort of electric processor or blender, as the results will be too liquid.

In a deep, preferably straight-sided bowl and using a wooden mallet (a meat tenderizer or a pestle for the drum-sieve known as a tamis), or a thick-bowled wooden spoon, pound mashed yams up and down against the side of the bowl for about 8 to 10 minutes, or until mixture forms a silky smooth and sticky mass.

Moisten your palms with a little cold water and form the mashed yams into balls, each made with about $^1/_4$ cup potato. Shape into balls about 1 $^1/_2$ to 2 inches in diameter. Arrange on a platter.

These balls are best served at once when they are warm and firm, but they can be prepared up to 1 hour in advance and kept uncovered at room temperature. If held longer, they become wet. If they become cold, place in individual portions of hot soup. Do not attempt to reheat them in any other way.

....

YIELD: 6 TO 8 BALLS; FOR 3 TO 8 SERVINGS

Potato Fufu

········◆·········

$^1/_2$ cup potato flour or starch
$^3/_4$ cup instant mashed potato flakes or powder
1 teaspoon salt, or to taste
3 cups hot water, just below boiling point

....

Combine potato flour and instant mashed potato mix with salt and stir into a 2$^1/_2$-quart saucepan of water with heat turned off. Using a thick wooden spoon or spatula, stir vigorously to combine, using one hand to keep pot steady, which will not be easy. Keep stirring until mixture forms a ball and lifts away from bottom and sides of pot, about 8 to 10 minutes.

Turn into a large ceramic bowl and roll around to form a smooth ball. Moisten your palms with a little cold water and pinch off pieces of dough measuring about $^1/_4$ cup. Roll into balls about 2 to 2$^1/_2$ inches in diameter.

Serve at once or keep uncovered at room temperature for up to 1 hour.

....

YIELD: ABOUT 12 BALLS; 6 TO 12 SERVINGS

Cassava or Gari Fufu

·········◆·········

Cassava, also known as manioc and in various processed forms as tapioca and yuca, is a tuberous root that produces a nourishing flour. When coarsely ground, it is gari, and that way provides a more interesting texture for *fufu*. In any form, it adds a slightly sharp and acidic accent to soups. Some recipes call for it to be prepared with hot water, but I find the cold water alternative less pasty.

···················

1 1/2 cups cassava or gari meal
1 teaspoon salt
1 1/2 to 2 cups cold water

···················

Combine flour and salt in a small, narrow mixing bowl. Gradually stir in enough water to come just to the level of the meal. Let stand to swell for about 15 minutes or until all water is absorbed and mixture has doubled in size. Add more water if it has not doubled, and let stand again.

Toss meal lightly with a fork until fluffy and serve as a side dish with soup.

···················

YIELD: 4 TO 6 SERVINGS

Chapter 11

ASIA

China, India, Indonesia, Japan,
Korea, Singapore and Malaysia,
Thailand, Vietnam

BASIC ASIAN
CHICKEN SOUP

········◆········

A sia's basic soup has very few flavors added to the long-simmering reduced combination of chicken, water, and salt. The seasonings most often added are fresh ginger root, scallions, and a little rice wine. That broth is really the starting point for the addition of a wide range of vegetables, meats, mushrooms, and exotic herbs and spices. Noodles and dumplings are cooked very quickly to retain color and texture, and added just before the soup is served.

···················

One 5-pound chicken, preferably a young fowl and freshly killed,
  with feet, or equivalent in smaller chickens
About 3¹/₂ quarts (14 cups) water
4 thin slices peeled fresh ginger (optional)
Green and white portions of 3 or 4 scallions (optional)
¹/₄ cup rice wine or pale dry sherry (optional)
1 tablespoon salt, or to taste

···················

If your chicken is fresh-killed, prepare according to instructions on pages 15 and 17 singeing and scalding feet as described.

To prepare any chicken, bring water (other than the 3¹/₂ quarts) to a boil in a 7-quart straight-sided stainless-steel soup pot and blanch whole chicken by boiling for 10 minutes. Lift chicken out and rinse in cold water. Discard water and rinse pot.

Return chicken to pot with feet, if any, and about 14 cups of water as needed to cover chicken, plus ginger, scallions, and wine if you are using them and half of the salt. Bring to a boil, reduce heat, and simmer very slowly, partly covered, for 3 hours. Turn chicken once in a while, but do not replenish water unless chicken is more than half uncovered.

Chicken meat will have no flavor and should be discarded. Reduce soup by about one-quarter, then strain and skim off as much fat as possible. Cool, uncovered, at room temperature, then cover in the refrigerator for up to 3 days.

The soup can be frozen for up to 2 months.

This soup can be served as is or prepared as in the following recipes.

···················

YIELD: ABOUT 2¹/₂ QUARTS

With the exception of India's, Asian soups are ladled out of big round porcelain bowls or tureens, family-style, into small conical or cup-shaped bowls, as shown here. Typical spoons traditionally made of porcelain are considered ideal because they get warm but not too hot and impart no metallic flavor. Large solids in the soup are usually eaten with chopsticks and dipping sauces are common for solids, especially chicken.

Basic Asian Chicken Soup from Canned Broth

........◆........

Simmer 10 cups canned, thoroughly degreased chicken broth (preferably low-sodium) and 5 cups of water with the ginger, scallions, and wine as in master recipe. Add chicken trimmings if you have any. Simmer, partly covered, for 30 minutes. Strain, skim, and use as called for. Do not add salt until serving.

....

YIELD: ABOUT 2¹/₂ QUARTS

ASIAN CHICKEN, VEGETABLE, AND NOODLE HOT POT

........◆........

Among the most restorative and delectable of Asian one-pot meals are soups that combine vegetables, meats, or in this case chicken, and one of the many varieties of noodles. Some of these soups are actually cooked by diners who choose ingredients from prettily arranged platters, cooking them for a few seconds by holding them on long chopsticks and dipping them into the broth that is kept bubbling in chimney-centered pots fueled with charcoal. With dishes such as Japanese *mizutaki* or *shabu-shabu*, the Korean or Mongolian hot pots, or the Chinese chrysanthemum pot, when the ingredients are cooked, they are dipped in a sauce, and at the end, the noodles are cooked and the reduced broth is drunk.

For other Asian one-bowl combinations of chicken, vegetables, and noodles, ingredients are sliced in advance and cooked all together, very briefly, in the kitchen before being ladled into big deep bowls. Among such dishes are Chinese *lo mein* or its Japanese adaptation, *ramen,* and the Japanese *torinabé.* Vietnamese *pho by* is yet another main course soup in this category.

With all of those delicious soups in mind, and at the risk of oversimplifying and offending purists, I devised the version below. It depends on your having prepared soup on hand, and the patience to cut all ingredients in advance so they can be added quickly for the almost instant final cooking. Use big Asian-shaped individual soup bowls for this, each of which should comfortably hold 3 to 4 cups of soup.

FOR THE SOUP
10 cups Basic Asian Chicken Soup (page 192) or prepared canned
*   variation (page 193)*
3 cups water
2 thin slices peeled fresh ginger
2 garlic cloves
2 large skinless and boneless chicken breasts
8 dried black Chinese mushrooms or fresh shiitake mushrooms
¹/₂ large head napa or Chinese celery cabbage
1 small head Chinese bok choy cabbage, or ¹/₂ pound fresh spinach
2 small squares (about ¹/₄ pound) tofu (fresh white bean curd)
¹/₃ pound cellophane or other Asian noodles (see page 196)
1 large onion, thinly sliced and separated into rings
2 medium carrots, scraped and thinly sliced (optional)
¹/₂ pound snow peas with strings removed (optional)
2 or 3 fresh cilantro (coriander) sprigs
5 watercress sprigs, or 8 to 10 pea shoots (optional)
Salt and pepper, to taste

FOR THE OPTIONAL GARNISH
Chopped green and white portions of scallions
Fresh cilantro leaves
Soy sauce
Chinese rice vinegar
Sesame oil
Hot red chili paste or oil
Steamed white rice

....

Do not cover pot during any of the following steps, as soup should reduce a little.

Combine soup and water with ginger and garlic in a 5-quart stainless-steel or enameled soup pot. Heat if you are going to cook soup immediately or let stand at room temperature if you are preparing other ingredients 1 or 2 hours in advance.

Slice chicken meat horizontally into thin scallopini-style slices or cut into julienne strips, removing tendons and membranes. Set aside at room temperature for up to 30 minutes, or chill for a longer period.

If using dried mushrooms, soak for 30 minutes in hot water, drain, discard steams, and cut caps into quarters. Reserve water, letting sediment settle. If using fresh mushrooms, wipe with a damp paper towel, discard stems, and slice caps. Set aside.

Wash cabbage and slice, or remove stems and wash spinach leaves. Blanch by boiling in plain water for 2 or 3 minutes, then drain well and set aside, discarding water.

Trim off dried edges of tofu and cut each cake crosswise, then slice down into julienne slivers. Set aside.

If using cellophane noodles, soak in cold water for 10 minutes, then drain and cut into convenient lengths. Set aside.

Just before serving, warm individual soup bowls in low oven or by rinsing in hot water. Bring soup to a boil, reduce heat, add dried mushrooms and their soaking water (but not fresh mushrooms) and simmer uncovered for about 8 minutes. Add napa cabbage and/or bok choy (but not spinach), onion, and noodles and simmer 5 minutes longer. Add chicken, tofu, carrots, spinach, fresh mushrooms, and snow peas and simmer for 3 or 4 minutes, then add any other greens and simmer 2 or 3 minutes, by which time all ingredients should be tender. Add salt and pepper to taste and serve immediately. Garnish each portion with scallions and/or cilantro and pass seasonings and sauces at the table.

....

YIELD: 4 MAIN-COURSE SERVINGS

VARIATIONS

Japanese-style soup: Add 10 or 12 thin half-round slices of white daikon radish or peeled white turnip with cabbage, and offer the seven-spice powder condiment shichimi (sold in little plastic shaker bottles). Thin slices of the compressed white fish cake, kameboko, is also favored in such a soup. Use soba, udon, or somen noodles, see below, and tamari soy sauce, if possible.

Korean-style soup: Add 1/4 pound of the very spicy pickled cabbage, kimchi, and use spinach and either cellophane or vermicelli egg noodles. Season with hot Szechuan or Korean chili paste.

Vietnamese *pho by*: Add 5 or 6 fresh cilantro (coriander) sprigs and cook 2 small, fresh hot chili peppers (seeds removed) along with the cabbage and mushrooms. Season midway through the cooking with 1 to 2 teaspoons of the fermented fish sauce, nam pla or nam prik. Use cellophane or vermicelli egg noodles and garnish with fresh cilantro, passing extra red chili paste at the table.

CHINA

◆ ◆ ◆

SHUN LEE'S BASIC CHINESE CHICKEN SOUP

Gee Tang

········◆········

Michael Tong, the proprietor of Shun Lee West and Shun Lee Palace, two of New York's best Chinese restaurants, and his talented, Hong Kong–born and trained chef, Man Sun Dav, allowed me to spend several hours in their kitchen so I could watch the preparation of the four soups plus my favorite, hot and sour chicken soup. Although the Chinese traditionally use a 5-pound chicken for full flavor, Michael Tong and his chef prefer one that is about 3½ pounds because it has less fat. I am partial to the 5-pounder, but you can choose for yourself.

ASIAN NOODLES

◆◆

Europeans, most notably Italians, vary their pastas by shape, but in Asia most noodles are classified by width, with additional variety coming from length and, most of all, different doughs based on grains such as rice, wheat, and buckwheat, as well as soybeans. Those noodles that follow are those most often used in soups throughout Asia, but with the exception of India. Soba and udon are particularly Japanese. Although each country (and many regions within each country) has its own names and varying widths and lengths, these are the basic types and suitable for the soup recipes here.

CELLOPHANE, GLASS NOODLES, or BEAN THREADS are sold dry in packages. They must be soaked and briefly cooked. They come in very long lengths and should be cut into convenient lengths with scissors after soaking.

EGG NOODLE VERMICELLI are much like the Italian style, which can be substituted. If fresh, cook directly in the soup for 5 minutes; if dried, cook for about 8 minutes.

RICE VERMICELLI are sold dried but are cooked and need only be soaked for 20 minutes in warm water, then rinsed and separated into portions. Hot soup can simply be ladled over them, but to develop more

flavor, simmer in soup for 2 or 3 minutes. Use only the thinnest for soup.

SOBA are buckwheat noodles usually tan in color but sometimes tinted with green tea. They are cooked right in the soup for 7 or 8 minutes, just as standard European pasta. They are sold fresh, dried, or frozen.

SOMEN are fresh or dried Japanese wheat noodles that are cooked directly in the soup for about 7 minutes.

UDON are thick, chewy fresh, frozen, or dried Japanese wheat noodles that have cut edges and a nice bite. They are cooked in soup for about 7 minutes.

Although ginger and scallions are traditionally the only flavorings for this soup, at Shun Lee, celery and onions are added. It is easy for a restaurant to have an uncooked chicken carcass since there is much use for the meat. If that is impractical for you, use chicken parts or cut most (but not all) of the meat off the bones. Slice whatever meat is needed for the soup you are making, then freeze the rest for future use.

Salt and monodosium glutamate are traditional in this, but at Shun Lee they use only salt, and add it just at the end of cooking.

....

FOR THE SOUP
Raw carcass, with some meat on it, of 3 1/2- to 5-pound chicken or
    young fowl
15 cups water
3 large celery stalks with leaves
1 small onion with a thin layer of outer yellow skin left on
4 large scallions, white and green portions
4 thin slices peeled fresh ginger
1/4 pound lean raw pork tenderloin, thinly sliced (optional)
Salt, to taste
Black pepper, to taste

FOR THE OPTIONAL GARNISH
Bits of cooked chicken meat from carcass
Egg Drops (page 38), Wontons (page 199), cooked rice, Chinese
    egg or cellophane noodles
Watercress sprigs; chopped green and white portions of scallions;
    shredded leaves of 1/2 pound spinach, lettuce or Chinese
    cabbage simmered in the soup for 3 minutes

....

Crack the carcass to flatten it slightly. Boil 3 quarts of water (other than the 15 cups) in a 5-quart stainless-steel pot. Blanch chicken carcass in it by boiling for 5 minutes, then rinsing under cold water. Discard the boiling water and rinse pot. Place blanched carcass and all remaining ingredients except salt and pepper in the pot. Bring to a boil, reduce to a simmer, and skim foam as it rises to the surface. Simmer very gently, partly covered, for 2 hours or until chicken meat is falling from the bones. Skim fat intermittently as it rises to the surface during cooking and season with salt and pepper.

When done, strain soup, discarding vegetables and bones and reserving chicken meat for another use. Cool and remove fat when congealed.

If stored in the refrigerator, covered, this soup will keep for 3 or 4 days. It can be frozen for up to 8 weeks.

YIELD: ABOUT 2 1/2 QUARTS

MY MOST MEMORABLE COOKING LESSON

◆◆◆

The most memorable cooking lesson I ever had came from a superb Chinese dental technician famous for the replacement teeth he made. I went to him to have a porcelain cap matched to my own teeth, and during the two hours I spent there as he tinted the tooth with a brush, then fired it, then retinted and refired, he explained with matching precision how to make the best chicken soup. He felt the meat very important, so to retain its moisture he plunged it whole into a deep potful of boiling water. Then, he explained, to have all of the water boiling at once, it was necessary to lift the chicken out of the water five times, each time draining the cavity back into the pot and bringing all back to a boil. Otherwise, he said, the water inside the chicken would not be boiling for a long time and the bird would not cook evenly.

CHICKEN VELVET AND CORN SOUP
Gae Lim Sook Mi Gai Tang

·········◆·········

The snowy cloudlets of chicken and souffléed egg white give this an especially gentle appeal.

FOR THE SOUP
1 skinless and boneless chicken breast
1 tablespoon rice wine (or light dry sherry if using canned creamed corn)
2 egg whites
6 cups Basic Asian Chicken Soup (page 192)
One 8-ounce can creamed corn or kernels cut from 2 ears fresh cooked corn
1 or 2 teaspoons soy sauce, to taste
1 or 2 teaspoons roasted sesame oil, to taste (optional)
Salt and pepper, to taste
1 1/2 tablespoons cornstarch blended into 2 tablespoons water (if using fresh corn)

FOR THE GARNISH
¹/₄ cup minced cooked ham
Minced green and white portions of scallions
Cilantro (coriander) leaves

....

Pound chicken breast with mallet or tenderizer until it is almost a paste. Chop or cut finely, removing tendons and membranes as you do so. Or, to puree in a food processor, remove as much of the tendon and membranes as possible, then process chicken meat for about 2 minutes, using the pulse several times, until you have a paste. Add sherry or rice wine to pureed chicken and set aside.

Beat egg whites with a fork until thick and frothy, then stir into chicken. In a food processor or blender, grind half of the creamed corn or corn kernels until completely smooth and add to the soup with remaining unground corn. Simmer in stock, partly covered, for 3 or 4 minutes.

Bring soup to a gentle boil and stir in chicken mixture. Simmer, uncovered, for 1 or 2 minutes. Season with soy sauce, sesame oil, salt, and pepper.

If using fresh corn, at this point stir in dissolved cornstarch and simmer for 1 minute, or until soup is slightly thickened. Garnish each portion with minced ham and scallions or cilantro.

....

YIELD: 4 SERVINGS

WONTON SOUP
Huntun Tang

..........◆..........

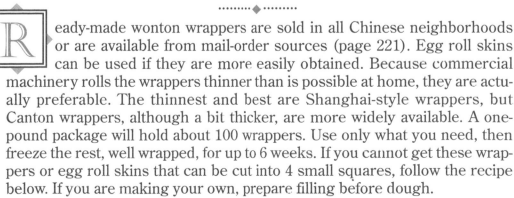

Ready-made wonton wrappers are sold in all Chinese neighborhoods or are available from mail-order sources (page 221). Egg roll skins can be used if they are more easily obtained. Because commercial machinery rolls the wrappers thinner than is possible at home, they are actually preferable. The thinnest and best are Shanghai-style wrappers, but Canton wrappers, although a bit thicker, are more widely available. A one-pound package will hold about 100 wrappers. Use only what you need, then freeze the rest, well wrapped, for up to 6 weeks. If you cannot get these wrappers or egg roll skins that can be cut into 4 small squares, follow the recipe below. If you are making your own, prepare filling before dough.

My favorite filling is this blend of pork, shrimp, and water chestnuts, but a mix of white and dark meat of chicken can be substituted for the pork. Instead of shrimp, add an extra $1/4$ pound of pork or chicken.

....

FOR THE WONTONS
$1/2$ pound lean ground pork
$1/2$ pound shrimp, shelled, deveined, and finely minced
$1/2$ teaspoon finely minced peeled ginger
5 or 6 fresh or canned water chestnuts, finely minced
2 tablespoons minced scallions, white portions only
2 to 3 teaspoons soy sauce, or to taste
$1/2$ teaspoon roasted sesame oil (optional)
Pinch of salt, or to taste
About 50 ready-made wonton wrappers or egg roll skins, or $1/2$
*   recipe Egg Noodles (page 33)*
Cornstarch, for rolling homemade wrappers

FOR THE SOUP
10 cups Basic Asian Chicken Soup (page 192)
10 to 12 watercress sprigs, or 10 leaves fresh or frozen spinach,
*   washed, stemmed, and sliced*

....

Combine pork, shrimp, ginger, water chestnuts, scallions, soy sauce, sesame oil, and salt in a large bowl and mix thoroughly with a wooden spoon or your hands so all can be smoothly kneaded. Do not taste for seasoning, as it contains raw pork. Instead, cook a $1/2$-inch ball of filling in a little boiling water for about 5 minutes, then taste, adding salt or soy sauce or oil as needed. Let stand for 30 minutes at room temperature; or prepare several hours in advance, and store, loosely covered, in the refrigerator, but let stand at room temperature for 30 minutes beforc filling wonton wrappers.

If using prepared wonton wrappers, lay them out and place $1^{1}/2$ teaspoons of filling on the lower half of each wrapper. Or cut egg roll skins into 4 square quarters and fill as for wrappers. Fold unfilled side over and tuck its edge under the filling. Moisten the open side of the wrapper with a little cold water and roll it over the filled portion, forming a cylinder but leaving a flap of loose wrapper at the top. Pull the 2 ends of the cylinder together under the roll and overlap slightly, pinching closed. Each filled and folded wonton should be placed under a dry towel or sheet of waxed paper to prevent drying until all are ready to be cooked.

If you are making your own wrappers, dough can be mixed, formed in a ball, covered with plastic wrap, and set aside until you are ready to fill. Just

Among foods that build physical strength, called ch'i in Chinese, chicken boiled in broth is foremost, according to Food in Chinese Culture: Anthropological and Historical Perspectives, *edited by K. C. Chang. Declaring this soup the most universal of all cure-alls, the book also points out its special benefits for new mothers, especially in Canton, and also in North China, where friends carry chicken, soup, noodles, and eggs to the nursing mother to eat during the first month after her delivery.*

before filling, roll out as thinly as possible, as described for Filled Noodle Dough, page 35. Use cornstarch to dust board and rolling pin. Cut into 3-inch squares and form as described above.

Wontons can be prepared up to this point 1 hour before cooking, but keep them covered with a towel at room temperature. Or they can be frozen in sealed plastic freezer bags for up to 6 weeks, then cooked without thawing.

To cook, drop wontons into about 3 quarts of lightly salted, boiling water. Boil, uncovered, for 5 to 7 minutes or until one tests done. Remove wontons with a slotted spoon or Chinese skimmer, or drain in a colander. Wontons can be cooked up to 30 minutes before serving if kept in a warm spot, but not in liquid.

Heat chicken soup and add cooked wontons and watercress sprigs or spinach leaves. Simmer for 2 minutes and serve immediately. Slivers of cooked chicken can be added to the soup.

YIELD: 6 TO 12 SERVINGS

STEAMED CHICKEN CUSTARD SOUP
Tang Deh

T his was a standard in our family," says Gene Young, a true friend and an adept editor. Her mother, Mrs. Juliana Koo, who is 89 as I write, still prepares this when the family comes to visit. "It is a Shanghai dish that we ate for comfort," Gene Young says. The chopped clam is optional but lends a stylish zing to this soup, which is served in the bowl in which it was steamed. A Chinese rice or soup bowl with about ³/₄ cup capacity is the most suitable for this, but standard custard cups that hold about ¹/₂ cup are also fine; just use 2 for each serving.

FOR EACH SERVING
1 or 2 shucked and chopped cherrystone clams, with juice (optional)
1 egg
³/₄ cup slightly warm Basic Asian Chicken Soup (page 192)
¹/₂ to 1 teaspoon soy sauce

FOR THE GARNISH
Green and white portions of 1 small scallion,
    finely minced

If you are using clams, put pieces and juice in the bottom of the soup bowl. In a small mixing bowl, beat egg with a fork until it is thin and frothy. Add chicken soup and soy sauce and beat again until frothy. Pour over clam in bowl, filling bowl to about ¹/₂ inch from the rim.

Place bowl, uncovered, in a Chinese bamboo steamer set over a wok half full of boiling water, or on a pierced metal vegetable steamer over boiling water. If you have neither, set bowl in a saucepan and add enough boiling water to come halfway up the sides of the bowl. Cover steamer or saucepan and steam for 6 to 8 minutes, or until egg sets in a creamy cap. (The steamer results in an airier custard.) Sprinkle with scallions and serve immediately.

If you prepare more than 1 bowl at a time, allow a little more time for steaming.

CHICKEN CONGEE OR CHICKEN-RICE
Chi'chu (in China)
Kai Chok (in Singapore)
·········◆·········

My first experience with this gently luscious, porridge or soup-gruel came many years ago in Singapore, where as "chicken-rice" it was sold from street stands along Middle Road and cost about 35 cents for a big bowl. One taste of the succulent rice mellowed in the rich, scallion- and ginger-scented chicken broth and fleshed out with bits of chicken, and I knew I would be addicted for life.

Delectable congees are also made with crabmeat or other seafood, all vegetables, or even with chicken livers and gizzards. It is standard breakfast food in China, available even in the most touristy hotel dining rooms and from street stands, and it is also relied on as a restorative for frayed nerves or those suffering colds and stomach upsets.

Although glutinous rice adds a pleasantly chewy stickiness when combined with regular long-grained rice, a satisfactory congee can be made without it. However, you will have much better results with absolutely raw, unconverted long-grain rice—not, for example, Uncle Ben's. That will do, however, if nothing else is available.

FOR THE SOUP
1 cup long-grain rice
¼ cup glutinous rice, or additional long-grain rice, or 1¼ cups
*   Uncle Ben's Converted rice*
8 to 10 cups Basic Asian Chicken Soup (page 192)
2 cups diced cooked white meat of chicken
Sugar, salt, and pepper, to taste

FOR THE OPTIONAL GARNISH
Chopped white and green portions of scallion
Soy sauce
Chinese salt-pickled turnips or kohlrabi

Wash glutinous rice in several changes of water until water is clear. Drain and combine with long-grain rice. Use Uncle Ben's unwashed.

Bring 8 cups of soup to a boil in a 4- to 5-quart stainless-steel saucepan or soup pot. Stir in rice and simmer, partly covered, for 1 to 1¼ hours, stirring occasionally to keep rice from scorching and adding soup to keep fairly liquid. If you have trouble preventing scorching, place pot over a flame insulator. Stir in chicken and season rice with sugar, salt, and pepper. Cook for a few minutes to heat chicken. Serve immediately in individual, deep Chinese-style soup bowls. Pass garnishes, if any, separately.

YIELD: 6 TO 8 SERVINGS

VARIATION

Indonesian Chicken Rice
Bubur Ayam

In his meticulous cookbook *The Indonesian Kitchen*, Copeland Marks suggests delicious garnishes of fried onion and garlic, fish sauce, chopped hot chili pepper, chopped celery leaves, and a fried egg. He also recommends adding a little lemon juice and peanut or corn oil to the rice during cooking. For the above amount, add 1 tablespoon lemon juice and ⅔ cup peanut, corn, or, preferably, roasted sesame oil.

YIELD: 6 TO 8 FIRST-COURSE SERVINGS;
4 MAIN-COURSE SERVINGS

HOT AND SOUR SOUP
Suanla Tang
·········◆·········

My own most favorite cure for colds and flu is this hottest of hot Szechuan soups as prepared at the two Shun Lee restaurants. It is guaranteed to clear heads and induce runny noses. Black pepper is the authentic spice for this, but I like to add a little chili oil at the table. It is a first-course soup, but a whole meal to cold victims.

···········

FOR THE SOUP
³/₄ cup dried tiger lily buds
²/₃ cup dried tree ear mushrooms
¹/₂ cup canned bamboo shoots
¹/₂ pound square salt-packed bean curd (dofu)
2 cooked skinless and boneless chicken breasts
¹/₄ pound minced lean pork tenderloin
¹/₂ cup sliced fresh white mushroom caps
8 cups Basic Asian Chicken Soup (page 192)
2 teaspoons salt, or to taste
2 extra-large eggs, lightly beaten
4 to 5 tablespoons distilled white vinegar
1 to 2 teaspoons white pepper
4 tablespoons cornstarch dissolved in 1 cup cold water
1 to 2 tablespoons roasted sesame oil, to taste
1 scallion, green and white portions, finely chopped

FOR THE OPTIONAL GARNISH
Red chili oil or paste
Cilantro (coriander) leaves

···········

Soak tiger lily buds and tree ear mushrooms in hot water for 20 minutes. Drain and set aside. Rinse bamboo shoots under cold running water and slice into slim julienne strips. Cut pillows of bean curd in half crosswise, then slice each half into slim julienne strips. Cut chicken breasts into julienne slivers. Blanch pork in 2 cups boiling water for 2 minutes. Drain and rinse pork under cold running water.

Bring soup to a boil in a 3-quart saucepan. Add chicken, pork, dried and fresh mushrooms, tiger lily buds, and bamboo shoots. Boil briskly, partly covered, for about 5 minutes or until mushrooms are tender. Add salt and boil for 5 minutes, adjusting seasonings. Stir in beaten eggs, vinegar, and pepper and slowly trickle in cornstarch liquid, stirring briskly. Cook 2 or 3 minutes, stirring, until you have a creamy consistency.

Remove from heat, adjust seasonings, and stir in sesame oil and scallions. Serve immediately, with garnishes.

YIELD: 8 TO 10 SERVINGS

SHUN LEE'S BANQUET OR BEST TASTE SOUP
Hau Teu Dong Gee Tang

Delicacies added to this soup—birds' nests, sharks' fins, and abalone—are prized primarily for their crunchy textures, according to Michael Tong, and so the rich soup provides the flavor. Those ingredients, however, are extremely costly and difficult to prepare and seem beyond the definition of a chicken soup.

FOR THE SOUP
One 3- to 4-pound whole chicken, preferably fresh-killed and
*   with feet*
¼ pound lean pork tenderloin, sliced
¼ pound Smithfield-type ham, sliced
1 tablespoon rice wine
4 thin slices peeled fresh ginger
15 cups water
Salt, only if needed

FOR THE GARNISH
Poached quail eggs
Thin slices of carrot cut into flower shapes and simmered 2 or 3
*   minutes in soup*
Minced chicken mixed with egg white, as in Chicken Velvet and
*   Corn Soup (page 198)*
Soaked and cooked birds' nests or sharks' fins

My good health is due to a soup made of white doves. It is simply wonderful.

—MADAME CHIANG KAI-SHEK

If you can get a chicken with feet, follow instructions for scalding and cleaning feet (page 14) and for singeing the rest of the chicken (page 17). Leave feet attached to chicken if possible.

Boil 3 quarts of water in a 5-quart wide casserole-shaped pot and blanch whole chicken by boiling for 5 minutes, then rinsing under cold water. Blanch pork for 3 minutes, then rinse in cold water. Empty and rinse pot. Lay blanched pork slices on bottom of pot, place chicken over that, and top with ham slices. Add rice wine, ginger, and water, which should cover chicken. Cover, bring to a boil, then simmer very gently, partly covered, for 3 hours. Do not replenish water as it evaporates.

Remove and discard chicken, meats, and ginger. Cool soup and skim off as much fat as possible. Serve clear in small cups or with 1 or 2 of the suggested garnishes.

....

YIELD: 8 TO 10 SERVINGS

BLACK OR SILKIE CHICKEN SOUP
Tsu bambu

..........◆..........

In *Chinese Gastronomy*, Hsiang Ju Lin and Tsuifeng Lin, the daughter and wife of China's poet-statesman, Lin Yutang, declare black chicken soup a "pseudo-rustic" dish suitable for "artists, gourmets and noted authors."

It is also given to nursing mothers and is made with black or "silkie" chicken, which has black feathers and pearl gray skin and bones. It is available frozen in Chinese markets and produces a dusky, smoke-haze of a broth. The warming, earthy overtones of medicinal herbs such as ginseng and fruity red medlar seeds or berries make it a soothing brew for sufferers of head colds and fever.

....

One 2½-pound black chicken that will probably come with feet and head
¼ pound lean pork tenderloin, sliced
5 thin oval slices of ginseng
6 thin slices peeled fresh ginger
½ cup medlar seeds or berries
5 cups water
1 tablespoon rice wine

....

The Chinese have a chicken soup hierarchy with a Basic (or Ordinary) Chicken Soup prepared for most uses and especially when served with wontons, noodles, egg drops, or as hot and sour soup or as lo mein, fleshed out with noodles, chicken and vegetables. The richer, clearer, and more complex Banquet (or Best Taste) Chicken Soup is reserved for luxurious and elegant garnishes such as bird's nests, shark's fins, and abalone. Most ethereally, there is steamed chicken soup, a virtual distillation of the bird's own juices, with very little water added. This can be made with a regular chicken, but for new, nursing mothers it is made with black or "silkie" chicken.

Cut off and discard head. Scald and clean feet as described on page 14 but leave them on the chicken. Boil water (other than the 5 cups) in a large pot and blanch chicken by boiling for 5 minutes, then rinsing under cold water. Blanch pork for 3 minutes, then rinse. Discard blanching water.

You will need a 3- to 4-quart heat-proof china or glass casserole that has a tight-fitting lid. In it place blanched pork and top with ginseng, ginger, and medlar seeds and chicken. Add water and wine. Cover casserole and wrap it, tightly—lid and all—with plastic wrap.

Place on a rack in a larger pot, adding boiling water to come one third up the sides of the casserole. Cover outside pot. Simmer gently for 3 1/2 hours, adding water to outside pot if level becomes low.

Lift casserole out of larger pot carefully and unwrap. Remove chicken and set aside. Ginger, ginseng, and seeds can be strained out, but are usually left in.

The chicken meat can be chopped in chunks, through skin and bones, and served on the side to be dipped into vinegar and soy sauce, separately or equal parts of each combined.

YIELD: 8 DEMITASSE CUPS OR 4 TO 8 FIRST-COURSE SERVINGS

VARIATION

The above recipe can be prepared in the Yunnan steamer, exactly as described below, but use 2 black chickens chopped in pieces before cooking.

YUNNAN STEAMED CHICKEN SOUP
Qiguo Ji

Scented with wine, ginger, and scallions, this eye-opening broth is one of the headiest in this collection, and the ultimate essence of chicken soup. It seems the most likely to cure whatever ails you. It is best prepared in a Yunnan chicken steamer—a covered terra-cotta or stoneware crock with a chimney in the center. It is set over a pot of boiling water, and the resultant steam extracts the juices of the chicken, creating an aromatic elixir, best sipped directly from small cups.

In place of such a steamer, use a deep, fairly narrow, heat-proof glass or ceramic casserole that has a tight-fitting lid and that will hold 3 to 4 quarts of combined solids and liquid. You will also need a larger pot that will hold the casserole, and a rack to set it on.

....

One 4- to 5-pound chicken
2 cups water
4 thin slices peeled fresh ginger
5 small scallions, green and white portions, sliced
2 to 3 tablespoons Chinese rice wine or dry sherry
$^1\!/_2$ to 1 teaspoon salt, to taste

....

Chicken should be chopped through bones and skin into 2- or 3-inch chunks. Blanch in boiling water for 5 minutes. Drain and rinse chicken.

Set steamer over saucepan that will hold it above the water level and that fits tightly enough so that steam does not escape at the sides. Distribute chicken pieces evenly inside the steamer or casserole and add water, ginger, scallions, wine, and a pinch of salt.

Cover steamer and bring water to a boil. If using a casserole, wrap it completely, lid and all, with plastic wrap and place on rack inside larger pot that has enough water to come one-third up to the sides of the casserole; cover outside pot. Whether using steamer or casserole, reduce heat so that water simmers steadily and creates steam. Keep a kettle of hot water ready to refill saucepan as water evaporates.

Steam for about 3 hours or until chicken is completely tender and well covered with broth. Strain soup, discarding ginger and scallions. Skim off fat and add salt as needed. Just before serving, reheat in a saucepan, preferably of enamel or glass.

Chicken can be nibbled on as a snack, or it can be served at room temperature with small bowls of vinegar and soy sauce for dipping.

....

YIELD: 10 DEMITASSE CUPS OR 6 FIRST-COURSE SERVINGS

INDONESIA AND MALAYSIA

◆◆◆

PUNGENT CELLOPHANE NOODLE AND CHICKEN SOUP
Soto Ayam

········◆········

The ingredients in this soup vary in different parts of Indonesia, but the combination below is typical. Kemiri or candlenuts, whether fresh, frozen, or vacuum-packed, are usually sold raw and cannot be eaten until cooked. Their texture and flavor match those of macadamia nuts. This soup can be a first or a main course.

··················

FOR THE SOUP
One 3- to 3¹/₂-pound chicken, cut and jointed into 8 pieces
8 to 10 cups water, as needed
2 to 3 teaspoons salt, to taste
2 tablespoons peanut oil
1 medium onion, coarsely chopped
2 fresh red or green hot chilies, seeded and chopped
2 garlic cloves, sliced
2 salam (manting or Indian bay) leaves, or 2 bay leaves, crushed
2 thin slices peeled fresh ginger, crushed to a paste
4 kemiri or candlenuts, or unsalted macadamia nuts, crushed
   (optional)
1 teaspoon dried shrimp paste (terasi) or anchovy paste
1 teaspoon turmeric
2 teaspoons ground coriander
1 teaspoon ground fennel
¹/₂ teaspoon ground black pepper
¹/₄ pound cellophane noodles
1 to 1¹/₂ tablespoons lemon juice, to taste

··················

FOR THE OPTIONAL GARNISH
1 cup fresh bean sprouts with ends pinched off
3 chopped hard-cooked eggs
Sliced and fried slices of 4 garlic cloves
6 scallions, green and white portions chopped
Sweet soy sauce
Hot chili paste such as Thai Red Curry paste, Moroccan harissa, or
    Szechuan chili paste

....

Cover chicken pieces with water in a 3- to 3$\frac{1}{2}$- quart enameled or stainless-steel saucepan. Add 2 teaspoons salt, bring to a boil, reduce to a simmer, and skim foam as it rises to the surface.

Simmer, partly covered, for about 40 minutes or until chicken is beginning to come away from the bone. Remove chicken and when cool enough to handle, trim off and discard bones and skin. Shred meat into spoon-size pieces and set aside. Skim fat from soup as it cools.

Heat peanut oil in a small skillet, and over low heat sauté onion, chilies, and garlic for about 5 minutes or until they begin to soften. Stir in selem leaves, ginger, nut and shrimp pastes, and all spices and fry gently for 2 to 3 minutes or until smoothly blended and spices lose their raw smell. Stir sautéed mixture into soup.

The soup can be prepared up to this point 1 or 2 hours before it is finished and served. Keep uncovered at room temperature until ready to finish.

Just before serving, soak cellophane noodles in cold water in a large bowl for 15 minutes or until completely limp. Drain and cut into convenient lengths with scissors. Bring soup to a simmer and add cellophane noodles along with shredded chicken. Simmer gently, uncovered, for 7 or 8 minutes or until noodles are done and chicken is hot.

Adjust seasonings, adding enough lemon juice to impart a gently sharp tang. To serve, lift out noodles and place at bottom of each soup bowl or in a tureen and add bean sprouts if you are using them, and chicken. Bring soup to a low boil and ladle it over other ingredients in each bowl. Top with garnishes such as egg, fried garlic, and raw scallions and pass sauces at the table.

....

YIELD: 6 TO 8 FIRST-COURSE SERVINGS;
4 MAIN-COURSE SERVINGS

JAPAN
◆◆◆

CRYSTAL CLEAR CHICKEN SOUP
Tori no Suimono
·········· ◆ ··········

C hicken soup plays a very minor role in Japanese culinary culture and is not imbued with any special magic. Nevertheless, there are a few chicken soups in the repertory, including the variation of Asian Chicken, Vegetable, and Noodle Hot Pot, page 193.

This is the Basic Asian Chicken Soup (page 192) made without rice wine, but with ginger and scallions and clarified with egg whites as described on page 23. In keeping with the Japanese appreciation of delicately arranged food, the soup should be a crystal clear backdrop for the few, artfully arranged garnishes.

The soup should have only 2 or 3 simple garnishes. Typical garnishes are thin slices of carrot or bamboo shoots cut into flower or fish forms; 1 or 2 sprigs of the green herb trefoil or Italian parsley or radish sprouts; 1 teaspoon diced tofu (fresh bean curd); 2 or 3 thin slivers of lemon rind; 1 thin slice of the fish cakes known as kameboko; 1 quail egg that is poached or hard-cooked and cut in half vertically.

CHICKEN,
POTATO, AND BLACK MUSHROOM
SOUP
Kenchin-jiru
·········· ◆ ··········

 I ntensely flavored dried black mushrooms lend a smoky luster to this soup that is accented by rice wine and daikon. Any potatoes will bolster its consistency, but the purple ones add a pleasant color.

6 cups Basic Asian Chicken Soup (page 192)
1 tablespoon sake rice wine
3 small Japanese potatoes (sato imo) or purple
    Peruvian-style potatoes or new potatoes, peeled and diced
    (optional)
4 dried black mushrooms, soaked in hot water for 30 minutes and sliced
A 3-inch piece Japanese white daikon radish, or 1 medium white
    turnip, peeled and cut into 1/2-inch-thick half-circles
1 small carrot, scraped and cut into julienne slivers
1 skinless and boneless chicken breast, finely diced
Salt, to taste

· · · · · · · · · · · · · · · · · ·

In a 2 1/2-quart stainless-steel or enameled cast-iron saucepan combine soup, sake, potatoes, and mushrooms. Simmer gently, partly covered, for 10 minutes. Add radish or turnip, carrot, and chicken and simmer 5 minutes more. Adjust seasoning and serve immediately.

· · · · · · · · · · · · · · · · · ·

YIELD: 6 SERVINGS

THAILAND
◆◆◆

CHICKEN, GALANGAL, AND COCONUT MILK SOUP
Gai Tom Ka
· · · · · · · · ◆ · · · · · · · ·

Creamy coconut milk and the pungent Thai ginger, galangal, make this elegant soup at once soothing and exciting. The supreme example in my experience is served at Vong, the New York restaurant where Jean-Georges Vongerichten works his Gallic culinary magic on exotic Thai specialties. He generously provided this recipe that is surprisingly quick and easy to prepare, considering the flavor wallop it packs. It is traditionally a first course, although a big bowlful would make a fine light lunch or supper.

New York is the world capital of chicken soup. You would have to travel across five continents to try all of the ethnic chicken soups you can get right here in five boroughs. That's just another reason why I'm proud to be the mayor of this city.

—MAYOR RUDOLPH W. GIULIANI

Generally, it is followed by Thai seafood or meat dishes that are grilled or fried rather than those such as curries that have abundant sauces, but any simple grilled fish or meat and a salad would be fine. The variety of rice known as jasmine lends an intriguing perfumed accent. If unavailable, use the Indian variety, basmati, or, if you must, ordinary converted white rice.

....

FOR THE SOUP
2 tablespoons peanut oil
$1/2$ medium onion, thinly sliced
2 garlic cloves, finely chopped
1 Thai bird chili, preferably red; or 1 serrano or jalapeño chili,
   seeded and chopped
2 slices peeled galangal or fresh ginger
1 dried lemongrass stalk, cut into 2-inch lengths and crushed
   (no substitute)
1 teaspoon Thai red chili paste (see Note, page 215)
4 cups Basic Asian Chicken Soup (page 192)
2 cups canned coconut milk
2 tablespoons fresh lime juice
2 skinless and boneless chicken breasts, cut into $1/2$-inch cubes
12 shiitake mushroom caps, sliced in strips
1 to 2 teaspoons Thai fish sauce (nam pla), or $1/2$ teaspoon
   salt, or to taste
2 scallions, white and green portions, sliced
4 fresh cilantro (coriander) sprigs

FOR THE GARNISH
2 cups steamed jasmine or basmati rice

....

Heat peanut oil in a $2^{1}/_{2}$- to 3-quart enameled or stainless-steel saucepan and slowly simmer or "sweat" onion, garlic, chili, galangal or ginger, lemongrass, and chili paste for 5 minutes, stirring once or twice until onion and garlic are soft but not colored. Add chicken soup and simmer for 30 minutes.

The soup can be prepared up to this point about 1 hour before serving and kept, partly covered, at room temperature.

Just before serving, skim thoroughly. Remove lemongrass and add chicken, mushrooms, and fish sauce. Cook at a gentle boil for 2 to 4 minutes, then add coconut milk and lime juice. Heat but do not boil, until chicken and mushrooms are just tender.

Ladle into 4 warm soup bowls, preferably of Asian shape, and garnish each portion with chopped scallions and cilantro. Serve each portion with ¹/₂ cup rice in a small side dish to be spooned into the soup or eaten along with it.

....

YIELD: 4 SERVINGS

SOUR LEMON-LIME CHICKEN SOUP
Tom Yam Gai
.........◆.........

This clear but headily spiced soup with its pungent overtones of citrus juices, lemongrass, and fiery chilies is bound to alleviate standard cold symptoms and lift spirits. Fresh straw mushrooms are preferable but are rarely available in this country.

....

FOR THE SOUP
6 cups Basic Asian Chicken Soup (page 192) made with ginger
*   and scallions, or prepared from canned broth (page 193)*
3 kaffir lime leaves, or 2 teaspoons fresh lime juice and a 1-inch-
*   long strip of lime peel*
A 4-inch length dried lemongrass, crushed
1 tablespoon bottled Thai fish sauce (nam pla), or to taste; or salt,
*   to taste*
3 to 4 tablespoons fresh lemon juice
2 small red or green chili peppers such as Thai bird, serranos, or
*   jalapeños, seeded and minced*
¹/₂ to 1 teaspoon Thai red chili paste (see Note)
10 to 12 whole canned straw mushrooms, rinsed
1 large skinless and boneless chicken breast, finely slivered
Sugar, to taste

FOR THE GARNISH
Fresh cilantro (coriander) leaves

....

Heat soup in a 2-quart enameled or stainless-steel saucepan and add lime leaves or juice and peel, lemongrass, half of the fish sauce or salt, 3 tablespoons of lemon juice, the chilies, and a bit of the red chili paste. Simmer gently for 3 minutes. Add straw mushrooms and the chicken and simmer for about 3 minutes or until mushrooms are hot and chicken is just tender. Remove lemongrass and adjust seasonings with salt, sugar, additional lemon juice, fish sauce, or chili paste.

Serve immediately in individual, Asian-style bowls, garnishing each portion with cilantro leaves.

....

YIELD: 4 SERVINGS

NOTE: Thai red chili paste (krung gaeng ped) is a rich and fiery condiment prepared from scratch at Vong. It is made of crushed dried red chili peppers, shallots, cumin, cilantro, ginger or galangal, lime peel, black pepper, kaffir lime powder, garlic, and shrimp paste, all ground and blended with vegetable or peanut oil. It is very time-consuming to make, and fortunately can be purchased prepared at stores featuring Asian ingredients such as the sources listed on page 221. But it can also be approximated by using a hot red chili paste such as the Moroccan harissa or Szechuan chili paste. For more authentic flavor blend in a pinch of powdered cumin, cilantro, ginger, black pepper, grated lime peel, and a bit of crushed garlic fried for 1 or 2 minutes in a little vegetable oil.

INDIA

◆◆◆

ISMAIL MERCHANT'S GINGERED CHICKEN SOUP
Murgh aur Adrak Shorba

......◆......

The pungent, intense ginger and chili pepper chicken soup is Ismail Merchant's cure for just about everything that might ail him, and he shares his recipe. Be warned that he likes this soup very highly spiced. He also likes it made with olive or vegetable oil and it's his recipe; I prefer butter and it's my book. Finally, it's your choice, but if you want to cut fat and calories, you can eliminate both.

FOR THE SOUP
1 whole 3-pound chicken
5 to 6 cups water, as needed
8 whole cloves
A 1-inch piece fresh ginger, peeled and very finely chopped or crushed
2 whole long or round, dried hot red chili peppers, or $1/2$ to $1^1/2$
*   teaspoons dried red pepper flakes, or to taste*
2 tablespoons light olive oil or other light vegetable oil, or 2 table
*   spoons ($1/4$ stick) unsalted butter*
2 small fresh or canned tomatoes, peeled, seeded, and coarsely chopped
$3/4$ to 1 teaspoon salt, to taste
$1/2$ teaspoon coarsely ground black pepper, or to taste

FOR THE GARNISH
Fresh cilantro (coriander) or parsley leaves

Place chicken in a straight-sided 3- to 5-quart enameled or stainless-steel soup pot and add just enough water to cover. It should not take more than 6 cups. If so, cut chicken in halves or quarters so no more water will be needed to cover. Add all other ingredients, using minimum amounts of chili peppers, salt, and black pepper for the first 25 minutes of cooking time. Simmer gently but steadily, partly covered, for about 25 minutes, adding water to maintain original level.

Taste for seasonings and cautiously add more chili, salt, and black pepper to taste. Continue to cook for another 20 to 25 minutes or until chicken is just about falling from the bone. Keep adding water to maintain original level. Adjust seasonings as you go along, keeping in mind that a fiery flavor is traditional. Remove cooked chicken, cloves, and stems from chili peppers if any;

SEDUCTIVE BUT SIMPLE

◆◆◆

The food of the Indian subcontinent resembles that of the Middle East somewhat more than it does that of the rest of Asia. In his latest and most inviting cookbook, Ismail Merchant's Passionate Meals, the author states that soup is not native to India's cuisine and is served primarily in Westernized households. Even the characteristic restaurant choice, mulligatawny—literally "pepper-water"—was created by Indian cooks to please Anglo employers.

Nevertheless, this producer of exquisitely seductive films such as Howard's End, Room with a View, and The Remains of the Day, loves to prepare equally seductive soups of the simplest sort, in contrast to his director-partner James Ivory, who prefers those that are more complex.

it is not necessary to strain or remove pepper seeds. Pick chicken meat from bones and skin, discarding the latter, and returning spoonable chunks of chicken to the soup.

The soup can be prepared up to 2 hours before serving and kept uncovered at room temperature.

To serve, reheat to just below the boiling point. Garnish each portion with cilantro or parsley.

....

YIELD: 2 TO 4 SERVINGS

CHICKEN MULLIGATAWNY
Murgh Mulligatunny Shorba
.........◆.........

owdered ginger can be substituted for the fresh, but it will not have nearly the sprightly bite. Use chickpea flour if available, as it adds a nutlike flavor. For a richly creamy result, add coconut milk.

....

FOR THE SOUP
One 3- to 3¹/₂-pound chicken, chopped into 10 or 12 pieces
6 to 8 cups water, as needed
2 tablespoons (¹/₄ stick) unsalted butter or light vegetable oil other
    than olive
1 medium onion, finely chopped
2 garlic cloves, minced
A 1-inch piece fresh ginger, peeled and minced or mashed; or 1
    teaspoon ground ginger
1 teaspoon turmeric
1 teaspoon ground coriander
¹/₂ teaspoon ground cumin
1 teaspoon salt, or to taste
¹/₂ teaspoon ground black pepper, or to taste
Pinch of cayenne pepper, or to taste
2 to 3 tablespoons canned coconut milk (optional)
2 tablespoons chickpea flour or all-purpose flour
2 to 3 tablespoons lemon juice, to taste

FOR THE GARNISH
Fresh cilantro (coriander) or parsley leaves

....

Place chicken in a straight-sided enameled or stainless-steel soup pot and add 6 cups of water, which should cover the chicken. Bring to a boil, reduce to a simmer, and cook, partly covered, for about 45 minutes or until chicken is completely tender. Add water to maintain original level. Chicken may be served as is, on the bone and with skin, or you can remove it from the soup, trim off skin and bones, and return meat to soup.

Heat butter or oil in a small, heavy skillet and sauté onion, garlic, and ginger over low heat for 5 to 7 minutes or until soft but not yet taking on color. Remove from heat and stir in turmeric, coriander, and cumin and sauté, stirring, over very low heat for a minute or two or until spices lose the raw smell. Stir this into simmering soup, using a little soup to rinse out sauté pan so all flavors are incorporated. Season with salt, pepper, and cayenne and add coconut milk if you use it. Simmer for 10 minutes.

The soup can be prepared up to this point 1 hour before serving and kept uncovered at room temperature.

A few minutes before serving, bring soup to a simmer. Blend chickpea or all-purpose flour into lemon juice and stir into soup. Simmer for 5 minutes or until slightly thickened. Adjust seasonings.

Garnish each portion with cilantro or parsley leaves.

....

Yield: 4 to 6 servings

BIBLIOGRAPHY

◆◆◆

The following are the books and periodicals that provided me with invaluable information and background material.

INTRODUCTION

Fisher, M. F. K. *With Bold Knife and Fork.* New York: G. P. Putnam, 1968.

Lévi-Strauss, Claude. "The Roast and the Boiled." In *The Anthropologist's Cookbook*, Jessica Kupfer, ed. New York: Universe, 1977.

Sendak, Maurice. *Chicken Soup and Rice.* The Nutshell Library. New York: HarperCollins, 1962.

Soyer, Alexis. *The Pantropheon.* London: Simpkin, Marshall & Co., 1853.

Tyler, Anne. *Dinner at the Homesick Restaurant.* New York: Alfred A. Knopf, 1982.

Visser, Margaret. *Much Depends on Dinner.* New York: Grove, 1986.

———. *The Rituals of Dinner.* New York: Grove, 1991.

CHAPTER 1: IS IT REALLY PENICILLIN?

Saketkhoo, Kiumars, M.D., Adolph Januszkiewicz, B.S., and Marvin A. Sackner, M.D., F.C.C.P. "Effects of Drinking Hot Water, Cold Water, and Chicken Soup on Nasal Mucus Velocity and Nasal Airflow Resistance." Mount Sinai Medical Center, Miami Beach, Fla. *Chest* 74:4 (October 1978).

CHAPTER 2: IN THE SOUP

Brillat-Savarin, Jean Anthelme. *The Physiology of Taste,* M. F. K. Fisher, trans. New York: Alfred A. Knopf, 1971.

Davis, Adelle. *Let's Cook It Right.* New York: Harcourt-Brace, 1947.

McGee, Harold. *On Food and Cooking: The Science and Lore of the Kitchen.* New York: Charles Scribner's Sons, 1984.

CHAPTER 3: BASIC SOUPMANSHIP

Frolich, Lucie Keyser. *Ola's Norwegian Cookbook.* Boston: Lucie Rist-Frohlich, 1946, 1951.

CHAPTER 4: THE MOTHER OF ALL CHICKEN SOUPS

Ginsberg, Allen. *"Yiddishe Kopf."* In *Cosmopolitan Greetings.* New York: HarperCollins, 1994.

Machlin, Edda Servi. *The Classic Cuisine of the Italian Jews.* New York: Everest House, 1981.

Marks, Copeland. *Sephardic Cooking.* New York: Donald I. Fine, 1992.

Sheraton, Mimi. *From My Mother's Kitchen.* New York: HarperCollins, 1984.

Weinreich, Uriel. *Modern English-Yiddish, Yiddish-English Dictionary.* New York: McGraw-Hill, 1968.

CHAPTER 5: UNITED STATES

Adams, Marcia. *Heartland: The Best of the Old and New from Midwest Kitchens.* New York: Clarkson Potter, 1991.

Hark, Ann, and Preston A. Barbra. *Pennsylvania Dutch Cookery.* Allentown, PA: Schlechter's, 1950.

Hibben, Sheila. *The National Cookbook.* New York: Harper & Bros., 1932.

Mitcham, Howard. *Creole Gumbo and All That Jazz.* Reading, MA: Addison-Wesley, 1978.

Rosenberg, Jay F. *The Impoverished Students' Book of Cookery, Drinkery & Housekeepery.* Portland, OR: Reed College Alumni Assoc., 1965.

Tyler, Anne. *Dinner at the Homesick Restaurant.* New York: Alfred A. Knopf, 1982.

Wauwatosa Junior Woman's Club. *The Ethnic Epicure.* Wauwatosa, WI: Junior Woman's Club, 1973.

Wilson, José. *America: The Eastern Heartland.* New York: Time-Life, 1971.

CHAPTER 6: LATIN AMERICA AND THE CARIBBEAN

Burt, Elinor. *Olla Podrida.* Caldwell, ID: Caxton, 1938.

Brown, Cora, Rose, and Bob. *The South American Cook Book.* Garden City, NY: Doubleday, 1939.

Green, Linette. *A Taste of Cuba.* New York: Plume-Penguin, 1994.

Harris, Jessica B. *Iron Pots and Wooden Spoons.* New York: Atheneum, 1989.

———. *Tasting Brazil.* New York: Macmillan, 1992.

Ritzberg, Charles. *Caribfrikan Portfolio.* Self-published, 1979.

Ritzberg, Charles, as Kudjo. *Classical Afrikan Cuisines.* Richmond, VA: Afrikan World InfoSystems, 1993 (Charles Ritzberg, 5901 F., Willow Oaks Drive, Richmond, VA 23225).

CHAPTER 7: EUROPE

Artusi, Pellegrino. *La Scienza in Cucina e L'Arte Di Mangiar Bene.* Florence: Accademia Italiana della Cucina, 1890; reprinted by Casa Editrice Morocco, 1950.

Bastianich, Lidia, and Jay Jacobs. *La Cucina di Lidia.* New York: Doubleday, 1990.

Bugialli, Giuliano. *The Fine Art of Italian Cooking.* New York: Quadrangle, New York Times, 1977.

Caminiti, M. L. Pasquini, and G. Quondamatteo. *Mangiari Di Romagna.* Milan: Garzanti, 1960.

Caron, Michel, and Ned Rival. *Dictionnaire des Potages.* Paris: Éditions De La Pensée Moderne, 1964.

Cucina Montovana, di Principe e di Popoli. Adapted from antique texts by Gino Brunetti. Mantua: Instituto Carlo D'Arte Per La Storia Di Montavana, 1963.

David, Elizabeth. *Italian Food.* New York: Alfred A. Knopf, 1958.

Digbie, Sir Kenelme. *The Closet of Sir Kenelme Digbie, Opened.* London, 1669. Facsimile by Mallinckrodt Chemical Works, 1967.

Garrett, Theodore Francis, ed. *The Encyclopedia of Practical Cookery,* Vol. VII. London, about 1900.

Glasse, Hannah. *The Art of Cookery.* London, about 1750.

Hale, William Harlan, and the editors of *Horizon* magazine. *The Horizon Cookbook and Illustrated History of Eating and Drinking Through the Ages.* New York: American Heritage, 1968.

Hartley, Dorothy. *Food in England.* London: Macdonald, 1954.

Montagné, Prosper. *Larousse Gastronomique.* New York: Crown, 1961.

Platina (Bartolomeo de Sacchi di Piadena). *De Honesta Voluptate.* Venice, 1475. Facsimile by Mallinckrodt Chemical Works, 1967.

Pohren, D. E. *Adventures in Taste: The Wines and Folk Food of Spain.* Morón de la Frontera, Spain: Society of Spanish Studies, 1972.

Ranhofer, Charles. *The Epicurean.* Evanston, IL: Hotel Monthly Press, 1920.

Sarvis, Shirley. *A Taste of Portugal.* New York: Charles Scribner's Sons, 1967.

Sheraton, Mimi. *The German Cookbook.* New York: Random House, 1965.

CHAPTER 8: EASTERN EUROPE AND RUSSIA

Benet, Sula. *How to Live to Be 100.* New York: Dial Press, 1976.

Chamberlain, Lesley. *The Food and Cooking of Russia.* New York: Penguin, 1982.

Goldstein, Darra. *The Georgian Feast.* New York: HarperCollins, 1993.

Kovi, Paul. *Transylvanian Cuisine.* New York: Crown, 1985.

Lang, George. *George Lang's Cuisine of Hungary.* New York: Atheneum, 1971.

Mirodan, Vladimir. *The Balkan Cookbook.* New York: Pelican, 1989.

Mrljies, Radajko. *The Balkan Cookbook.* Belgrade: Jugoslovenska Knjiga, 1987.

Stechishin, Savella. *The Ukrainian Cookbook.* Winnipeg: Trident Press, 1967.

Yugoslav Cookbook. Belgrade: Izdavacki Zavod, 1963.

CHAPTER 9: MIDDLE EAST, NORTH AFRICA, AND CULINARY COUSINS

Guinaudeau-Franc, Zette. *Fez—Traditional Moroccan Cooking.* Rabat: Édition J.E. Laurent, 1964.

Khalil, Nagwa E. *Egyptian Cuisine.* Washington, D.C.: World Wide Graphics, 1980.

Khayat, Marie Karam, and Margaret Clark Keatinge. *Food from the Arab World.* Lebanon: Khayat's, 1959.

Mardikian, George. *Dinner at Omar Khayyam's.* New York: Viking, 1944.

Weiss-Armushu, Anne Marie. *The Arabian Delights.* Los Angeles: Lowell House, 1994.

CHAPTER 10: SUB-SAHARAN AFRICA

Copage, Eric V. *Kwanzaa: An African-American Celebration of Culture and Cooking.* New York: Quill-Morrow, 1991.

Ghana Government Medical and Educational Departments. *Ghana Nutrition and Cookery.* Edinburgh: Thomas Nelson and Sons.

Hafner, Dorinda. *A Taste of Africa.* Berkeley: Ten Speed Press, 1993.

Harris, Jessica B. *Iron Pots and Wooden Spoons*. New York: Atheneum, 1989.

Hultman, Tami, ed. *The African News Cookbook*. New York: Africa News Service, Inc. Penguin, 1985.

Kuper, Jessica, ed. *The Anthropologists' Cookbook*. New York: Universe, 1977.

Mesfin, Daniel J. *Exotic Ethiopian Cooking*. Falls Church, VA: Ethiopian Cookbook Enterprises, 1990.

Osseo-Asare, Fran. *A Good Soup Attracts Chairs*. Gretna, Louisiana: Pelican, 1993.

CHAPTER 11: ASIA

Brackman, Agnes de Keijzer. *The Art of Indonesian Cooking: The ABC's*. Singapore: Asian Pacific Press, 1970.

Chang, K.C., ed. *Food in Chinese Culture: Anthropological and Historical Perspectives*. New Haven: Yale University Press, 1977.

Lin, Hsiang Ju, and Tsuifeng Lin. *Chinese Gastronomy*. New York: Hastings House, 1969.

Marks, Copeland, with Mintari Soeharjo. *The Indonesian Kitchen*. New York: Atheneum, 1981.

Merchant, Ismail. *Ismail Merchant's Passionate Meals*. Westport, CT: Hyperion, 1994.

Solomon, Charmaine. *The Complete Asian Cookbook*. New York: McGraw-Hill, 1976.

MAIL-ORDER FOOD SOURCES

GENERAL

Almost all of the ethnic seasonings and ingredients in these recipes (with the exception of highly perishable meats, poultry, and seafood, and some fruits and vegetables) can be ordered from the following sources:

Adriana's Caravan
409 Vanderbilt Street
Brooklyn, NY 11218
1-800-316-0820 or 718-436-8565
Catalog on request.

Dean & DeLuca
560 Broadway
New York, NY 10012
1-800-221-7714
Catalog for $3 by check or money order.

Penzeys, Ltd. Spice House
P.O. Box 1448
Waukesha, WI 53187
414-574-0277
Catalog on request.

AFRICAN, WEST INDIAN, AND CARIBBEAN INGREDIENTS

Authentic African Imports
568 Flatbush Avenue
Brooklyn, NY 11225
718-287-9080
Ask for Kenny or Mohammed.

MIDDLE EASTERN, NORTH AFRICAN, AND INDIAN INGREDIENTS

Sultan's Delight
P.O. Box 090302
Brooklyn, NY 11209
1-800-852-5046
Minimum order $20; catalog on request.

ASIAN INGREDIENTS

Anzen Oriental Food and Imports
736 Martin Luther King, Jr., Boulevard
Portland, OR 97232
503-233-5111
Price list on request.

LATIN AMERICAN, MEXICAN, AND SOUTHWESTERN INGREDIENTS

The Kitchen
218 Eighth Avenue
New York, NY 10011
212-243-4433
Catalog on request.

The Chile Shop
109 East Water Street
Santa Fe, NM 87501
505-983-6080
Catalog on request.

CONVERSION CHARTS

LIQUID MEASURES

FLUID OUNCES	U.S. MEASURES	IMPERIAL MEASURES	MILLILITERS
	1 tsp.	1 tsp.	5
¼	2 tsp.	1 dessert spoon	7
½	1 T.	1 T.	15
1	2 T.	2 T.	28
2	¼ cup	4 T.	56
4	½ cup or ¼ pint	–	110
5	–	¼ pint or 1 gill	140
6	¼ cup	–	170
8	1 cup or ½ pint	–	225
9	–	–	250 (¼ liter)
10	1¼ cups	½ pint	280
12	1½ cups or ¾ pint	¾ pint	340
15	–	–	420
16	2 cups or 1 pint	–	450
18	2¼ cups	1 pint	500 (½ liter)
20	2½ cups	–	560
24	3 cups or 1½ pints	1¼ pints	675
25	–	–	700
27	3½ cups	1½ pints	750
30	3¾ cups	–	840
32	4 cups or 2 pints or 1 quart	1¾ pints	900
35	–	–	980
36	4 ½ cups		1000 (1 liter)

SOLID MEASURES

U.S. AND IMPERIAL MEASURES		METRIC MEASURES	
OUNCES	POUNDS	GRAMS	KILOS
1	–	28	–
2	–	56	–
3½	–	100	–
4	¼	112	–
5		140	–

SOLD MEASURES (CONTINUED)

U.S. AND IMPERIAL MEASURES		METRIC MEASURES	
6	–	168	–
8	½	225	–
9	–	250	¼
12	¾	340	–
16	1	450	–
18	–	500	½
20	1¼	560	–
24	1½	675	–
27	–	750	¾
28	1¾	780	–
32	2	900	–
36	2¼	1000	1
40	2½	1100	–
48	3	1350	–
54	–	1500	1½

OVEN TEMPERATURE EQUIVALENTS

FAHRENHEIT	GAS MARK	CELSIUS	HEAT OF OVEN
225	¼	107	Very Cool
250	½	121	Very Cool
275	1	135	Cool
300	2	148	Cool
325	3	163	Moderate
350	4	177	Moderate
375	5	190	Fairly Hot
400	6	204	Fairly Hot
425	7	218	Hot
450	8	232	Very Hot
475	9	246	Very Hot

INDEX

❖◆❖